EBO

NORDIC SAILORS' & FISHERMEN'S SWEATERS

MODERN KNITWEAR INSPIRED BY HISTORICAL PATTERNS

Lotte Rahbek
and
Gitte Verner Jensen

ABRAMS, NEW YORK

Contents

Foreword

A couple of years ago, we at the M/S Maritime Museum put on an exhibit, titled OCEANISTA—The Sea and Fashion, where we traced the influence of the sea and maritime traditions on modern fashion. Sailors' collars, work shirts, uniform jackets, corals, and images of tattoos filled the rooms. And, of course, seafarers' knitwear was also included. Historically, for a working fisherman, it was imperative to have the strongest, most practical, and most durable clothing. Our exhibit displayed everyday garments and clothes for an absolutely exhausting life—a seafarer's typical knitwear suits the latter.

There is something genuine about sailors' knitwear. It goes back centuries to men who in many ways were like us, but at the same time, lived a life very different from our own. A life that was simultaneously a pact with and a fight against nature; steeped in the scents of waves, salt water, and air so fresh one can scarcely imagine it today.

In truth, seamen's knitwear does not go as far back as we would like to believe. Knitting as a general phenomenon first appeared in Europe in the late Middle Ages, but we don't know precisely when it found its way to the maritime community. Vikings did not sail over the Atlantic Ocean in knitted garments—their clothing was both woven and needle-woven (nålbinding) rather than knit.

What we think of as Nordic "seamen's knitwear" was relatively well defined and popularized by nineteenth-century folklorists who traveled to remote regions of Scandinavia, Iceland, Finland, and elsewhere in Europe to do their research. What they discovered and recorded became part of a national awakening, spreading throughout each region and inspiring great interest in not just mapping states as a source of power (*magtenhed*), but viewing nations as a community of people (*folkefaellesskab*). Folklorists were very interested in clothing, and they described local customs as they saw them and as they understood them through conversations with local people. But, in so doing, they froze the traditions, so they remained static, staying just as they were at the time they were documented. Moreover, to a high degree, the pictures of seamen's knitwear they recorded have continued to dominate our understanding of it today.

Because folklorists traveled and researched in the 1800s, we don't necessarily know what seamen's knitwear looked like in the 1600s or how it would have looked today if it had been allowed to develop without intervention. That doesn't mean older traditions cannot be traced. In seafaring and fishing communities, knitting was part of everyday life, custom, and community identity. The knitting of these places (particularly the Guernsey, Aran, and Faroe Island traditions) shows deep roots in time and a living history.

Both yesterday and today, knits are the product of a lot of work. Sheep can care for themselves, but they must be shorn, and the wool carded, spun, and dyed before one may begin knitting a sweater that is warm and useful.

I am happy that we had the OCEANISTA—The Sea and Fashion exhibit, as it opened my eyes to a world that I had not known much about beforehand. And now with this book in hand, I am even more knowledgeable. I will probably never be a big knitter, but I am happy to be a good reader.

—Thorbjørn Thaarup, historian and museum inspector at the M/S Maritime Museum of Denmark

Introduction

In this book, we honor seamen's knitwear and life on the water. Knitting's essence is as rhythmic as the pounding of the waves. A pattern of repeated stitches can become a sweater if one is patient and navigates the "ocean" of time.

The knits in this book are based on classic maritime traditions and pastimes. Inspiration came from the colors, patterns, and design details of garments worn by windblown seamen, fishermen, and their wives. Our designs honor the hands that crafted these classic maritime knits, while offering a connection to the present day. We developed these twenty-three patterns with the hope that they will excite you (and anyone with a soft spot for sailors' knitwear) as much as they did us. Each chapter offers patterns inspired by various historic sources, including photographs found in the archives of the M/S Maritime Museum of Denmark, in Helsingør. By updating both the patterns and the models, we shifted these classic knits to a contemporary gender- and age-neutral style that can be worn by anyone (three months old and up!). The historic pictures reproduced in the book document life by the sea and a seagoing people. These same photos—wonderful authentic portraits of working men and women filled with pride and strength—inspired the names of each design and the style in which we photographed them.

The book is divided into four chapters: Two-Color Stranded Knits and Iconic Cables; Knits Inspired by Fishing Nets and Sailor Collars; Bubble and Textured Knits; and Classic Striped Knits. Each includes patterns and variations—and all are simple and Scandinavian in style. We drew on our fashion and knitwear design experience to develop these garments, focusing on varied silhouettes, details, techniques, colors, and materials. In the process, we used mood boards, color history, and many checklists to corral our research and wild ideas. The finished collection includes sweaters, caps, and accessories for adults and children of all ages and genders. In the patterns using colorwork, there are references to history and the sea, but readers can, of course, choose their own colors. It was important for us to present designs that a knitter can build upon. The patterns are easy to follow and also show beginner knitters the path to a completed design.

We are truly thankful to the contributors who offered their time, energy, and needles to make these knits. We are grateful, too, to the makers of the lovely yarns we used: Isager, Filcolana, Krea Deluxe, Sandnes, and Rauma. The work you hold in your hands represents a close collaboration between two passionate knitters, one from the clothing industry and the other from the world of hand knitting. We found each other when the publisher Bogoo invited us to co-author. Together with photographer Sibel Rønstrup we chose local models for the photoshoots. We found a neighbor's daughter, a café owner and one of his employees, a single colleague, a dog-walking architect, a test knitter's grandchild, as well as friends and family in Snekkersten and Århus. Each model helped us create these lovely photos—taken in Denmark in Snekkersten, Helsingør, and Rønde and on the Fregatten Jutland in Ebeltoft. We hope that our readers will be inspired—not only by the knitting but also by the historic photos—to set course for the horizon.

Colors of the Sea and Coast, set in Color History

Abbreviations

BO	bind off
BOR	beginning of round
cb	center back
CC	contrast or pattern color
cf	center front
cm	centimeters
cn	cable needle
CO	cast on
dpns	double-pointed needle(s)
est	established
in	inch(es)
k	knit
M1L	make 1 left: With left needle, lift strand between 2 sts from front to back and knit into back loop = left-leaning increase.
M1R	make 1 left: With left needle, lift strand between 2 sts from back to front and knit into front loop = right-leaning increase.
m	meters
MC	main or background color
mm	millimeters
p	purl
pm	place marker
psso	pass slipped st(s) over
rep	repeat
rnd(s)	round(s)
RS	right side
sl	slip
slm	slip marker
st(s)	stitch(es)
tbl	through back loop(s)
tog	together
WS	wrong side
yd	yards
yo(s)	yarnover(s)

Levels of Difficulty

BEGINNER	INTERMEDIATE	EXPERIENCED
A knitter who has practiced the knitting techniques of knit and purl stitches, decreases, increases, and binding off.	A knitter who has practiced the knitting techniques of knit and purl stitches for texture patterns, decreases, increases, binding off, I-cord edgings, and picking up and knitting stitches.	A knitter who has practiced the knitting techniques of texture patterns, stranded colorwork, brioche, cables, attaching a zipper, and picking up and knitting stitches for striped sleeves.

Techniques

Patterns	knit/purl/increase/decrease/bind off	I-cord/pick up and knit stitches	texture patterns, stranded colorwork, etc.
TWO-COLOR STRANDED COLORWORK AND CABLES			
Fisherman, Adult Version	x	x	x
Fisherman, Child Version	x	x	x
Haddock	x	x	x
Cordage	x	x	x
Mate	x	x	x
KNITS INSPIRED BY FISHING NET AND SAILOR COLLARS			
Able Seaman	x	x	x
Nettie	x	x	x
Martha	x	x	x
Maren	x	x	
Wellies	x	x	x
BUBBLE AND TEXTURED KNITS			
Snekkersten	x	x	x
Storm, Adult Version	x	x	
Storm, Child Version	x	x	
Ruth	x	x	
Willow		x	x
Sail	x	x	x
CLASSIC STRIPED KNITS			
Sailor, Oversize Version	x	x	x
Sailor, Adult Version	x	x	x
Sailor, Child Version	x	x	x
Captain	x	x	x
Ocean	x	x	x
King Jens	x	x	x
Cousteau	x	x	x

Motifs and Their Meanings

In our research, we found a Dutch book on Gansey sweaters. Gansey refers to the wool sweaters traditionally worn by fishermen on the island of Guernsey or Gansey in the English Channel. Ganseys have texture patterns often unique to local areas or families. We have received permission to reproduce those motifs and descriptions here.

Motifs and Patterns

A knitwear motif is a combination of stitches used to create a repeated pattern. Because of the harsh conditions and long journeys that fishermen face, they attached great significance to the symbols visible in the textures and patterns of their sweaters—which often represented talismans, or their background, or membership in a certain community. All of the traditional motifs listed below can be found in endless variations and combinations in classic fishermen's knits.

TIDEWATER

Ebb and flow. Alternating horizontal bands of Stockinette and texture knitting is called tidewater.

FISHERMEN'S HOUSE

The blocks can represent fishing nets or the walls of a fisherman's house. This motif can be found in many types of blocks.

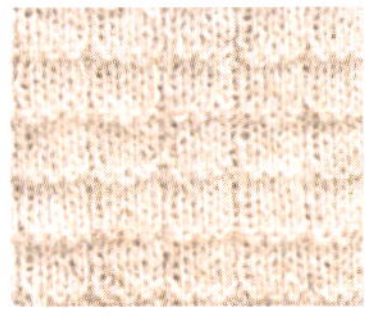  

FISHING NET

These variations of continuous and linked rhomboids are inspired by fishing nets.

LIGHTNING

If lightning strikes land, it is frightening and terrifying, but that's nothing compared to a thunderstorm at sea.

GOD'S EYE

God's all-seeing eye is a motif dating to ancient times and found in many different cultures. The motif has also been called a flower or diamond, symbolizing prosperity. It protected fishermen and was used "to keep the eye on them" when they were in foreign waters—at least, that is what their wives hoped.

  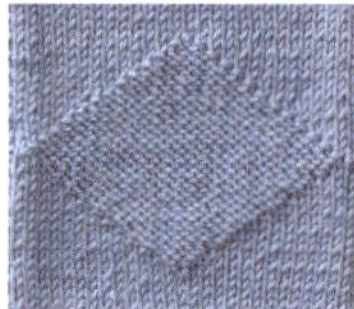

WAVES

Waves are a constant on the sea and can be very dangerous in combination with strong winds.

HAIL

Hail is represented by seed stitches and variations of this texture pattern (such as moss and double moss stitches).

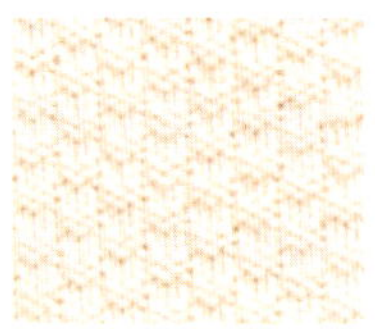  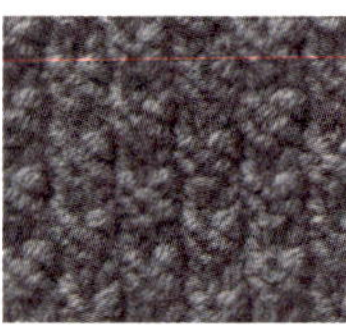

CORDS AND ROPE

Cords are used to give stability and a good grip. Rope and rigging are used to hoist the sails and moor the ship. They are rendered in knitting as various types of cables.

FLAG

Flags were very important for communication at sea. The manner in which the flags were raised and the number of flags all had a specific meaning. Both elements could signify whether they had pulled in a large or small catch.

TREE OF LIFE

The tree of life symbolized the relationship of father to sons. Mothers and daughters were not part of this lineage, but were considered a separate entity. The trunk of the tree could be styled like a herringbone with branches close together.

STEPS

Out at sea, there are many rope steps to clatter up on a sloop or to crawl onboard a ship. The "steps" of reverse Stockinette can be knit with various amount of space between them.

ARROWS

Arrows and harpoons were used at sea to kill and pull in large fish.

CHAINS

Chains were used to hold the anchor. In knitting, chains are usually represented by a cable pattern variation but can also be knit as horizontal bands of purl stitches.

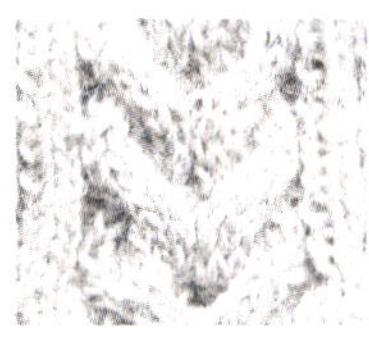  

RIGGING

A ship's rigging is, in marine terminology, a collective term for the masts, cordage, and sails. In knitting, it is a combination of cable and vertical texture patterns embellishing gansey yokes.

SANDBANKS

Straight and diagonal garter stitch lines represent ridges of sand on the beach.

DIAMONDS

There are various types of diamonds representing "God's eye."

Historic Photographs from the M/S Maritime Museum

FISH
OR
DIE

TWO-COLOR STRANDED KNITTING AND ICONIC CABLES

INSPIRATION

Aran Cables
Cables and Texture
Focus on Collars
Recycled Yarn
Stranded Colorwork

HADDOCK

Roll-Neck Sweater with Cables

Designed for sailors, fishermen, port visitors, and townspeople, HADDOCK is the perfect choice for a cool evening, on either land or water. This roll-neck sweater is designed with an allover cable pattern.

HADDOCK has set-in sleeves and ribbing for the sleeve cuffs and lower edge of the body. The sweater was knit with a recycled tweed yarn, respun from extra-fine wool blended with cashmere. The tweed effect from small bits of wool gives the sweater its distinctive look.

HADDOCK

PATTERN SUITABLE FOR EXPERIENCED KNITTERS

SIZES	S (M, L, XL, 2XL)
FINISHED MEASUREMENTS	
Chest Circumference	39½ (42½, 45¾, 47½, 52) in / 100 (108, 116, 124, 132) cm
Length	25½ (26½, 27¼, 28, 28) in / 65 (67, 69, 71, 71) cm
Sleeve Length	20½ (21, 21¼, 21¾, 22) in / 52 (53, 54, 55, 56) cm
GAUGE	21 sts × 32 rnds = 4 × 4 in / 10 × 10 cm in Stockinette with larger-size needles. Make a gauge swatch before you begin knitting to ensure that you are working at the correct gauge. Adjust needle size if necessary to obtain correct gauge.
MATERIALS	
Yarn	Tweed Recycled by Sandnes Garn (80% wool, 20% cashmere, approx. 191 yd / 175 m per 50 g)
Yarn Amounts	9 (10, 11, 12, 13) balls
Needles	US sizes 4 and 6 / 3.5 and 4 mm: 32 in / 80 cm circulars and sets of 5 dpns if you are not using magic loop
Notions	4 stitch markers; cable needle

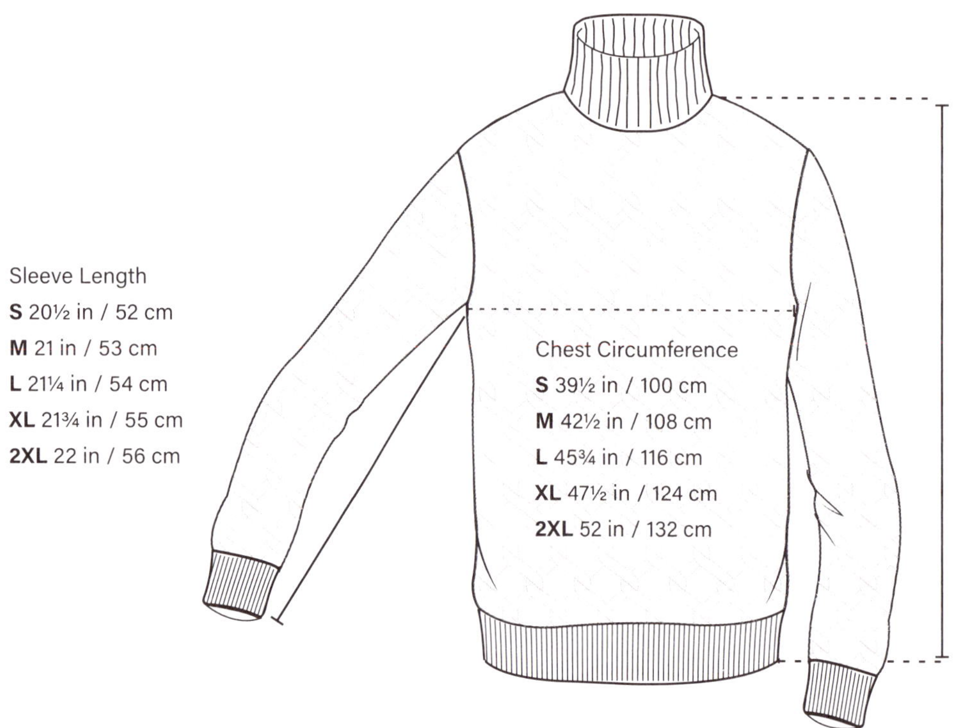

Garment Construction

The sweater is worked from the bottom up. Once the body is divided at the underarms, the front and back are each worked separately. The body is worked first and then the sleeves. Finally, stitches are picked up and knit around the neckline for the neckband.

Body

With smaller-size circular needle, CO 210 (224, 238, 266, 280) sts. Join to work in the rnd, being careful not to twist cast-on row. Begin with ribbing and, *at the same time*, place markers: Pm for beginning of rnd; work k1, p1 ribbing for 105 (112, 119, 133, 140) sts; pm; continue in ribbing as est to end of rnd.

Work in ribbing as est for 2½ in / 6 cm. On the last rnd, increase 70 (84, 84, 84, 98) sts evenly spaced as follows:
Size S: (K3, M1L) 70 times.
Size M: *(K2, M1L, k3, M1L) 10 times, k6, M1L*; work from * to * 4 times.
Size L: *M1L, (k2, M1L) 3 times, (k3, M1L) 18 times; (k2, M1L) 2 times, (k3, M1L) 18 times, k1*; work from * to * 2 times.
Size XL: K7, (k3, M1L) 84 times, k7.
Size 2XL: Work *M1L, (k3, M1L) 23 times; k1, M1, (k3, M1L) 23 times; k1, M1R*; work from * to * a total of 2 times.

= a total of 280 (308, 322, 350, 378) sts. Change to larger-size circular needle and begin Cable Pattern in the Round (see below).

Cable Pattern (in the Round)

Worked over a multiple of 14 sts / 20 rnds
NOTE: Work stitches on even-numbered rows/rounds as each stitch shows when facing you.

Rnd 1: *P4, k6, p4*; rep from * to *.
Rnd 2: Work sts as they appear.

Rnd 3: *P4, sl 3 sts onto cn and hold in front of work, k3, k3 from cn, p4*; rep from * to *.
Rnd 4: Work sts as they appear.

Rnd 5: *P2, sl 2 sts onto cn and hold in back of work, k3, p2 from cn, sl 3 sts onto cn and hold in front of work, p2, k3 from cn, p2*; rep from * to *.
Rnd 6: Work sts as they appear.

Rnd 7: *Sl 2 sts onto cn and hold in back of work, k3, p2 from cn, p4, sl 3 sts onto cn and hold in front of work, p2, k3 from cn*; rep from * to *.
Rnd 8: Work sts as they appear.

Rnd 9: At beg of rnd, remove BOR marker, sl 3 sts purlwise to right needle and pm for new BOR. *P8, sl 3 sts onto cn and hold in front of work, k3, k3 from cn*;' rep from * to *.
Rnd 10: Work sts as they appear.

Rnd 11: Work sts as they appear.
Rnd 12: Work sts as they appear.

Rnd 13: *P8, sl 3 sts onto cn and hold in front of work, k3, k3 from cn;* rep from * to *. On final rep, after completing cable, remove BOR marker, sl 3 sts from right needle to left needle, pm on right needle for new BOR, slip 3 sts from left needle back to right needle..
Rnd 14: Work sts as they appear.

Rnd 15: *Sl 3 sts onto cn and hold in front of work, p2, k3 from cn, p4, sl 2 sts onto cn and hold in back of work, k3, p2 from cn*; rep from * to *.
Rnd 16: Work sts as they appear.

Rnd 17: *P2, sl 3 sts onto cn and hold in front of work, p2, k3 from cn, sl 2 sts onto cn and hold in back of work, k3, p2 from cn, p2*; rep from * to *.
Rnd 18: Work sts as they appear.

HADDOCK Chart Symbols

(blank square)	Knit on RS, purl on WS
(dot)	Purl on RS, knit on WS
(5-st left cable)	5-st left cable: Slip 3 sts onto cn and hold in front of work, p2, k3 from cn
(5-st right cable)	5-st right cable: Slip 3 sts onto cn and hold in back of work, k3, p2 from cn
(6-st left cable)	6-st left cable: Slip 3 sts onto cn and hold in back of work, k3, k3 from cn
(orange 6-st left cable)	6-st left cable: Slip 3 sts onto cn and hold in back of work, k3, k3 from cn. After working final rep, remove BOR marker, slip 3 sts from right needle to left needle, pm on right needle for new BOR, slip 3 sts from left needle back to right needle.
(yellow)	At beg of rnd only, remove BOR marker, slip 3 sts purlwise to right needle and pm for new BOR. Omit them st for remainder of rnd.

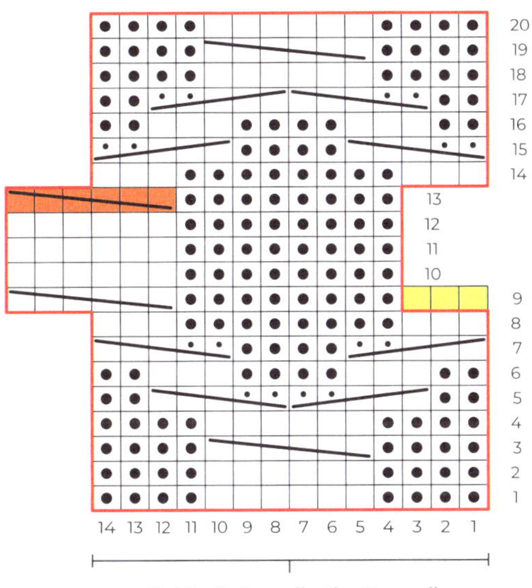

Cable Pattern (in the Round)
14-st repeat

Cables drawn as for the pattern

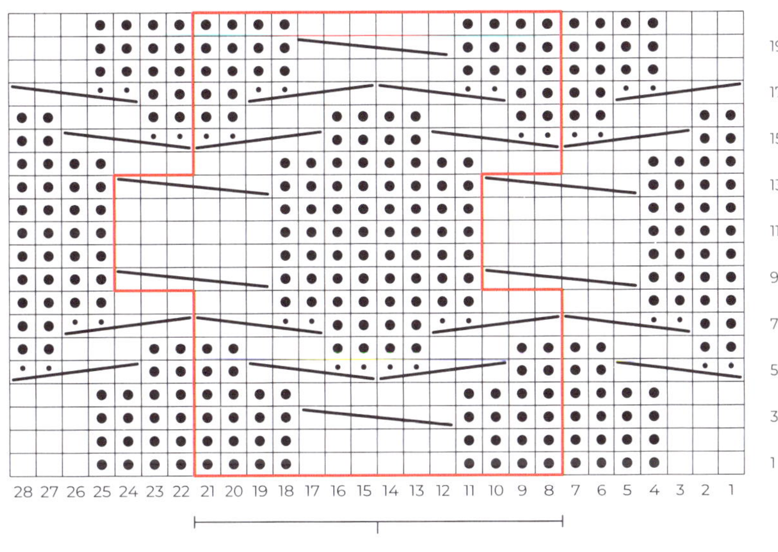

Cable Pattern (Flat)
14-st repeat

Rnd 19: *P4, sl 3 sts onto cn and hold in front of work, k3, k3 from cn, p4*; rep from * to *.
Rnd 20: Work sts as they appear.
Rep Rows 1–20 as instructed in pattern.

Cable Pattern (Flat)

Worked over 4 sts / 20 rows
Row 1 (RS): K3, p8, *k6, p8*; rep from * to * to last 3 sts, k3.
Row 2 and all WS rows: Work sts as they appear.

Row 3: K3, p8, *sl 3 sts onto cn and hold in front of work, k3, k3 from cn, p8*; rep from * to * to last 3 sts, k3.
Row 5: Sl 3 sts onto cn and hold in front of work, p2, k3 from cn, p4, *sl 2 sts onto cn and hold in back of work, k3, p2 from cn, sl 3 sts onto cn and hold in front of work, p2, k3 from cn, p4*: rep from * to * to last 5 sts, sl 2 sts onto cn and hold in back of work, k3, p2 from cn.

Row 7: P2, sl 3 sts onto cn and hold in front of work, p2, k3 from cn, *sl 2 sts onto cn and hold in back of work, k3, p2 from cn, p4, sl 3 sts onto cn and hold in front of work, p2, k3 from cn*; rep from * to * to last 7 sts, sl 2 sts onto cn and hold in back of work, k3, p2 from cn, p2.
Row 9: P4, sl 3 sts onto cn and hold in front of work, k3, k3 from cn, *p8, sl 3 sts onto cn and hold in front of work, k3, k3 from cn*; rep from * to * to last 4 sts, p4.

Row 11: Rep Row 2.
Row 13: Rep Row 9.

Row 15: P2, sl 2 sts onto cn and hold in back of work, k3, p2 from cn, *sl 3 sts onto cn and hold in front of work, p2, k3 from cn, p4, sl 2 sts onto cn and hold in back of work, k3, p2 from cn*; rep from * to * to last 7 sts, sl 3 sts onto cn and hold in front of work, p2, k3 from cn, p2.
Row 17: *Sl 2 sts onto cn and hold in back of work, k3, p2 from cn, p4, sl 3 sts onto cn and hold in front of work, p2, k3 from cn*; rep from * to *.

Row 19: Rep Row 3.
Row 20: Rep Row 2.
Rep Rows 1–20 for pattern.

When body measures 13½ (13¾, 14½, 15, 15) in / 34 (35, 37, 38, 38) cm, BO 2 (2, 2, 3, 3) sts centered on each side for underarms = 276 (304, 318, 344, 372) sts rem. Place 138 (152, 159, 172, 186) front sts on a holder.

Back

The back is worked back and forth over 138 (152, 159, 172, 186) sts and pattern continuing as est.
NOTE: The first st at each side is an edge st that is always knit on both RS and WS. When decreasing, make sure to continue the cable pattern as well as possible; if there aren't enough sts for a cable crossing, work the sts as they show. Work decrease rows on every RS row as follows: K1 (edge st), work 2tog as sts shown, work to last 3 sts of row, work 2tog as sts present, k1 (edge st). Work decrease row a total of 3 (3, 4, 4, 4) times = a total of 132 (146, 151, 164, 178) sts rem.

Continue in cable pattern as est until body measures 24¾ (25½, 26½, 27¼, 27¼) in / 63 (65, 67, 69, 69) cm. BO the center 38 (46, 47, 48, 48) sts as follows:

Size S: Work 47 sts, BO 38, work 46 sts.
Size M: Work 50 sts, BO 46, work 49 sts.
Size L: Work 52 sts, BO 47, work 51 sts.
Size XL: Work 58 sts, BO 48, work 57 sts.
Size 2XL: Work 65 sts, BO 48, work 66 sts.

NOTE ALL SIZES: 1 stitch remains from last bind-off.

Now work each shoulder separately, beginning with the left. BOs for the left side of the neck begin on RS and are worked on every other row while pattern continues. At the neck edge, BO 2 sts, then 1 st, and then 1 st = 43 (46, 48, 54, 61) sts rem for shoulder. Continue in pattern until piece measure 25½ (26½, 27¼, 28, 28) in / 65 (67, 69, 71, 71) cm, ending with a WS row. Make note of last row worked in pattern. Place rem sts on holder. Make the opposite shoulder the same way, binding off at neck edge as above so shaping mirrors the first shoulder.

Front

The front is worked as for the back until piece measures 22¾ (23¾, 24½, 25¼, 25¼) in / 58 (60, 62, 64, 64) cm. BO the center 40 (48, 49, 50, 50) sts as follows:

Size S: Work 46 sts, BO 40, work 45 sts.
Size M: Work 49 sts, BO 48, work 48 sts.
Size L: Work 51 sts, BO 49, work 50 sts.
Size XL: Work 57 sts, BO 50, work 56 sts.
Size 2XL: Work 64 sts, BO 50, work 63 sts.

NOTE ALL SIZES: 1 stitch remains from last bind-off.

Now work each shoulder separately. BOs for the right side of the neck beg on RS and are worked on every other row at the neck edge, while continuing in cable pattern as est: At the neck edge, BO 2 (2, 2, 2, 2) sts, then 1 (1, 1, 1, 1) st = 43 (46, 48, 54, 61) sts rem for shoulder.

Continue in cable pattern until piece measure 25½ (26½, 27¼, 28, 28) in / 65 (67, 69, 71, 71) cm, ending on same row as for back. Place rem sts on holder. Make the opposite shoulder the same way, binding off at neck edge as above to mirror shaping.

Sleeves

With smaller-size dpns, CO 42 (42, 46, 46, 46) sts. Divide sts onto dpns, pm for BOR, and join to work in the round, being careful not to twist cast-on row. Work k1, p1 ribbing until cuff measures 2½ in / 6 cm long. On the last rnd of ribbing, increase 18 (18, 20, 20, 20) sts evenly spaced as follows: Work 3 sts, (2 sts, M1L) 18 (18, 20, 20, 20) times, work 3 sts = 60 (60, 66, 66, 66) sts. Pm after first st and before last st. Change to larger-size dpns. Begin cable pattern, making sure that the pattern is centered on the sleeve (see Cable Pattern above):

Sizes S and M: K2, work (14 sts of cable) 4 times, k2.

Sizes L, XL, and 2XL: K5, work (14 sts of cable) 4 times, k5.

After 1¼ in / 3 cm, begin increasing to shape sleeve as follows: Work in pattern, and, *at the same time*, increase 1 st after the first marker and before the last marker with M1L every ¾ in / 2 cm a total of 15 (16, 13, 15, 18) times = 90 (92, 92, 96, 102) sts. Maintain pattern when possible; if not enough stitches for a cable, work the stitches as they appear.

Continue in pattern without further increases until sleeve measures 20½ (21, 21¼, 21¾, 22) in / 52 (53, 54, 55, 56) cm long. BO 4 (4, 6, 6, 6) sts centered on underarm = 86 (88, 86, 90, 96) sts rem. Now work the sleeve back and forth, continuing cable pattern as est. BO to shape top of sleeve on RS as follows: BO 1 st at beginning of next 2 rows. Work this BO a total of 8 (8, 8, 8, 7) times. Then, BO 2 sts at beginning of next 2 rows; BO 3 (3, 2, 1, 1) sts at beginning of next 2 rows. BO 3 sts each at beginning of next 2 rows; BO 4 sts each at beginning of next 2 rows = a total of 46 (48, 48, 54, 62) sts rem. BO all sts. Set sleeve aside while you make the second sleeve the same way.

Shoulders

Join shoulders with Kitchener st.

Neckband

With smaller-size circular needle and RS facing, pick up and knit an even number of stitches, approx. 86 (90, 90, 94, 94) sts, around neckline. PM for BOR and join to work in the rnd. Work k1, p1 ribbing for 6¼ in / 16 cm. BO in ribbing.

Finishing

Weave in all ends neatly on WS by sewing into the tops of the sts so the yarn won't show on RS. Attach sleeves.

Wash sweater following instructions on ball band. Lay sweater on a dry towel, pat it out to finished measurements, and leave until completely dry.

FISHERMAN

Shawl Collar Sweater with Cables

A group photo of the crew of a freighter in the 1930s. Among the cranes and ropes, the men take a break from loading wood to be photographed. One of the workers stands in a sweater with a shawl collar and cable pattern—the inspiration for FISHERMAN.

FISHERMAN has wide raglan bands. It is designed with a cable pattern at the center of the sweater, combined with a texture pattern on each side of the cable. The sleeves have the same texture pattern. The shawl collar is a folded rib and the sweater also has ribbing for the sleeve cuffs and bottom edge of the sweater.

The FISHERMAN sweater was knit with a recycled tweed yarn, respun from extra-fine wool blended with cashmere. The tweed effect from small bits of wool gives the sweater its distinctive look.

FISHERMAN, Adult Version

PATTERN SUITABLE FOR EXPERIENCED KNITTERS

SIZES	S (M, L, XL, 2XL)
FINISHED MEASUREMENTS	
Chest Circumference	39½ (42½, 45¾, 47½, 52) in / 100 (108, 116, 124, 132) cm
Length	25½ (26½, 27¼, 28, 28¾) in / 65 (67, 69, 71, 73) cm
Sleeve Length	18¼ (19, 19¾, 20½, 21¼) in / 46 (48, 50, 52, 54) cm
GAUGE	21 sts × 30 rnds = 4 × 4 in / 10 × 10 cm in Stockinette with larger-size needles. Make a gauge swatch before you begin knitting to ensure that you are working at the correct gauge. Adjust needle size if necessary to obtain correct gauge.
MATERIALS	
Yarn	Tweed Recycled by Sandnes Garn (80% wool, 20% cashmere, 191 yd/175 m / 50 g)
Yarn Amounts	10 (11, 12, 13, 14) balls
Needles	US sizes 4 and 6 / 3.5 and 4 mm: 24 in / 60 cm circulars and sets of 5 dpns if you are not using magic loop
Notions	8 stitch markers; cable needle

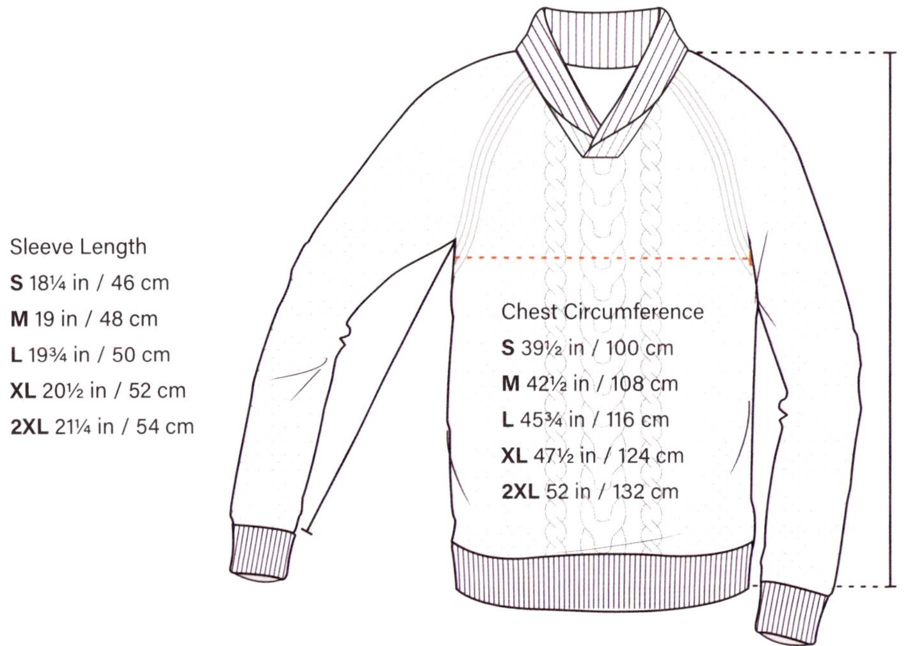

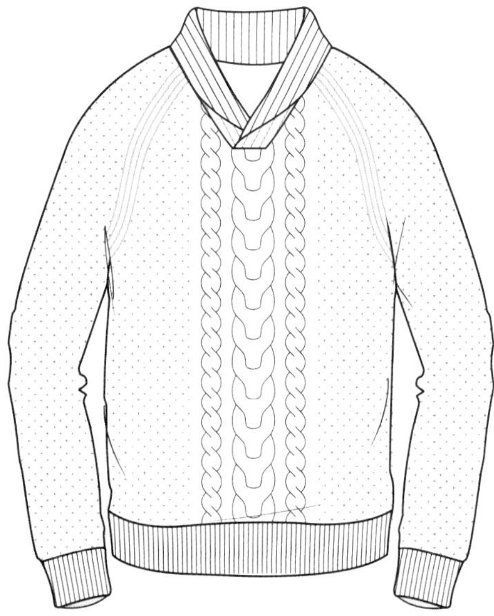

Garment Construction

The body of the sweater is worked from the bottom up. The body is worked first and then the sleeves. The body and sleeves are placed together on a circular needle for the yoke. Finally, stitches are picked up and knit around the neckline for the shawl collar. The stitch pattern can be worked from the chart or the written patterns.

Body

With smaller-size circular needle, CO 184 (208, 224, 240, 256) sts. Join to work in the rnd, being careful not to twist cast-on row. Begin with ribbing and, *at the same time*, place markers: Pm for beginning of rnd; work k2, p2 ribbing for 92 (104, 112, 120, 128) sts; pm; continue in ribbing to end of rnd. The markers divide for the front and back. Work in ribbing for 2½ in / 6 cm. On the last rnd, increase 12 (8, 4, 4, 4) sts evenly spaced *each* for front and back as follows:

Size S: K4, (k7, M1L) 12 times, k4.
Size M: (K13, M1L) 8 times.
Size L: (K28, M1L) 4 times.
Size XL: (K30, M1L) 4 times.
Size 2XL: (K32, M1L) 4 times.

= 104 (112, 116, 124, 132) sts each on front and back for a total of 208 (224, 232, 248, 264) sts.

Change to larger-size circular needle and place markers for the pattern as follows: sl 32 (36, 38, 42, 46) sts, pm, sl 40 sts, pm, sl rem sts to beginning of rnd.

Begin pattern as follows: *Work 32 (36, 38, 42, 46) sts in Fishing Net pattern; p1; work 10-stitch cable; work 18-stitch cable; work 10 stitch cable; p1; work Fishing Net to end of rnd. Continue in pattern as est until body measures approx. 13½ (13¾, 14½, 15, 15) in / 34 (35, 37, 38, 38) cm.

On the next rnd, BO to shape underarms, *at the same time*, continue in pattern as est: At beginning of rnd, BO 4 (5, 5, 5, 5) sts, work until 4 (5, 5, 5, 5) sts before next marker, BO 8 (10, 10, 10, 10) sts, work until 4 (5, 5, 5, 5) sts before BOR marker, BO 4 (5, 5, 5, 5) sts; cut yarn = 192 (204, 212, 228, 244) sts rem. Make note of last rnd worked in Fishing Net. Set body aside while you make the sleeves.

Patterns

Fishing Net (worked over a multiple of 4 sts / 4 rnds/rows)
Rnd/Row 1: *P2, k2*; rep from * to *.
Rnd/Row 2: Work sts as they appear.
Rnd/Row 3: Knit the purl sts and purl the knit sts as they appear.
Rnd/Row 4: Work sts as they appear.
Rep Rnds/Rows 1–4 for pattern.

10-Stitch Cable (worked over 10 rnds)
Rnd 1: P2, sl 3 sts onto cn and hold in front of work, k3, k3 from cn, p2.
Rnds 2–10: P2, k6, p2.
Rep Rnds 1–10 for pattern.

18-Stitch Cable (worked over 8 rnds)
Rnd/Row 1: P1, k16, p1.
Rnds/Rows 2–6 and 8: Work sts as they appear.
Rnd/Row 7: P1, sl 3 sts onto cn and hold in back of work, k3, k3 from cn, sl 3 sts onto cn and hold in front of work, k3, k3 from cn.
Rnd/Row 8: Work sts as they appear.
Rep Rnds/Rows 1–8 for pattern.

Sleeves

With smaller-size dpns, CO 44 (48, 52, 52, 56) sts. Divide sts onto 4 dpns and join to work in the round, being careful not to twist cast-on row. Work in k2, p2 ribbing until cuff measures 1½ in / 4 cm long. Pm after first and before last st. Change to larger-size dpns and begin sleeve shaping: K1, slm, M1L, knit to next marker, M1R, slm, k1.

Now begin working in Fishing Net pattern. Increase the same way, working new sts in Fishing Net pattern as est between markers, every 1¼ in / 3 cm a total of 14 (14, 14, 16, 16) times = 72 (76, 80, 84, 88) sts.

FISHERMAN Chart Symbols

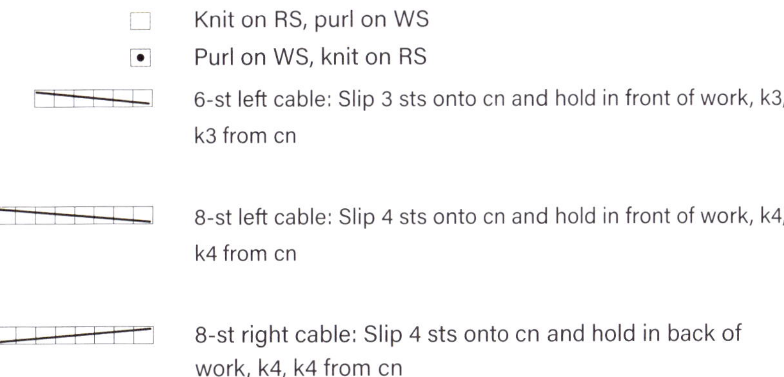

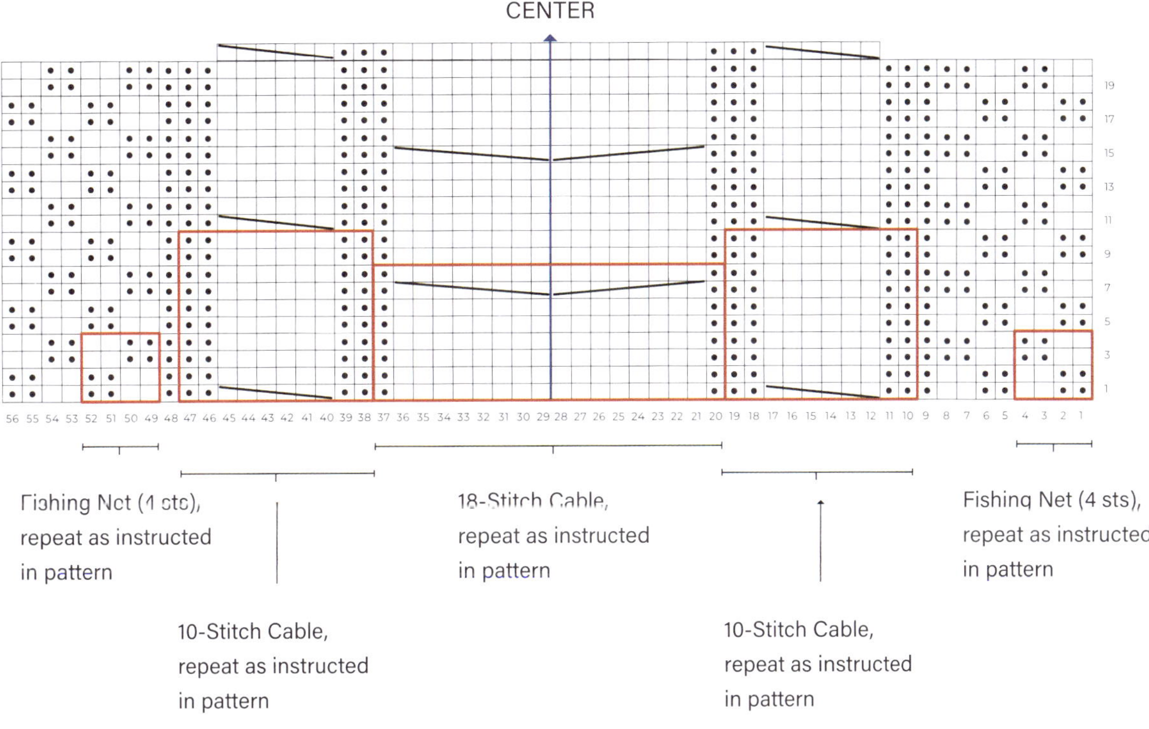

Continue in pattern as est until sleeve measures 18¼ (19, 19¾, 20½, 21¼) in / 46 (48, 50, 52, 54) cm, ending with same rnd of Fishing Net as for body. Bind off a total of 8 (10, 10, 10, 10) sts for underarm: BO 4 (5, 5, 5, 5) sts on each side of BOR (= center of underarm) = 64 (66, 70, 74, 78) sts rem.

Set first sleeve aside while you make the second sleeve the same way.

FISHERMAN Cable

Cable crossing (3 knit sts over 3 knit sts)

Cable crossing (3 knit sts over 3 knit sts)

Cable crossing (two cables, each 4 knit sts over 4 knit sts)

Fishing Net Pattern

Fishing Net Pattern

3 purl sts

3 purl sts

3 purl sts

Joining Body and Sleeves

NOTE: The Fishing Net pattern should match on sleeves and body—that is, they should end on the same round in the pattern on all pieces.

Place all pieces on larger-size circular needle, matching underarms. Begin by placing 8 raglan markers. The round begins at left shoulder on the back of the sweater:

Marker 1: K1, pm, work in pattern to last st before next piece intersection.

Marker 2: Pm, k1, yo, k1.

Marker 3: Pm, work in pattern to last st before next piece intersection.

Marker 4: Pm, k1, yo, k1.

Marker 5: Pm, work in pattern to last st before next piece intersection.

Marker 6: Pm, k1, yo, k1.

Marker 7: Pm, work in pattern to last st before next piece intersection.

Marker 8: Pm, k1, yo.

There should now be 324 (340, 356, 380, 404) sts total, including yos. On the next rnd, work each yo as k1tbl.

Raglan Shaping

Begin decreasing at every marker as follows: *Work until 2 sts before marker; sl 1, k1, psso, k3, k2tog*; rep from * to *.

A total of 8 sts are decreased on every dec rnd. Continuing to work in pattern as est, rep the raglan decreases on every third rnd a total of 28 (30, 31, 34, 37) times = 224 (240, 248, 272, 296) sts to be decreased for raglan shaping. *At the same time*, after 13 (14, 14, 16, 18) rnds of raglan decreases (= 220 (228, 244, 252, 260) sts rem), begin shaping the neckline, while *at the same time* continuing the raglan decreases and texture pattern.

NOTE: After splitting for the collar and working in rows, the raglan decreases are worked in the opposite way on the WS so they will look the same all along the raglan lines on RS.

On WS: *Purl until 2 sts before marker, p2tog, p3, p2tog tbl*; rep from * to *.

Split for the neck on a rnd without any raglan decreases as follows:

Next rnd: Work to front stitches (after marker 3), BO the center 18 sts for front neck, and finish rnd as est. Cut yarn and rejoin yarn at left side of neck. Now work back and forth in pattern, continuing the raglan decreases while also shaping neck at beginning of every row. *BO 1 st at beg of next 2 rows. Work 2 rows even.* Rep from * to * until raglan decreases are complete. BO rem sts.

Shawl Collar

NOTE: The shawl collar is worked in ribbing for 5½ (6, 6¼, 6¾, 7) in / 14 (15, 16, 17, 18) cm, worked in 3 steps: First, vertical ribbing along the back neck. Then, pick up and knit along the left side of the shawl collar edge *at the same time* as the edges are joined down along the edge of left side of neck. Finally, rep the sequence on the right side of the neck, but mirrored.

Step 1, Back Neck: Begin at the left side of back neck. With smaller-size circular needle, pick up and knit an even number of sts, approx. 44 (44, 46, 46, 46) sts across back neck. Work back and forth in k1, p1 ribbing until collar measures 5½ (6, 6¼, 6¾, 7) in / 14 (15, 16, 17, 18) cm. BO all sts.

Step 2, Left Side of Shawl Collar: Pick up and knit approx. 16 sts along the left side of back neck ribbing, from WS of work, so the picked-up edge lies in toward the back when the collar is folded. Work k1, p1 ribbing while *at the same time* incorporating sts from the neck edge to connect the collar to the body of the sweater. To prevent a wavy edge, skip about every 4th st when incorporating sts from the edge as follows: *Work k1, p1 ribbing at the body side to last 3 sts of row, work 2tog (knit or purl depending on ribbing sequence), k1, pick up 1 st from neck edge; turn, work 2tog (knit or purl depending on ribbing), continue in ribbing to end of row*; rep from * to * until you've picked up sts to the bottom of the neckline. BO rem sts.

Step 3, Right Side of Shawl Collar: Work as for left side of collar, but mirrored.

Finishing

Weave in all ends neatly on WS by sewing into the tops of the sts so the yarn won't show on RS. Sew the bound-off left edge of shawl collar to sweater on WS of work. Sew bound-off right edge behind left edge.

Wash sweater following instructions on ball band. Lay sweater on a dry towel, pat it out to finished measurements, and leave until completely dry.

FISHERMAN, Child Version

PATTERN SUITABLE FOR EXPERIENCED KNITTERS

SIZES	4 (6, 8, 10, 12) years
FINISHED MEASUREMENTS	
Chest Circumference	23¾ (26¾, 30, 33, 36¼) in / 60 (68, 76, 84, 92) cm
Length	16½ (17¾, 19, 20, 22) in / 42 (45, 48, 51, 56) cm
Sleeve Length	12¼ (13½, 14½, 15¾, 17) in / 31 (34, 37, 40, 43) cm
GAUGE	21 sts × 30 rnds = 4 × 4 in / 10 × 10 cm in Stockinette with larger-size needles. Make a gauge swatch before you begin knitting to ensure that you are working at the correct gauge. Adjust needle size if necessary to obtain correct gauge.
MATERIALS	
Yarn	Tweed Recycled by Sandnes Garn (80% wool, 20% cashmere, approx. 191 yd/175 m / 50 g)
Yarn Amounts	4 (6, 6, 6, 8) balls
Needles	US sizes 4 and 6 / 3.5 and 4 mm: 24 in / 60 cm circulars and sets of 5 dpns if you are not using magic loop
Notions	8 stitch markers; cable needle

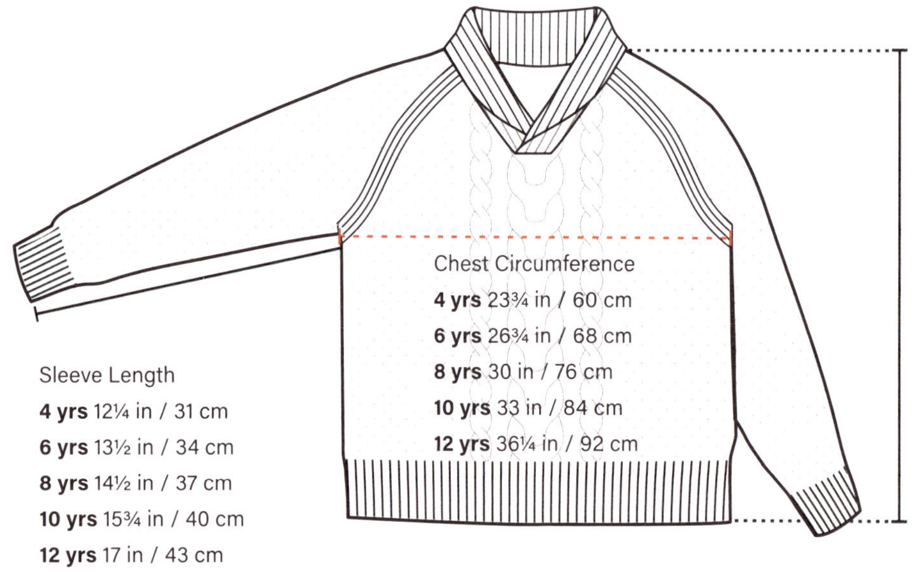

Garment Construction

The body of the sweater is worked from the bottom up. The body is worked first and then the sleeves. The body and sleeves are placed together on a circular needle for the yoke. Finally, stitches are picked up and knit around the neckline for the shawl collar. The stitch pattern can be worked from the chart or the written patterns.

Body

With smaller-size circular needle, CO 128 (144, 160, 176, 192) sts. Join to work in the rnd, being careful not to twist cast-on row. Begin with ribbing and, *at the same time*, place markers: Pm for beginning of rnd, work k2, p2 ribbing for 64 (72, 80, 88, 96) sts, pm (left side), continue in k2, p2 ribbing to end of rnd. The markers divide for the front and back. Work in ribbing for 1½ in / 4 cm. On the last rnd, pm for pattern: Work 12 (16, 20, 24, 28) sts, pm, work 40 (40, 40, 40, 40) sts, pm, work until beginning of rnd.

Change to larger-size circular needle and begin pattern: Work 12 (16, 20, 24, 28) sts in Fishing Net pattern; p1; work 10-stitch cable; work 18-stitch cable; work 10-stitch cable; p1; work Fishing Net to end of rnd. Continue in pattern as est until body measures approx. 9 (10¼, 11½, 11 ¾, 12¼) in / 23 (26, 29, 30, 31) cm.

On the next rnd, BO to shape underarms, *at the same time*, continue in pattern as est: At beginning of rnd, BO 4 (4, 4, 4, 4) sts, work until 4 sts before next marker, BO 8 (8, 8, 8, 8) sts, work until 4 sts before BOR marker, BO 4 (4, 4, 4, 4) sts; cut yarn = 112 (128, 144, 160, 176) sts rem. Make note of last rnd worked in Fishing Net. Set body aside while you make the sleeves.

Patterns

Fishing Net (worked over a multiple of 4 sts / 4 rnds)
Rnd/Row 1: *P2, k2*; rep from * to *.
Rnd/Row 2: Work sts as they appear.
Rnd/Row 3: Knit the purl sts and purl the knit sts as they appear.
Rnd/Row 4: Work sts as they appear.
Rep Rnds/Rows 1–4 for pattern.

10-Stitch Cable (worked over 10 rnds)
Rnd 1: P2, sl 3 sts onto cn and hold in front of work, k3, k3 from cn, p2.
Rnds 2–10: P2, k6, p2.
Rep Rnds 1–10 for pattern.

18-Stitch Cable (worked over 8 rnds)
Rnd/Row 1: P1, k16, p1.
Rnds/Rows 2–6: Work sts as they appear.
Rnd/Row 7: P1, sl 3 sts onto cn and hold in back of work, k3, k3 from cn, sl 3 sts onto cn and hold in front of work, k3, k3 from cn.
Rnd/Row 8: Work sts as they appear.
Rep Rnds/Rows 1–8 for pattern.

FISHERMAN Chart Symbols

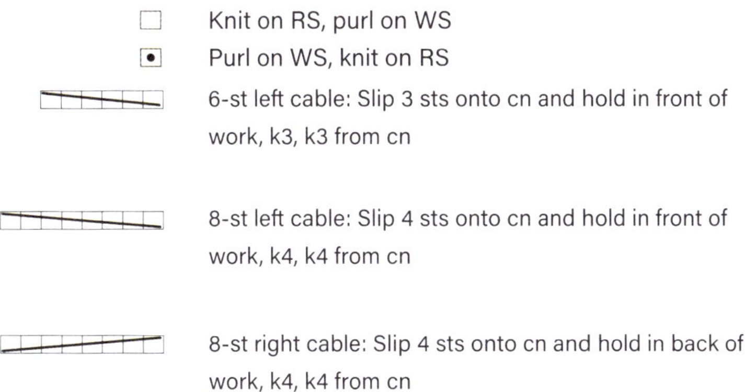

Knit on RS, purl on WS

Purl on WS, knit on RS

6-st left cable: Slip 3 sts onto cn and hold in front of work, k3, k3 from cn

8-st left cable: Slip 4 sts onto cn and hold in front of work, k4, k4 from cn

8-st right cable: Slip 4 sts onto cn and hold in back of work, k4, k4 from cn

CENTER

Fishing Net repeat, 4 sts, repeat as instructed in pattern

Cable (18 sts), work as instructed in pattern

Fishing Net repeat, 4 sts, repeat as instructed in pattern

Cable (10 sts), work as instructed in pattern

Cable (10 sts), work as instructed in pattern

Sleeves

With smaller-size dpns, CO 32 (32, 32, 40, 48) sts. Divide sts onto 4 dpns and join to work in the round, being careful not to twist cast-on row. Work k2, p2 ribbing until cuff measures 1½ in / 4 cm long. Pm after first and before last st. Change to larger-size dpns and begin sleeve shaping: Knit and, *at the same time*, increase with M1L after/before two marked sts: K1, M1L, knit to next marker, M1R, k1. On the next rnd, begin Fishing Net pattern. Increase the same way every ¾ in / 2 cm a total of 12 (13, 13, 14, 15) times, working new sts in Fishing Net = 56 (58, 58, 68, 78) sts. Continue in pattern as est until sleeve measures 12¼ (13½, 14½, 15¾, 17) in / 31 (34, 37, 40, 43) cm long, ending with same rnd of Fishing Net as for body.

Bind off a total of 8 sts for underarm as follows: BO the last 4 sts of one round and the first 4 sts of the next (= center of underarm) = 48 (50, 50, 60, 70) sts rem.

Set first sleeve aside while you make the second sleeve the same way.

Joining Body and Sleeves

Place all pieces on larger-size circular needle, matching underarms, and start raglan shaping. Begin by placing 8 raglan markers. The round begins at left shoulder on the back of the sweater:
Marker 1: K1, pm, work in pattern to last st before next piece intersection.
Marker 2: Pm, k1, yo, k1.
Marker 3: Pm, work in pattern until 1 st before next piece intersection.
Marker 4: Pm, k1, yo, k1.
Marker 5: Pm, work in pattern until 1 st before next piece intersection.
Marker 6: Pm, k1, yo, k1.
Marker 7: Pm, work in pattern until 1 st before next piece intersection.
Marker 8: Pm, k1, yo.
There should now be 212 (232, 248, 284, 320) sts total, including yos. On the next rnd, work each yo as k1tbl.

Raglan Shaping

Begin decreasing at every marker as follows: Work until 2 sts before marker. Sl 1, k1, psso, k3, k2tog. A total of 8 sts are decreased on every decrease rnd. Continuing to work in pattern as est, rep the raglan decreases on every third rnd a total of 16 (18, 20, 24, 28) times = 128 (144, 160, 192, 224) sts to be decreased for raglan shaping. *At the same time*, after 8 (9, 10, 13, 16) raglan decrease rounds [= 148 (160, 168, 180, 192) sts rem], begin shaping the neckline, while also continuing raglan decreases and texture pattern.

NOTE The raglan decreases are worked in the opposite way on the WS of the work so they will look the same all along the raglan lines on RS.
On WS: Purl until 2 sts before marker, p2tog, p3, p2tog tbl.

Decrease for the neck on rnds without any raglan decreases: Work to marker 3, BO the center 16 sts for front neck and finish rnd as est. Cut yarn. Now work back and forth in pattern, also shaping neck at beginning of every row. The sequence begins at the left side of the neck. BO 1 st at beginning of next 14 (16, 18, 18, 18) rows, still continuing pattern as est. After the last raglan decrease, BO rem sts.

Shawl Collar

NOTE: The shawl collar is worked in ribbing for 3¼ in / 8 cm, worked in 3 steps: First, vertical ribbing along the back neck. Then pick up and knit along the left side of the shawl collar edge *at the same time* as the edges are joined down along the edge of left side of neck. Finally, rep the sequence on the right side of the neck, but mirrored.

Step 1, Back Neck: Begin at the left side of back neck. With smaller-size circular needle, pick up and knit an even number of sts, approx. 32 (36, 36, 40, 40) across back neck. Work back and forth in k1, p1 ribbing until collar measures 3¼ (3¼, 3¼, 3¼, 3¼) in / 8 (8, 8, 8, 8) cm. BO all sts.
Step 2, Left Side of Shawl Collar: Pick up and knit 16 sts along the left side of ribbing, from WS of work, so the picked-up edge lies toward the back when the collar is folded. Work k1, p1 ribbing while *at the same time* incorporating sts from the neck edge to connect the collar to the body of the sweater.
To prevent a wavy edge, skip about every 4th st when incorporating sts from the edge as follows: *Work k1, p1 ribbing at the body side to last 3 sts of row, work 2tog (knit or purl depending on ribbing sequence), k1, pick up 1 st from neck edge; turn, work 2tog (knit or purl depending on ribbing), continue in ribbing to end of row*; rep from * to * until you've picked up sts to the bottom of the neckline. BO rem sts.

Step 3, Right Side of Collar: Work as for first side of collar, but mirrored.

Finishing

Weave in all ends neatly on WS by sewing into the tops of the sts so the yarn won't show on RS. Sew the bound-off right edge of shawl collar to sweater on WS of work. Sew bound-off left edge behind right edge.

Wash sweater following instructions on ball band. Lay sweater on a dry towel, pat it out to finished measurements, and leave until completely dry.

FISHERMAN Cable

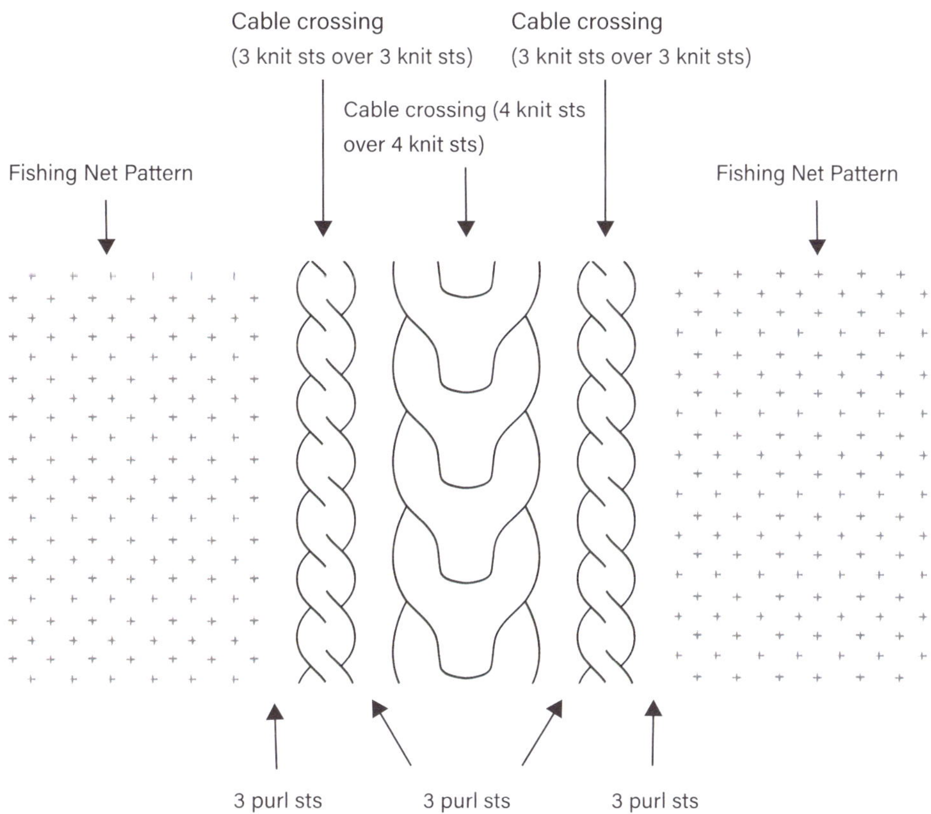

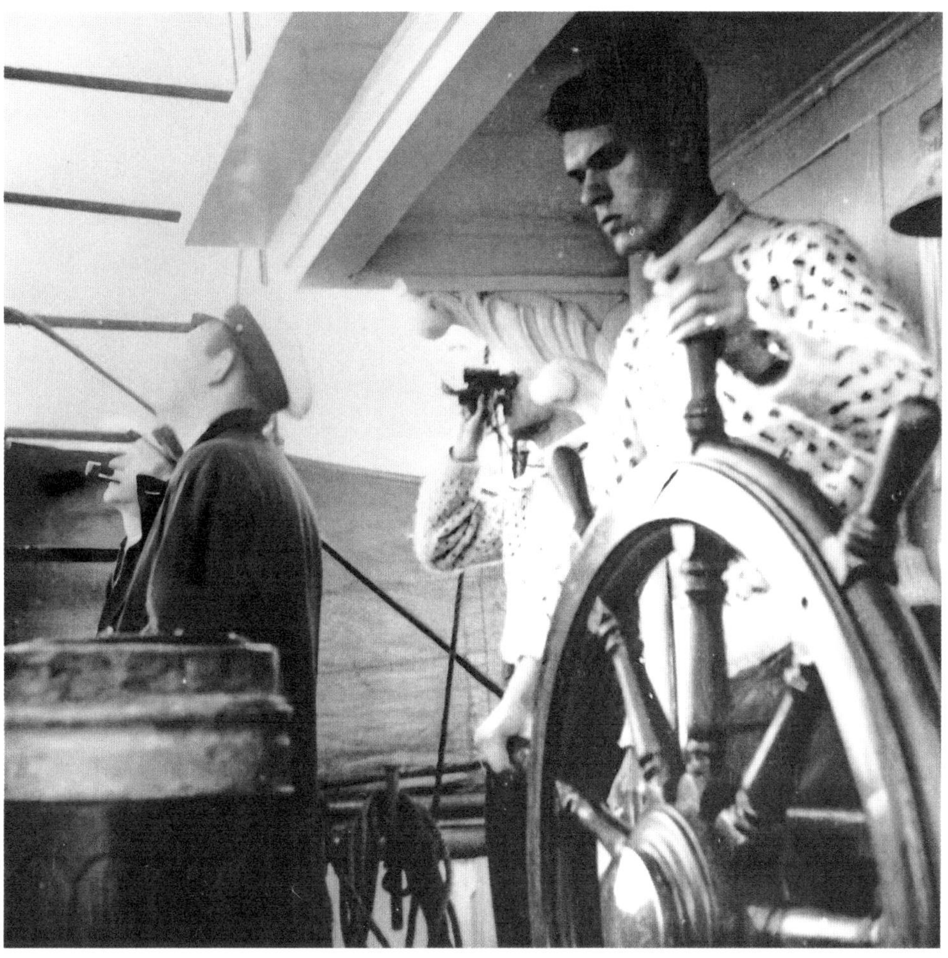

MATE

Pullover with Stranded Colorwork

MATE was inspired by classic Scandinavian fishermen's sweaters with a simple pattern, such as this one worn by the mate on the SS *Godthåb* in a photo from the 1940s.

The sweater has a two-color stranded knitting motif of staggered "lice." Easy to knit, this pullover was designed with raglan sleeves, a doubled ribbed neckband, and ribbing to edge the sleeves and body.

The MATE sweater was knit with Norwegian 3-ply worsted-spun wool from Rauma Garn. The yarn is lofty and strong, so it holds the sweater shaping and ribbing well.

MATE

PATTERN SUITABLE FOR EXPERIENCED KNITTERS

SIZES	S (M, L, XL, 2XL)
FINISHED MEASUREMENTS	
Chest Circumference	40¼ (42½, 45, 47¼, 49¾) in / 102 (108, 114, 120, 126) cm
Length	25½ (26½, 27¼, 28, 28¾) in / 65 (67, 69, 71, 73) cm
Sleeve Length	21 (21¼, 21¾, 22, 22½) in / 53 (54, 55, 56, 57) cm
GAUGE	21 sts × 30 rnds = 4 × 4 in / 10 × 10 cm in Stockinette with larger-size needles. Make a gauge swatch before you begin knitting to ensure that you are working at the correct gauge. Adjust needle size if necessary to obtain correct gauge.
MATERIALS	
Yarn	3-ply Strikkegarn by Rauma Garn (100% Norwegian wool, 118 yd [108 m] / 50 g)
Yarn Amounts	**MC:** 159 Navy Blue: 8 (9, 10, 11, 12) skeins / **CC:** 101 Natural White: 2 (3, 3, 4, 4) skeins
Needles	US sizes 2½ and 4 (3 and 3.5 mm): 32 in (80 cm) circulars and sets of 5 dpns if you are not using magic loop
Notions	8 stitch markers

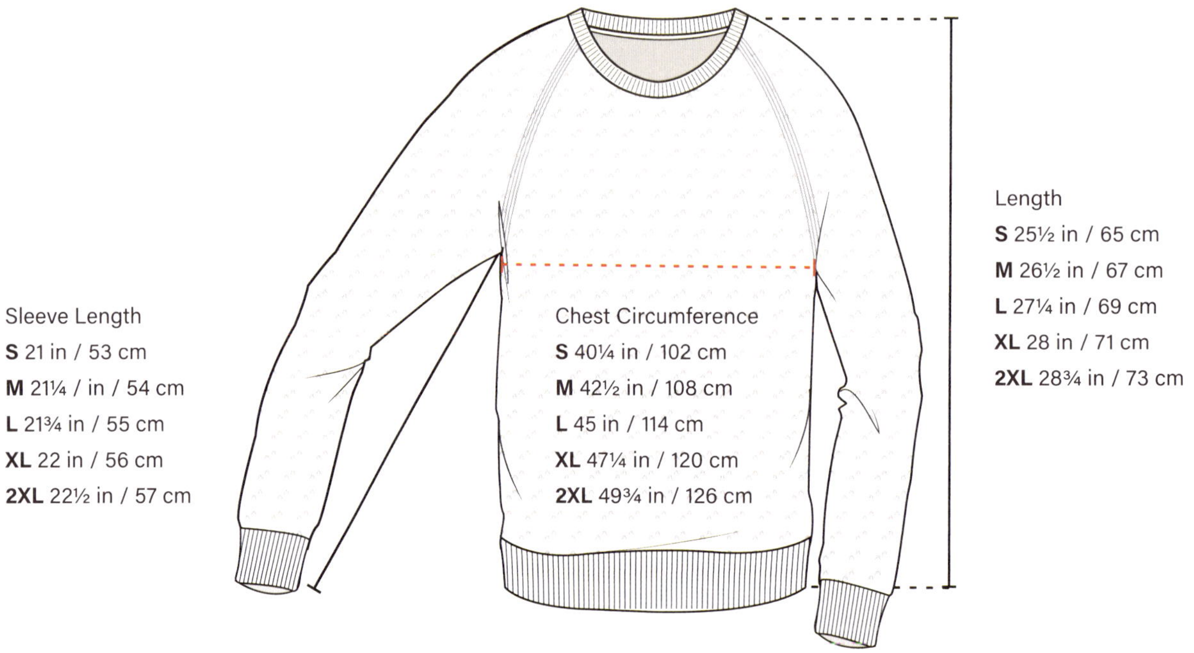

Garment Construction

The sweater is worked from the top down in two-color stranded knitting. It begins with the yoke and shoulders worked back and forth flat, while shaping the neck with increases. Then the pieces are joined and the yoke is knit in the round. After the yoke is complete, the piece is divided for body and sleeves, which are then each worked separately. The body and sleeves are worked straight down and finished with ribbed edgings. Finally, you'll pick up and knit stitches around the neckline for the doubled neckband. The pullover is worked in Stockinette with simple 3-stitch-wide raglan bands. The colorwork motif is an easily repeated pattern.

Yoke

With MC and larger-size circular needle, CO 74 (80, 82, 86, 88) sts. The yoke begins on WS and is worked back and forth following chart for two-color pattern. Purl 1 row. Begin Pattern Chart in the lower right corner. When the raglan shaping begins, work new sts into color pattern. The raglan increases are always made on RS and worked in MC. The three raglan sts between the raglan increases are always worked in MC in Stockinette.

Pattern Chart

Row 1 (WS): With MC, purl, and, *at the same* time, place markers: P1, pm, p3 (raglan sts), pm, p10 (11, 11, 12, 12) (left sleeve), pm, p3 (raglan sts), pm, p40 (44, 46, 48, 50) (back), pm, p3 (raglan sts), pm, p10 (11, 11, 12, 12) (right sleeve), pm, p3 (raglan sts), pm, p1.

Row 2 (RS): Work in Color Pattern to next marker, *M1R, k3 (raglan sts), M1L, work in Color Pattern to next marker*; rep from * to * 2 more times, M1R, k3 (raglan sts), M1L, work in Color Pattern to end = 8 sts increased.
Row 3: Purl, working new sts into Color Pattern.
Row 4: Work as for Row 2.
Rep Rows 3–4 a total of 8 times, ending with a WS row = 138 (144, 146, 150, 152) sts.

Now begin increasing for the neck, continuing the raglan increases as est on RS of work:
Row 1, Neck Increases: K1, M1L, *knit to next marker, M1R, k3, M1L*; rep from * to * until 1 st rem, M1R, k1.
Row 2, Neck Increases: Purl.
Rep Rows 1 and 2 a total of 4 (4, 4, 5, 5) times.

Continuing in pattern, CO 30 (34, 36, 36, 38) sts with MC and join to work in the round = a total of 208 (218, 222, 236, 240) sts; pm for beginning of rnd. Continue raglan shaping on every other rnd as est until you've worked a total of 22 (22, 24, 27, 32) rnds of raglan shaping = a total of 288 (298, 318, 348, 392) sts. Now begin working raglan increases only on every third rnd.

Continue until you've worked a total of 32 (34, 37, 38, 41) raglan increase rows/rnds = a total of 368 (394, 422, 436, 464) sts. Divide piece for body and sleeves: Place the two sets of sleeve sts on separate holders = 74 (79, 85, 88, 94) sts + 0 (3, 1, 0, 3) raglan sts for each sleeve (the last rem raglan sts will go to the body) = 220 (230, 250, 260, 270) sts rem for body.

Body

Now work body separately. Pm at each side. Continue working Color Pattern as est until piece measures 12¼ (12¾, 13, 13½, 13¾) in / 31 (32, 33, 34, 35) cm from underarm, finishing with 4 rnds in MC. Cut CC and continue with only MC. Knit 1 rnd, decreasing 12 (14, 18, 19, 22) sts evenly spaced as follows:
Size S: (K15, k2tog) 12 times.
Size M: K3, (k14, k2tog) 14 times, k3.
Size L: K5, (k11, k2tog) 18 times, k5.
Size XL: K2, (k11, k2tog) 19 times, k1.
Size 2XL: K2, (k10, k2tog) 22 times, k2.
= 192 (216, 226, 231, 246) sts rem.

Begin ribbing: Change to smaller-size circular needle and work k1, p1 ribbing for 2½ in / 6 cm. BO with your favorite stretchy bind-off method.

Two-Color Stranded Knitting Pattern

Colors

Navy Blue 159

Natural White 101

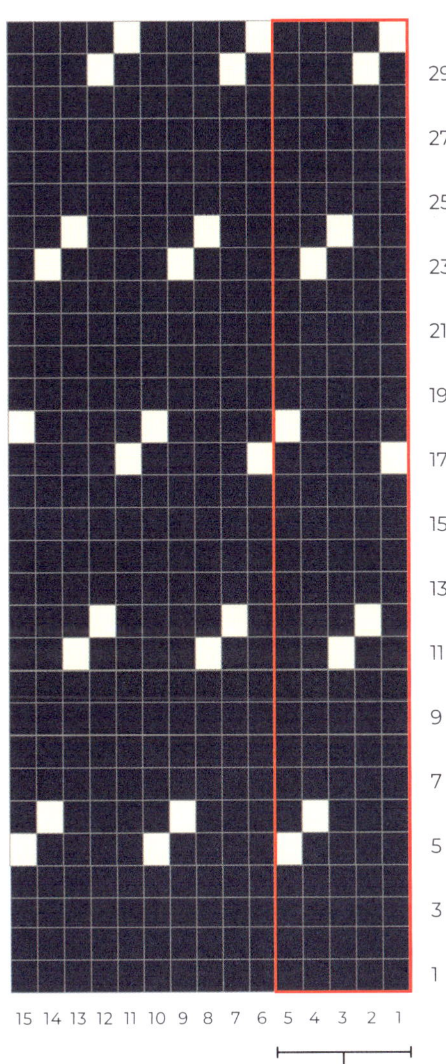

Begin working the chart in the lower right corner.

Sleeves

Make both sleeves alike. Divide the 74 (82, 86, 88, 97) sts onto larger-size dpns. Join yarn at center of underarm. Pm and join for working in the round, and increase 0 (0, 0, 0, 1) st at beginning of rnd = 74 (82, 86, 88, 98) sts. Continuing in Color Pattern as est, decrease at the markers as follows: *K1, slm, k2tog, knit until 2 sts before marker, k2tog tbl, slm, k1*; rep from * to * every ¾ in / 2 cm 18 (20, 22, 22, 27) times = 38 (42, 42, 44, 46) sts rem. Continue in pattern as est until sleeve measures 21 (21¼, 21¾, 22, 22½) in / 53 (54, 55, 56, 57) cm long. Change to smaller-size dpns and work k1, p1 ribbing until cuff measures 2½ in / 6 cm. BO with your favorite stretchy BO method. Make the second sleeve the same way.

Neckband

The neckband is folded double. With MC, smaller-size circular needle, and RS facing, pick up and knit an even number of sts, approx. 96 (96, 96, 104, 104) sts around neckline. Pm for BOR, join, and work k1, p1 ribbing until neckband measures 2½ in / 6 cm (all sizes). Fold neckband and sew down on WS.

Finishing

Weave in all ends neatly on WS by sewing into the tops of the sts so the yarn won't show on RS.

Wash sweater following instructions on ball band. Lay sweater on a dry towel, pat it out to finished measurements, and leave until completely dry.

CORDAGE

Loose-Fitting Pullover with Cables

Cordage is the word used for three or four cords twisted into a rope—and it is invaluable equipment for a boat.

The CORDAGE pullover features a combination of cables and texture patterns, with the cables as precisely twisted as cord ropes.

Cabled or Aran sweaters, as this type of knitwear design is called, originated on the islands off the west coast of Ireland, the Aran Islands. These warm, durable, cabled sweaters protected outdoor workers and fishermen against the often harsh and stormy Atlantic weather. It has been said that the visual look of the patterns and sweaters was connected to particular locales, which had their own methods of combining the cables and patterns. A cable sweater is an iconic symbol of classic marine and fishermen's clothing—and from the 1950s on, was a huge source of inspiration and a standard of the fashion scene.

CORDAGE has a relaxed silhouette. It is designed with alternating texture patterns of half-brioche, ribbing, and cables. It has raglan sleeves, a wide, medium-tall collar, and ribbing on the sleeve cuffs and lower edge of the body. CORDAGE is knit with a 100% Norwegian three-ply wool yarn.

CORDAGE

PATTERN SUITABLE FOR EXPERIENCED KNITTERS

SIZES	S (M, L, XL, 2XL)
FINISHED MEASUREMENTS	
Chest Circumference	39½ (42½, 45¾, 48¾, 52) in / 100 (108, 116, 124, 132) cm
Length	20½ (21¼, 22, 22¾, 23¾) in / 52 (54, 56, 58, 60) cm
Sleeve Length	17 (17¾, 18½, 19¼, 20) in / 43 (45, 47, 49, 51) cm
GAUGE	27 sts × 32 rnds = 4 × 4 in / 10 × 10 cm in Stockinette with larger-size needles. Make a gauge swatch before you begin knitting to ensure that you are working at the correct gauge. Adjust needle size if necessary to obtain correct gauge.
MATERIALS	
Yarn	Tynn Peer Gynt by Sandnes Garn (100% Norwegian wool, 224 yd / 205 m per 50 g)
Yarn Amounts	7 (8, 9, 10, 11) skeins
Needles	US sizes 1.5 and 2.5 / 2.5 and 3 mm: 32 in / 80 cm circulars and sets of 5 dpns if you are not using magic loop
Notions	15 stitch markers; cable needle

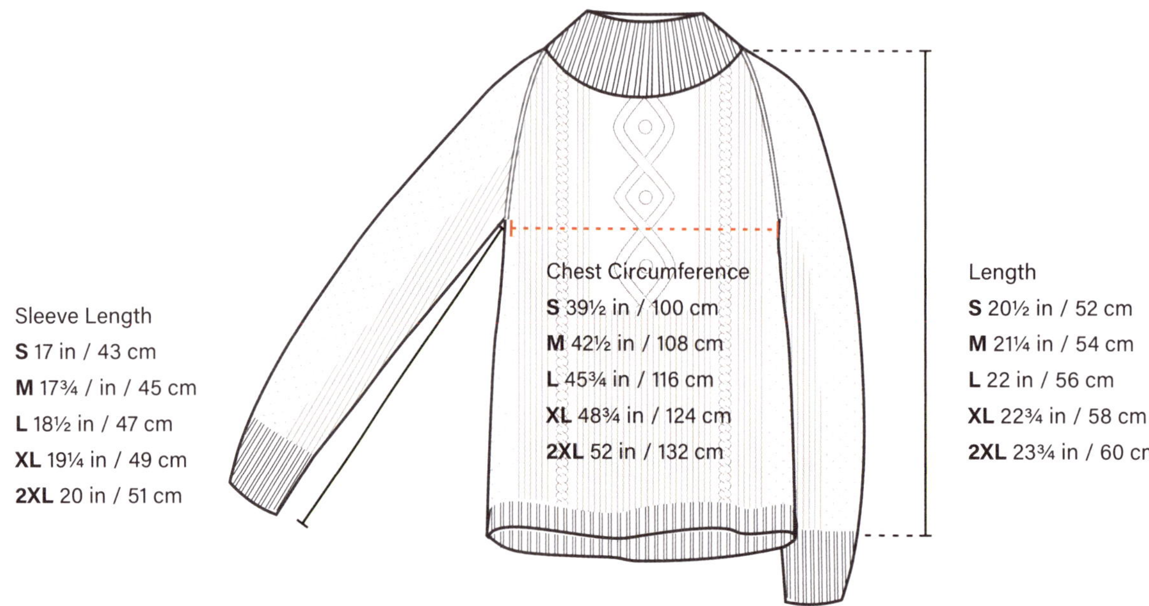

Garment Construction

CORDAGE is worked from the bottom up. The body is worked first and then the sleeves before they are all joined on a circular needle for the yoke. Finally, stitches are picked up and knit for the collar around the neckline.

Body

With smaller-size circular needle, CO 302 (322, 346, 354, 386) sts. Join to work in the rnd, being careful not to twist cast-on row. Place markers and begin ribbing: Pm (right side, BOR), work k1, p1 ribbing for 151 (161, 173, 177, 193) sts, pm (left side), work ribbing to end of rnd. Continue in ribbing for 2½ in / 6 cm. On the last rnd of ribbing, decrease 26 (22, 30, 14, 30) sts evenly spaced as follows:
Size S: K2tog, (k10, k2tog) 25 times.
Size M: K13, k2tog, (k12, k2tog) 21 times, k13.
Size L: K3, k2tog, (k10, k2tog) 28 times, k3, k2tog.
Size XL: K6, k2tog, (k24, k2tog) 13 times, k8.
Size 2XL: K9, k2tog, (k11, k2tog) 28 times, k9, k2tog.
= 276 (300, 316, 340, 356) sts rem.

Change to larger-size circular needle and, *at the same time,* place markers for pattern as you slip sts to the larger needle: *Sl 24 (30, 34, 40, 44) sts (Moss st), pm, sl 15 sts (Half-Brioche), pm, sl 10 sts (Cable), pm, sl 41 sts (Half-Brioche), pm, sl 10 sts (Cable), pm, sl 15 sts (Half-Brioche), pm, sl 23 (29, 33, 39, 43) sts (Moss st)*; rep from * to * on back.

Now begin patterns: See Pattern 1, Worked up to Yoke for stitch patterns. *Work 24 (30, 34, 40, 44) sts in Moss st, 15 sts Half-Brioche, 10 sts Cable, 41 sts Half-Brioche, 10 sts Cable, 15 sts in Half-Brioche, 23 (29, 33, 39, 43) sts in Moss st*; rep from * to * on back. Continue in pattern as est until body measures approx. 8¼ (9, 9½, 9¾, 10¾) in / 21 (23, 24, 25, 27) cm.

Begin front yoke pattern as follows (keeping back pattern as est): Work 24 (30, 34, 40, 44) sts Moss st, 15 sts Half-Brioche, 10 sts Cable, 5 sts Half-Brioche, pm, work 2 purl sts, work 27 sts Diamond pattern, work 2 purl sts, pm, 5 sts Half-Brioche, 10 sts Cable, 15 sts Half-Brioche, 23 (29, 33, 39, 43) sts Moss st, slm, work in pattern as est across back sts.

Continue in pattern as est until body measures approx. 10¼ (11, 11½, 11¾, 12¾) in / 26 (28, 29, 30, 32) cm, ending with Rnd 21 of Diamond pattern. On next rnd, continuing in pattern as est, BO for underarms as follows: At beginning of rnd, BO 5 sts, work to 5 sts before left side marker, BO 10 sts, work to 5 sts before BOR, BO 5 sts = 256 (280, 296, 320, 336) sts rem. Make note of last rnd of Moss st worked. Cut yarn and set body side.

Pattern 1, Worked up to Yoke

Moss Stitch (worked over a multiple of 2 sts / 4 rnds or rows)
Rnd/Row 1: *P1, k1*; rep from * to *.
Rnds/Rows 2 and 4: Work sts as they appear.
Rnds 3–4: *K1, p1*; rep from * to *.
Rep Rnds/Rows 1–4 for pattern.

Half-Brioche in the Round worked over a multiple of 2 sts / 2 rnds or rows)
Rnd/Row 1: *K1 in st below, p1*; rep from * to * until 1 st rem, k1 in st below.
Rnd/Row 2: Work sts as they appear.
Rep Rnds/Rows 1 and 2 for pattern.

6-st Left Cable (worked over 10 sts / 4 rnds or rows)
Rnd/Row 1: P2, slip 3 sts onto cn and hold in front of work, k3, k3 from cn.
Rnds/Rows 2–4: Work sts as they appear.
Rep Rnds 1–4 for pattern.

CORDAGE Chart Symbols

Half-Brioche st: knit 1 in st below

Knit on RS, purl on WS

Purl on RS, knit on WS

6-st left cable: Slip 3 sts onto cn and hold in front of work, k3, k3 from cn.

4-st left cable: Slip 3 sts onto cn and hold in front of work, p1, k3 from cn.

4-st right cable: Slip 1 purl st onto cn and hold in back of work, k3, p1 from cn.

7-st left cable: Slip 3 sts onto cn and hold in front of work, k3, p1, k3 from cn.

Bobble: (P1, k1, p1, k1) in same st; turn. P4; turn, k4; turn, p4; turn. Sl 2 sts to right needle, k2tog, pass 2 slipped sts over; tighten.

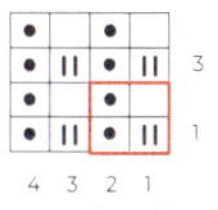

Half-Brioche repeat 2 sts
Repeat as instructed in pattern.

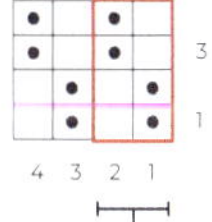

Moss repeat 2 sts
Work as instructed in pattern.

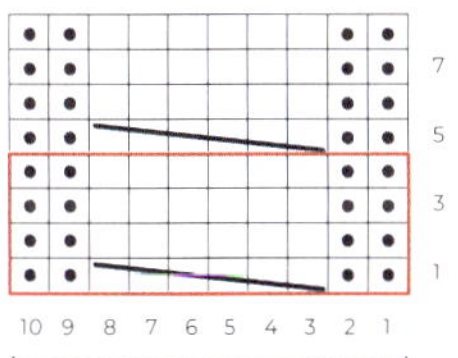

Cable 10 sts
Work as instructed in pattern.

Pattern 2

Diamond Pattern (worked over 27 sts and 31 rnds or rows)

Rnd/Row 1: P10, k3, p1, k3, p10.

Rnd/Row 2 and all following even-numbered rnds: Work sts as they face you.

Rnd/Row 3: P10, sl 3 sts onto cn and hold in front of work, p1, k3, k3 from cn, p10.

Rnd/Row 5: P9, sl 1 purl st onto cn and hold in back of work, k3, p1 from cn, p1, sl 3 knit sts onto cn and hold in front of work, p1, k3 from cn, p9.

Rnd/Row 7: P8, sl 1 purl st onto cn and hold in back of work, k3, p1 from cn, p3, sl 3 knit sts onto cn and hold in front of work, p1, k3 from cn, p8.

Rnd/Row 9: P7, sl 1 purl st onto cn and hold in back of work, k3, p1 from cn, p5, sl 3 knit sts onto cn and hold in front of work, p1, k3 from cn, p7.

Rnd/Row 11: P6, sl 1 purl st onto cn and hold in back of work, k3, p1 from cn, p7, sl 3 knit sts onto cn and hold in front of work, p1, k3 from cn, p6.

Rnd/Row 13: P5, sl 1 purl st onto cn and hold in back of work, k3, p1 from cn, p9, sl 3 knit sts onto cn and hold in front of work, p1, k3 from cn, p5.

Rnd/Row 15: P4, sl 1 purl st onto cn and hold in back of work, k3, p1 from cn, p11, sl 3 knit sts onto cn and hold in front of work, p1, k3 from cn, p4.

Rnd/Row 17: P3, sl 1 purl st onto cn and hold in back of work, k3, p1 from cn, p13, sl 3 knit sts onto cn and hold in front of work, p1, k3 from cn, p3.

Rnd/Row 19: P2, sl 1 purl st onto cn and hold in back of work, k3, p1 from cn, p15, sl 3 knit sts onto cn and hold in front of work, p1, k3 from cn, p2.

Rnd/Row 21: P2, k3, p8, work bobble (see below), p8, k3, p2.

Rnd/Row 23: P2, sl 3 knit sts onto cn and hold in front of work, p1, k3 from cn, p15, sl 1 purl st onto cn and hold in back of work, k3, p1 from cn, p2.

Rnd/Row 25: P3, sl 3 knit sts onto cn and hold in front of work, p1, k3 from cn, p13, sl 1 purl st onto cn and hold in back of work, k3, p1 from cn, p3.

Rnd/Row 27: P4, sl 3 knit sts onto cn and hold in front of work, p1, k3 from cn, p11, sl 1 purl st onto cn and hold in back of work, k3, p1 from cn, p4.

Rnd/Row 29: P5, sl 3 knit sts onto cn and hold in front of work, p1, k3 from cn, p9, sl 1 purl st onto cn and hold in back of work, k3, p1 from cn, p5.

Rnd/Row 31: P6, sl 3 knit sts onto cn and hold in front of work, p1, k3 from cn, p7, sl 1 purl st onto cn and hold in back of work, k3, p1 from cn, p6.

Rnd/Row 33: P7, sl 3 knit sts onto cn and hold in front of work, p1, k3 from cn, p5, sl 1 purl st onto cn and hold in back of work, k3, p1 from cn, p7.

Rnd/Row 35: P8, sl 3 knit sts onto cn and hold in front of work, p1, k3 from cn, p3, sl 1 purl st onto cn and hold in back of work, k3, p1 from cn, p8.

Rnd/Row 37: P9, sl 3 knit sts onto cn and hold in front of work, p1, k3 from cn, p1, sl 1 purl st onto cn and hold in back of work, k3, p1 from cn, p9.

Rnd/Row 38: Work sts as they appear.

Rep Rnds 3–38 for pattern.

Bobble

(P1, k1, p1, k1) in same st; turn. P4; turn, k4; turn, p4; turn. Sl 2 sts to right needle, k2tog, pass 2 slipped sts over; tighten.

Sleeves

With smaller-size dpns, CO 48 (48, 56, 56, 60) sts. Divide sts onto 4 dpns and join to work in the rnd, being careful not to twist cast-on row. Work k1, p1 ribbing for 3½ in / 9 cm. On the last rnd, increase 4 (4, 8, 8, 8) sts evenly spaced = 52 (52, 64, 64, 68) sts. Change to larger-size dpns; pm for BOR. Now begin pattern (see Sleeve Pattern below): Work 13 (13, 16, 16, 17) sts Half-Brioche, 26 (26, 32, 32, 34) sts in Moss st, 13 (13, 16, 16, 17) sts Half-Brioche (see Sleeve Patterns). *At the same time*, begin shaping sleeve: K1, M1L, work in pattern as est to last st, M1R, k1. Working new sts into Half-Brioche pattern, increase the same way every 1 (1, 1¼, 1¼, 1¼) in / 2.5 (2.5, 3, 3, 3) cm 13 (13, 12, 12, 13) times = 78 (78, 88, 88, 94) sts. Continue in pattern until sleeve measures 17 (17¾, 18½, 19¼, 20) in / 43 (45, 47, 49, 51) cm long, ending with same rnd of Moss st as for body. BO 10 sts for underarm as follows: BO 5 sts, work to 5 sts from end, BO 5 sts = 68 (68, 78, 78, 84) sts rem. Set sleeve aside while you make the second sleeve the same way.

Sleeve Patterns

Half-Brioche in the Round (worked over a multiple of 2 sts / 2 rnds)

Rnd 1: *K1 in st below, p1*; rep from * to *.

Rnd 2: *K1, p1*; rep from * to *.

Rep Rnds 1 and 2.

Moss Stitch (worked over a multiple of 2 sts / 4 rnds)

Rnds 1–2: *P1, k1*; rep from * to *.

Rnds 3–4: *K1, p1*; rep from * to *.

Rep Rnds 1–4.

CORDAGE

☐	Knit on RS, purl on WS
●	Purl on RS, knit on WS
B	Bobble: (Pl, kl, pl, kl) in same st; turn. P4; turn, k4; turn, p4; turn. Sl 2 sts to right needle, k2tog, pass 2 slipped sts over; tighten.
	4-st left cable: Slip 3 sts onto cn and hold in front of work, pl, k3 from cn
	4-st right cable: Slip l st onto cn and hold in back of work, k3, pl from cn
	7-st left cable: Slip 3 sts onto cn and in front of work, k3, pl, k3 from cn

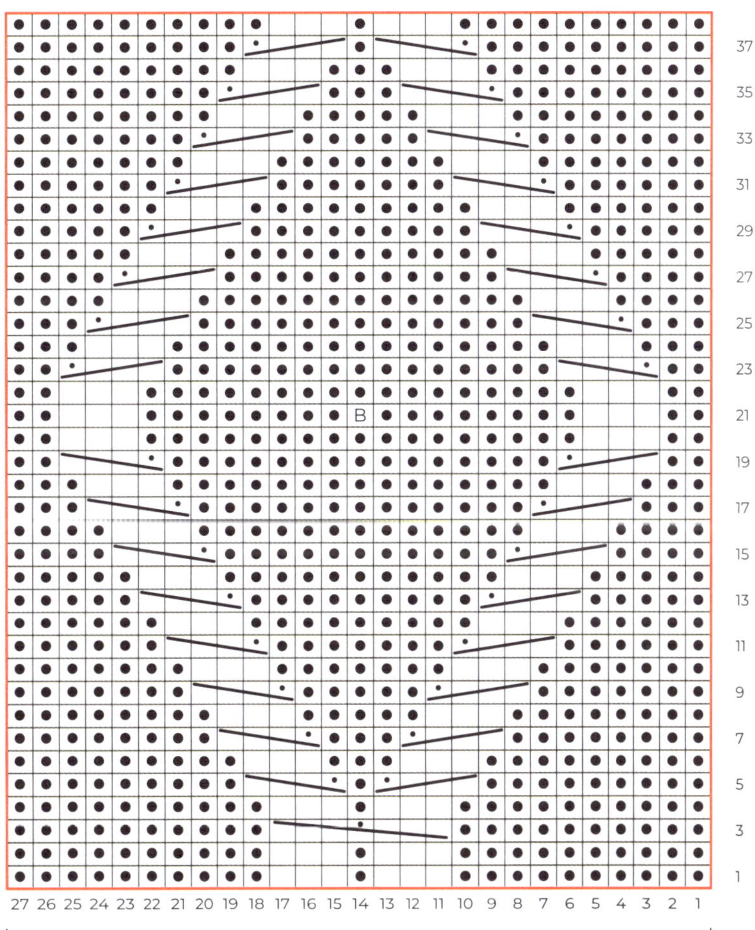

Diamond Pattern 27 sts

Join Body and Sleeves for Yoke

The Moss st patterns should align on the sleeves and body. Arrange the body and sleeves on larger-size circular needle, matching underarms. The rnd begins at the left shoulder on back of sweater. Begin raglan shaping by placing 4 markers, 1 between each intersection of body and sleeve:
Marker 1: Work pattern to next intersection, pm.
Marker 2: Work pattern to next intersection, pm.
Marker 3: Work pattern to next intersection, pm.
Marker 4: Work pattern to last intersection, pm.
= a total of 402 (426, 462, 486, 514) sts.

Raglan Shaping

Work 1 rnd in pattern as est. Begin decreasing at each marker, working Moss st between the raglan decreases on the sleeves, while the pattern on the front and back continues as est.
NOTE: The raglan st is always knit on rounds without decreases.
Raglan decrease rnd: Work as est until 1 st before marker, sl st to right needle, remove marker, move slipped st back to left needle, pm on right needle, sl 2 sts to right needle as if to k2tog, k1, pass the 2 slipped sts over the knit st; decrease the same way at each marker = 8 sts decreased.

Work a total of 32 (32, 34, 36, 38) raglan decrease rnds, decreasing on every 3rd rnd.

NOTE: Once you are working back and forth after binding off for the neck, raglan decreases are worked the opposite way on WS so the raglan lines will look the same on the front all the way through.
On WS: Purl until 2 sts before marker, p2tog, p3, p2tog tbl.

When the sweater measures 17¾ (18½, 19, 19¼, 20¼) in / 45 (47, 48, 49, 51) cm, begin neck shaping while continuing raglan decreases and pattern as est.

Neck Shaping

Decrease for the neckline on a round without raglan shaping as follows: Work to marker 3, BO the center 41 (41, 41, 41, 41) sts for front neck and continue to end of rnd in pattern as est. Cut yarn. Now work back and forth in pattern, and, *at the same time*, BO for neck shaping at the beginning of every row. Begin at neck on left side: BO 1 st at beginning of next 16 (18, 38, 42, 50) rows. After the last raglan decrease, BO rem sts.

Neckband

The neckband is worked in ribbing. With smaller-size dpns, pick up and knit an even number of sts, approx. 132 (138, 138, 144, 144) sts around neck. Pm for BOR, join, and work k1, p1 ribbing for 3½ in / 9 cm. BO using your favorite stretchy BO method.

Finishing

Weave in all ends neatly on WS by sewing into the tops of the sts so the yarn won't show on RS.

Seam underarms with WS facing.

Wash sweater following instructions on ball band. Lay sweater on a dry towel, pat it out to finished measurements, and leave until completely dry.

KNITS INSPIRED BY FISHING NETS AND SAILOR COLLARS

INSPIRATION

Fishing Nets
Net Structure
Airy Look
Sailor Collar
Oversize Silhouette

NETTIE

Pullover with Fishing Net Texture

A fishing net, with its open structure, was the inspiration for both NETTIE's name and its somewhat see-through and airy look. From raw to delicate!

NETTIE is a textured sweater with drop-shoulder sleeves, a wide neckline, and oversize silhouette. The shoulders are broad; the sleeves are attached farther down than on a classic sweater. The neckline, sleeves, and body are all edged with a narrow band of ribbing.

NETTIE is a loose-fitting and very soft sweater knit with a 45 percent silk, 33 percent mohair, 22 percent baby alpaca yarn. It can be worn with a T-shirt or, for more festive occasions, over a little top.

NETTIE

PATTERN SUITABLE FOR EXPERIENCED KNITTERS

SIZES	S (M, L, XL, 2XL)
FINISHED MEASUREMENTS	
Chest Circumference	44 (47¼, 50½, 53½, 56¾) in / 112 (120, 128, 136, 144) cm
Length	19¾ (21¼, 22¾, 23¾, 24½, 26) in / 50 (54, 58, 60, 62, 66) cm
Sleeve Length	17¾ (18¼, 18½, 19, 19¼) in / 45 (46, 47, 48, 49) cm
GAUGE	30 sts × 40 rnds = 4 × 4 in / 10 × 10 cm in ribbing and 24 sts × 40 rnds = 4 × 4 in / 10 × 10 cm in Fishing Net pattern, with two strands of Deluxe Silk Mohair held together. Make a gauge swatch before you begin knitting to ensure that you are working at the correct gauge. Adjust needle size if necessary to obtain correct gauge.
MATERIALS	
Yarn	Deluxe Silk Mohair by Krea Deluxe (45% silk, 33% mohair, 22% baby alpaca, 262 yd / 240 m / 20 g)
Yarn Amounts	8 (9, 10, 12, 13) balls
Needles	US size 2½ / 3 mm: 32 in / 80 cm circular and set of 5 dpns if you are not using magic loop
Notions	4 stitch markers; cable needle

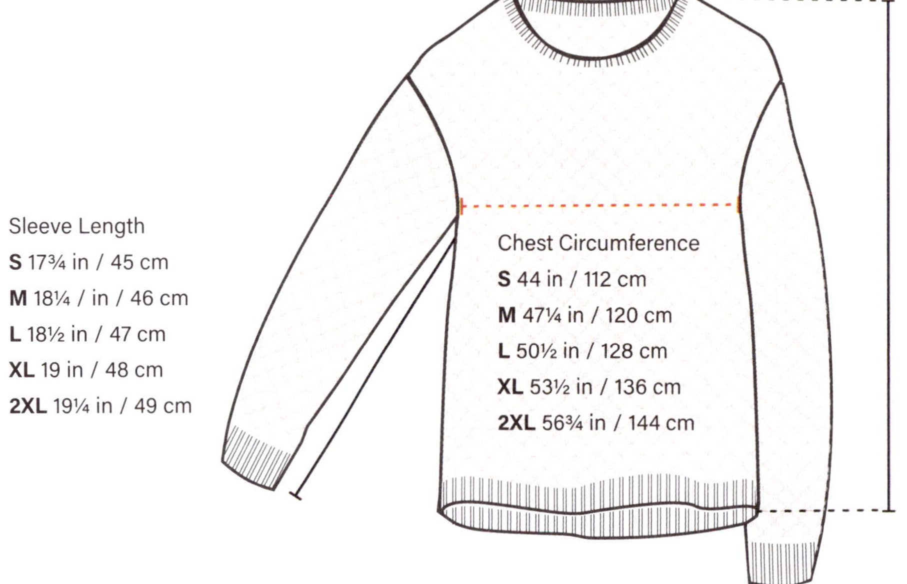

Garment Construction

NETTIE is worked from the bottom up. The body is divided at the underarms and then the back and front are worked separately. Finally, stitches are picked up and knit for the sleeves, which are worked top down.

Body

With circular needle and holding two strands of Deluxe Silk Mohair together, CO 276 (300, 324, 348, 372) sts. Join to work in the rnd, being careful not to twist cast-on row. Place markers and begin ribbing: Pm (BOR), work k1, p1 ribbing for 138 (150, 162, 174, 186) sts, pm, work k1, p1 ribbing for 138 (150, 162, 174, 186) sts. Continue in ribbing for 1½ in / 4 cm. On the last rnd of ribbing, pm on both sides of sweater for 8-st bands as follows: Work 4 sts in ribbing, pm, work 130 (142, 154, 166, 178) sts in ribbing, pm, work 8 sts in ribbing, pm, continue in ribbing to last 4 sts, pm, work 4 sts in ribbing.

Knit 1 rnd, *at the same time* decreasing 12 (12, 12, 12, 12) sts evenly spaced on front and back *between markers* = decrease 6 (6, 6, 6, 6) sts each on front and back as follows:
Size S: K9, (k2tog, k20) 5 times, k2tog, k9.
Size M: K10, (k2tog, k22) 5 times, k2tog, k10.
Size L: K14, (k2tog, k23) 5 times, k2tog, k13.
Size XL: K17, (k2tog, k24) 5 times, k2tog, k17.
Size 2XL: *K21, (k2tog, k25) 5 times, k2tog, k20*, rep from * to *.
= 264 (288, 312, 336, 360) sts total and 132 (144, 156, 168, 180) sts each for front and back rem.

Now begin pattern on front and back (see Fishing Net—Body). Always knit the 8 marked-off sts; work Fishing Net between the inner markers on front and back as follows:

Fishing Net—Body (in the Round)

Worked over a multiple of 4 sts / 8 rnds
Rnd 1: K1, yo, *sl 1 knitwise, k1, psso, k2tog, yo 2 times*; rep from * to * to last 5 sts, sl 1 knitwise, k1, psso, k2tog, yo, k1.
Rnd 2: P2, k1, *k1, k1 in front of yarnover, k1 in back of yarnover, k1*; rep from * to * to last 3 sts, k1, p2.
Rnd 3: K1, p1, *sl 1 onto cn and hold in front of work, k1, k1 from cn, p2*; rep from * to * to last 4 sts, sl 1 onto cn and hold in front of work, k1, k1 from cn, p1, k1.
Rnd 4: P2, *k2, p2*; rep from * to *.
Rnd 5: K1, *k2tog, yo 2 times, sl 1 knitwise, k1, psso*; rep from * to * to last st, k1.
Rnd 6: P1, k1, *k1 in front of yarnover, k1 in back of yarnover, k2*; rep from * to * to last 3 sts, k1 in front of yarnover, k1 in back of yarnover, k1, p1.
Rnd 7: K2, p2, *sl 1 onto cn and hold in front of work, k1, k1 from cn, p2*; rep from * to * to last 2 sts, k2.
Rnd 8: P1, k1, *p2, k2*; rep from * to * to last 4 sts, p2, k1, p1.
Rep Rnds 1–8 for pattern.

Work Rnds 1–8 of Fishing Net—Body (in the Round) until body measures 12¾ (13½, 14¼, 15, 15¾) in / 32 (34, 36, 38, 40) cm and then divide for back and front, each to be worked back and forth. Make note of last round worked in Fishing Net pattern. *At the same time,* divide the side bands so there are 4 sts at each side of front and back = 132 (144, 156, 168, 180) sts, including side bands.

Back

Working back and forth on back sts only, continue in Fishing Net (Round), beginning with row following last rnd worked in Fishing Net (in the Round). CO 1 new st at beginning of rnd and 1 st at end of rnd for edge sts along armholes on front and back. Edge sts are always knit on every row. Edge sts are not included in stitch counts.

Fishing Net (Flat)

Worked over a multiple of 4 sts + 2 / 8 rows
Rnd 1 (RS): K1, yo, *sl 1 knitwise, k1, psso, k2tog, yo twice*; rep from * to * to last 5 sts, sl 1 knitwise, k1, psso, k2tog, yo, k1.
Row 2: K2, p2, *p1 into front and back of double yo, p2*; rep from * to * to last 2 sts, k2.
Row 3: K1, p1, *LC, p2*; rep from * to * to last 4 sts, LC, p1, k1.
Row 4: K2, *p2, k2*; rep from * to *.
Row 5: K1, *k2tog, yo twice, sl 1 knitwise, k1, psso*; rep from * to * last st, k1.
Row 6: K1, p1, p1 into front and back of double yo, *p2, p1 into front and back of double yo*; rep from * to * to last 2 sts, p1, k1.
Row 7: K2, *p2, LC*; rep from * to * to last 4 sts, p2, k2.
Row 8: K1, p1, k2, *p2, k2*; rep from * to * to last 2 sts, p1, k1.
Rep. Rows 1–8 for pattern.

Work even in Fishing Net (Flat) until piece measures 18½ (20, 21¾, 23¼, 24¾) in / 47 (51, 55, 59, 63) cm, then place the center 50 (56, 60, 66, 72) sts on a holder as follows:
Size S: Work 41 sts, set aside 50 sts, work 41 sts.
Size M: Work 44 sts, set aside 56 sts, work 44 sts.
Size L: Work 48 sts, set aside 60 sts, work 48 sts.
Size XL: Work 51 sts, set aside 66 sts, work 51 sts.
Size 2XL: Work 54 sts, set aside 72 sts, work 54 sts.
= 41 (44, 48, 51, 54) sts rem for each shoulder.
Now work each shoulder separately, *at the same time*, shaping neckline at the beginning of each row: BO 2 sts at neck edge once, then BO 1 st at neck edge = a total of 38 (41, 45, 48, 51) sts rem. Work even as est until piece measures 19¾ (21¼, 22¾, 23¾, 24½, 26) in / 50 (54, 58, 62, 66) cm. Place the rem 38 (41, 45, 48, 51) shoulder sts on a spare needle. Work the opposite shoulder the same way, binding off at neck edge to mirror shaping.

Front

When piece measures 17¼ (19, 20½, 21¼, 22¾) in / 44 (48, 52, 54, 58) cm, place the center 44 (50, 50, 54, 58) sts on a holder for front neck as follows:
Size S: Work 44 sts, set aside 44 sts, work 44 sts.
Size M: Work 47 sts, set aside 50 sts, work 47 sts.
Size L: Work 53 sts, set aside 50 sts, work 53 sts.
Size XL: Work 57 sts, set aside 54 sts, work 57 sts.
Size 2XL: Work 61 sts, set aside 58 sts, work 61 sts.
= 44 (47, 53, 57, 61) sts rem for each shoulder.

Work each shoulder separately. BO for neck shaping at beginning of row as follows: *BO 2 sts at neck edge once, then BO 1 st at neck edge 4 (4, 6, 5, 6) times = 38 (41, 45, 48, 51) sts rem. Continue until piece measures 19¾ (21¼, 22¾, 23¾, 24½, 26) in / 50 (54, 58, 62, 66) cm. Place the rem 38 (41, 45, 48, 51) shoulder sts on a spare needle. Work the opposite shoulder the same way, decreasing at neck edge to mirror shaping.

Shoulders

Join each shoulder as follows: Turn work to WS. With left hand, hold the two needles so that RS of the shoulders are together. Join with three-needle bind-off.

Sleeves

With RS facing, beginning at center underarm, pick up and knit approx. 108 (108, 120, 132, 144) sts around armhole. Join, pm for BOR, and beg Fishing Net (Sleeves). *At the same time*, decrease 1 st on each side of marker every ⅜ in / 1 cm as follows: K2tog, work in pattern to last 2 sts, k2tog. Decrease the same way 27 (27, 29, 35, 39) times = 52 (52, 60, 60, 64) sts rem. When sleeve measures 16¼ (16½, 17, 17¼, 17¾) in / 41 (42, 43, 44, 45) cm long, continue in k1, p1 ribbing until cuff measures 1½ in / 4 cm. BO using your favorite stretchy BO method. Make the second sleeve the same way.

You can work the LC on Rnds/Rows 3 and 7 without a cable needle for faster knitting; see page 98.

Fishing Net—Sleeves

Worked over a multiple of 4 sts / 8 rnds

Rnd 1: *Sl 1 knitwise, k1, psso, k2tog, yo 2 times*; rep from * to *.

Rnd 2: *K1, k1 in front of yarnover, k1 in back of yarnover, k1*; rep from * to *.

Rnd 3: *Sl 1 onto cn and hold in front of work, k1, k1 from cn, p2*; rep from * to *.

Rnd 4: *K2, p2*; rep from * to *.

Rnd 5: *K2tog, yo 2 times, sl 1 knitwise, k1, psso*; rep from * to *.

Rnd 6: *K1 in front of yarnover, k1 in back of yarnover, k2*; rep from * to *.

Rnd 7: *Sl 1 onto cn and hold in front of work, k1, k1 from cn, p2*; rep from * to *.

Rnd 8: *K2, p2*; rep from * to *.

Rep Rnds 1–8.

Neckband

Beginning at front with RS facing, pick up and knit an even number of sts, approx. 110 (116, 122, 128, 134) sts around neck, picking up 3 sts for every 4 rows. Join, pm for BOR, and work k1, p1 ribbing for ¾ in / 2 cm. BO using your favorite stretchy BO method.

Finishing

Weave in all ends neatly on WS by sewing into the tops of the sts so the yarn won't show on RS.

Wash sweater following instructions on ball band. Lay sweater on a dry towel, pat it out to finished measurements, and leave until completely dry.

NETTIE Chart Symbols

- Knit on RS, purl on WS
- Purl on RS, knit on WS
- Yo
- K2tog
- Sl 1 knitwise, k1, psso
- Kl into front and back of double yo
- LC (left cross): Knit second st on left needle into back of st and then knit into front of first st.
- Knit this st for all reps except final rep; at end of rnd only, sl this st to right needle, remove BOR marker, sl st back to left needle to be worked at beginning of next rnd, pm for new BOR.

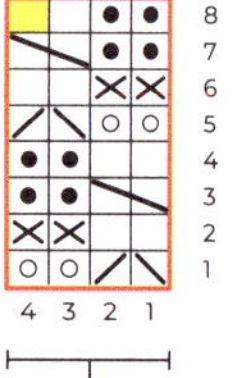

Fishing Net (in the Round)
4-st repeat
work as instructed in pattern

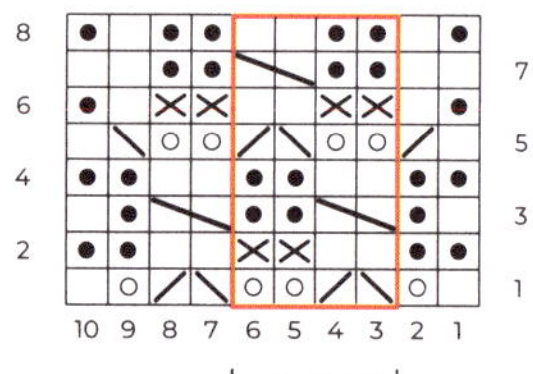

Fishing Net (Flat)
4-st repeat
work as instructed in pattern

ABLE SEAMAN

Textured Sweater with a Sailor's Collar

Sailors' garments, in particular the sailor's collar, are an iconic and an easily recognizable part of the fleet uniform. The ABLE SEAMAN sweater was inspired by both the name and rank of a sailor's post.

ABLE SEAMAN is a textured sweater with a wide sailor's collar, deep neckline, and long ribbing on the sleeve cuffs. The pullover is designed with slits at the sides, and the body has a loose silhouette. Classic and yet totally modern. ABLE SEAMAN is knit with a sunken texture in a blended rope-like yarn, which gives a net-like look.

The yarn for ABLE SEAMAN is an undyed, high-quality eco yarn, a mix of pima cotton and baby alpaca from Isager—a super soft material.

ABLE SEAMAN

PATTERN SUITABLE FOR EXPERIENCED KNITTERS

SIZES	S (M, L, XL, 2XL)
FINISHED MEASUREMENTS	
Chest Circumference	39½ (42½, 45¾, 48¾, 52) in / 100 (108, 116, 124, 132) cm
Length (back)	23¾ (24, 24½, 25¼, 26) in / 60 (61, 62, 64, 66) cm
Sleeve Length	17 (17¾, 18½, 19¼, 20½) in / 43 (45, 47, 49, 51) cm
GAUGE	30 sts × 40 rnds = 4 × 4 in / 10 × 10 cm in Block Pattern. Make a gauge swatch before you begin knitting to ensure that you are working at the correct gauge. Adjust needle size if necessary to obtain correct gauge.
MATERIALS	
Yarn	ECO BABY by Isager (68% baby alpaca, 32% cotton, 164 yd/150 m / 50 g)
Yarn Amounts	9 (10, 11, 2, 13) skeins
Needles	US size 6 / 4 mm: 32 in / 80 cm circular and set of 5 dpns if you are not using magic loop
Notions	4 stitch markers

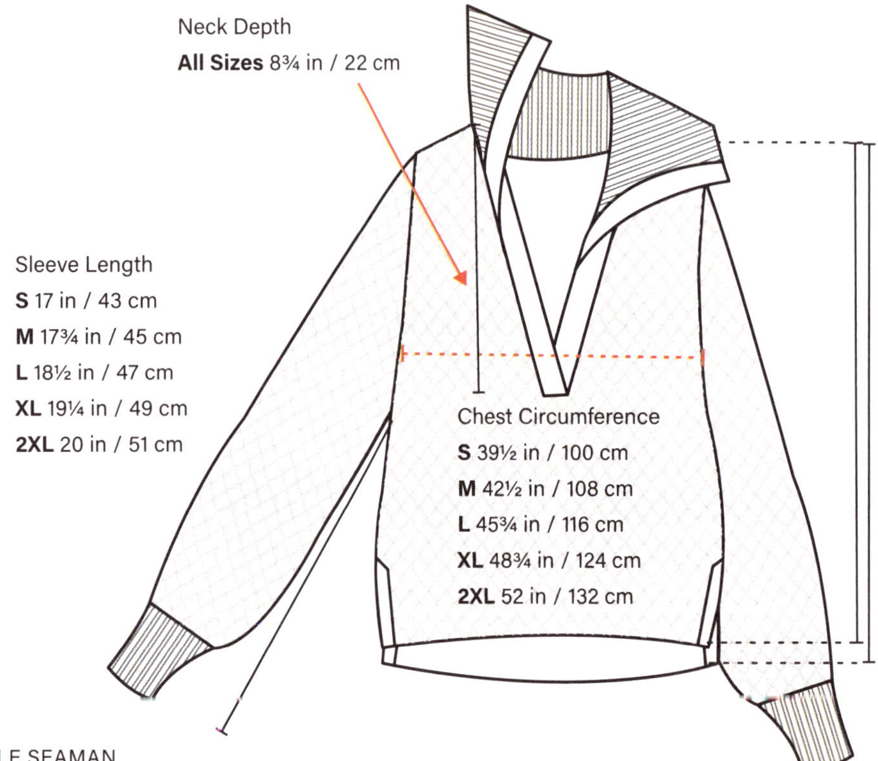

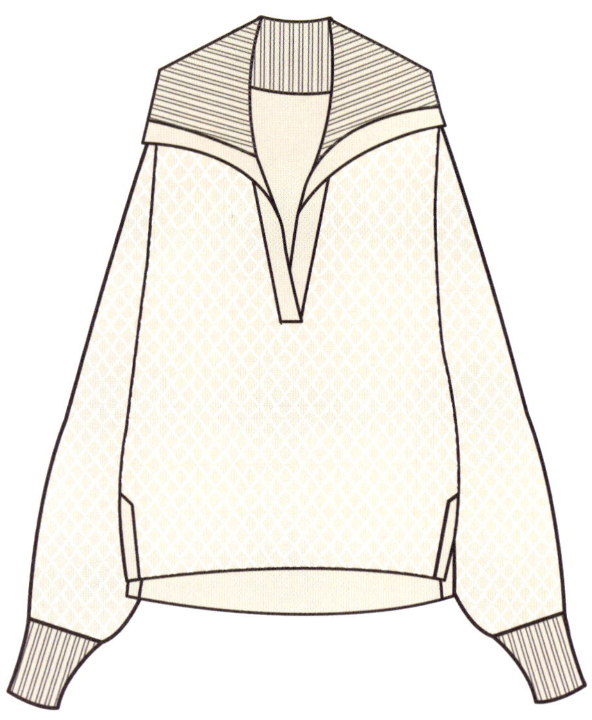

Garment Construction

The body of the sweater is worked from the bottom up. It begins with a split hem in different lengths for the lower edge. The two pieces are then joined for the front and back of the body and knit in the round. The body is divided at the neck opening and then the back and front are worked separately. The sailor's collar is worked last.

Back

With circular needle, CO 150 (162, 174, 186, 198) sts. Work back and forth. The first and last 6 sts are a ribbed edging. Begin back as follows: *k1, p1*, repeat from * to * 3 times total, M1L, then work Row 1 of Block Pattern (Flat) until there are 6 sts left on the needle, M1R, *k1, p1*, repeat from * to * 3 times total. Continue as est, without the increases, until piece measures 5¼ in / 13 cm, ending with Row 12 of pattern. Set back piece aside.

Front

Work as for back until piece measures 4 in / 10 cm, ending with Row 12 of pattern. Leave sts on needle.

Block Pattern (Flat)

NOTE: The odd-numbered rows are the front/RS of the work, while the even-numbered rows are the back or WS. Carefully work the right and left crosses without a cable needle as follows:
RC: Knit the second st on left needle into front of st and then knit first st into front of st.
LC: Knit second st on left needle into back of st and then knit into front of first st.

Worked over a multiple of 6 sts +2 / 12 rows
Row 1: P3, *RC, p4*; rep from * to * to last 5 sts, RC, p3.
Row 2: K3, *p2, k4*; rep from * to * to last 5 sts, p2, k3.

Row 3: *P2, RC, LC*; rep from * to * to last 2 sts, p2.
Row 4: K2, *p1, k2*; rep from * to *.

Row 5: P1, *RC, p2, LC*; rep from * to * to last st, p1.
Row 6: K1, p1, *k4, p2*; rep from * to * to last 6 sts, k4, p1, k1.

Row 7: RC, *p4, RC*; rep from * to *.
Row 8: K1, p1, k4, *p2, k4*; rep from * to * to last 2 sts, p1, k1.

Row 9: P1, *LC, p2, RC*; rep from * to * to last st, p1.
Row 10: K2, *p1, k2*; rep from * to *.

Row 11: *P2, LC, RC*; rep from * to * to last 2 sts, p2.
Row 12: K3, *p2, k4*; rep from * to * to last 5 sts, p2, k3.
Rep Rows 1–12.

Body

Now join the front and back lower edges. Make sure that you begin with the same pattern row on both pieces. The ribbing at the sides is discontinued, and those sts are now included in the Block Pattern. Place back sts to the left of front sts on same needle. Join to work in the rnd and pm for BOR = a total of 300 (324, 348, 372, 396) sts. Now work in pattern over all sts (see Block Pattern in the Round), making sure that motifs align. Continue in pattern as est until body measures 13¾ (14¼, 14½, 15½, 16¼) in / 35 (36, 37, 39, 41) cm on front of body. Now divide body for front and back with a total of 150 (162, 174, 186, 198) sts on each side and begin working back and forth.

Block Pattern (in the Round)

Worked over a multiple of 6 sts / 12 rnds
Rnd 1: P3, *RC, p4*; rep from * to * to last 3 sts, RC, p1.
Rnd 2: P3, *k2, p4*; rep from * to * to last 3 sts, k2, p1.
Rnd 3: *P2, RC, LC*; rep from * to *.
Rnd 4: *P2, k1*; rep from * to *.
Rnd 5: P1, *RC, p2, LC*; rep from * to * to last 5 sts, p1, RC, p2, LC (removing BOR marker and placing it between sts of LC).
Rnd 6: K1, p4, *k2, p4*; rep from * to *.
Rnd 7: *RC, p4*; rep from * to *.
Rnd 8: P1, *k1, p5*; rep from * to * to last 5 sts, k1, p4.
Rnd 9: P1, *LC, p2, RC*; rep from * to * to last 6 sts, p1, LC, p2, RC (working RC over last st of current rnd and first st of following rnd, removing BOR marker and placing it between sts of RC).
Rnd 10: *P2, k1*; rep from * to *.
Rnd 11: *P2, LC, RC*; rep from * to *.
Rnd 12: P3, *k2, p4*; rep from * to * to last 3 sts, k2, p1.
Rep Rnds 1–12 for pattern.

Front

Work decreases for neck and armholes on front of work and, *at the same time*, continue in pattern as est. Begin by placing markers as follows: Work 72 (78, 84, 90, 96) sts in pattern, pm, BO the center 6 front sts and work in pattern to end of rnd = 144 (156, 168, 180, 192) sts rem. Work each side separately = 72 (78, 84, 90, 96) sts on each side. Shape armhole at side: BO 3 sts = 69 (75, 81, 87, 93) sts rem. Begin neck decreases: Use the last st at neck edge as an edge st and knit it on every row: On RS rows, work in pattern to last 3 sts at neck edge, k2tog, k1 (edge st); on WS rows, k1 (edge st), p2tog, work in pattern to end. Rep neck decrease row every 5th (4th, 4th, 3rd, 3rd) row until 51 (54, 57, 60, 63) sts rem and piece measures 22½ (22¾, 23¼, 24, 24¾) in / 57 (58, 59, 61, 63) cm, ending with a WS row. Make note of last row worked in pattern. Place rem sts on a spare needle. Make the opposite side the same way, decreasing at neck edge as above to mirror shaping, and ending with same row as for first side.

Back

Work back and forth, continuing pattern as est. Begin armhole shaping on RS: BO 3 sts at beginning of next 2 rows = 144 (156, 168, 180, 192) sts rem. Continue in pattern until back measures 21¾ (22, 22½, 23¼, 24) in / 55 (56, 57, 59, 61) cm and then BO the center 38 (44, 50, 56, 62) sts for back neck as follows:

Size S: Work 53 sts, BO 38 sts, work 52 sts.
Size M: Work 56 sts, BO 44, work 55 sts.
Size L: Work 59 sts, BO 50, work 58 sts.
Size XL: Work 62 sts, BO 56, work 61 sts.
Size 2XL: Work 65 sts, BO 62, work 64 sts.
NOTE: 1 st remains from last bind-off.
= 53 (56, 59, 62, 65) sts rem for each shoulder.

Work each shoulder separately and shape neck as follows: BO 2 sts at neck edge = a total of 51 (54, 57, 60, 63) sts rem for shoulder. Continue in pattern until back measures 23¾ (24, 24½, 25¼, 26) in / 60 (61, 62, 64, 66) cm, ending with same row of pattern as for front. Place rem 51 (54, 57, 60, 63) shoulder sts on a spare needle. Make the opposite side the same way, decreasing at neck edge as above to mirror shaping.

Shoulders

Join each shoulder as follows: Turn work to WS. With left hand, hold the two needles so that RS of the shoulders are together. Join with three-needle bind-off.

Sleeves

Beginning on front at center of underarm (= BOR), pick up and knit 114 (120, 126, 132, 132) sts around armhole edge; pm for BOR. Begin pattern. Work in pattern until sleeve measures 9 (9½, 9¾, 10¼, 10¾) in / 23 (24, 25, 26, 27) cm long. Now begin decreasing 1 st each side of marker as follows: K2tog, work in pattern to last 2 sts, k2tog. Decrease the same way on every other rnd a total of 21 times = 42 sts decreased and 72 (78, 84, 90, 90) sts rem. When sleeve measures 13¾ (14¼, 14½, 15, 15½) in / 35 (36, 37, 38, 39) cm long, decrease 30 (30, 30, 30, 24) sts evenly spaced as follows:
Size S: K3tog, (k1, k2tog, k2tog) 13 times, k2tog, k2tog.
Size M: K3, k3tog, (k1, k2tog, k2tog) 14 times, k2.
Size L: K4, (k1, k2tog, k2tog) 15 times, k5.
Size XL: (K1, k2tog) 30 times.
Size 2XL: K3, (k1, k2tog, k2, k2tog) 12 times, k3.
NOTE: 1 st remains from last bind-off.
= 42 (48, 54, 60, 66) sts rem.

Continue in k1, p1 ribbing for 3¼, 3½, 4, 4¼, 4¾) in / 8 (9, 10, 11, 12) cm. BO using your favorite stretchy BO method. Make the second sleeve the same way.

Neckband

We recommend using two dpns for this. With RS facing, pick up and knit 1 st at lower edge of neck on left side, slide st to tip of needle. CO 8 sts. Work p1, k1 ribbing to last 3 sts, p1, k2tog, pick up and knit 1 st from neck edge with yarn on left side of work*; turn and work 9 sts as they show, to beginning of row; rep from * to * until you've worked an edging from the beginning of neck to 4¼ in / 11 cm from top of shoulder. When picking up sts along neck edge, pick up 3 sts for every 4 rows so the band lies flat. Place the rem 9 sts on a spare needle. Make the opposite side of neck to match.

Sailor's Collar

With RS of sweater facing, pick up and knit sts starting at right side for the sailor's collar. Begin by slipping the 9 sts on holder to circular needle and then pick up and knit approx. 129 (131, 131, 135, 135) sts around rest of neckline from end of edging to right side; end by working ribbing on the 9 sts on holder. Work k1, p1 ribbing until collar measures 5½ in / 14 cm. BO using your favorite stretchy BO method.

Finishing

Weave in all ends neatly on WS by sewing into the tops of the sts so the yarn won't show on RS.

Sew the left edge of neckband down at base of neck so the 2 edges overlap.

Wash sweater following instructions on ball band. Lay sweater on a dry towel, pat it out to finished measurements, and leave until completely dry.

ABLE SEAMAN Chart Symbols

- Kn t on RS, purl on WS
- Purl on RS, kn t on WS"
- RC (right cross): Knit second st on left needle into front of st and then knit first st into front of st.
- LC (left cross): Knit second st on left needle into back of st and then knit into front of first st.
- Omit this st on first rep of rnd only (it was knit at the end of previous rnd); knit this st on rem reps.
- Purl this st at beginning of rnd only; omit this st for remainder of rnd.
- Omit this st on first rep of rnd only (it was knit at the end of previous rnd); purl this st on rem reps.
- LC; on final rep of rnd only, work LC over last st of current rnd and first st of following rnd, removing BOR marker and placing it between sts of LC.
- RC; on final rep of rnd only, work RC over last st of current rnd and first st of following rnd, removing BOR marker and placing it between sts of RC.

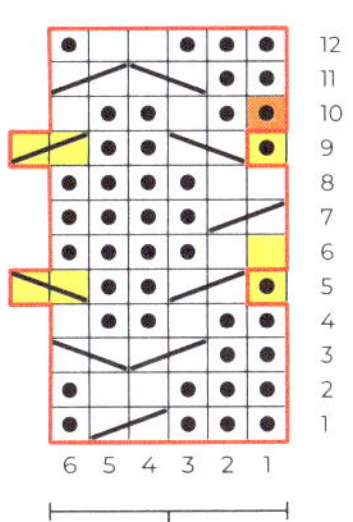

Block Pattern (in the Round)
6-st repeat
work as instructed in pattern

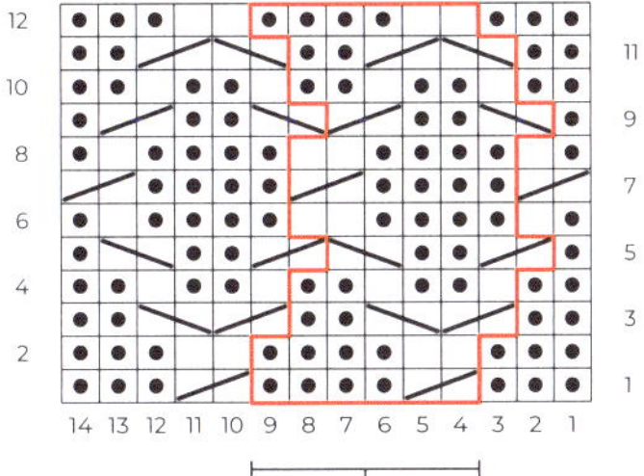

Block Pattern (Flat)
6-st repeat
work as instructed in pattern

Fishing Net texture pattern

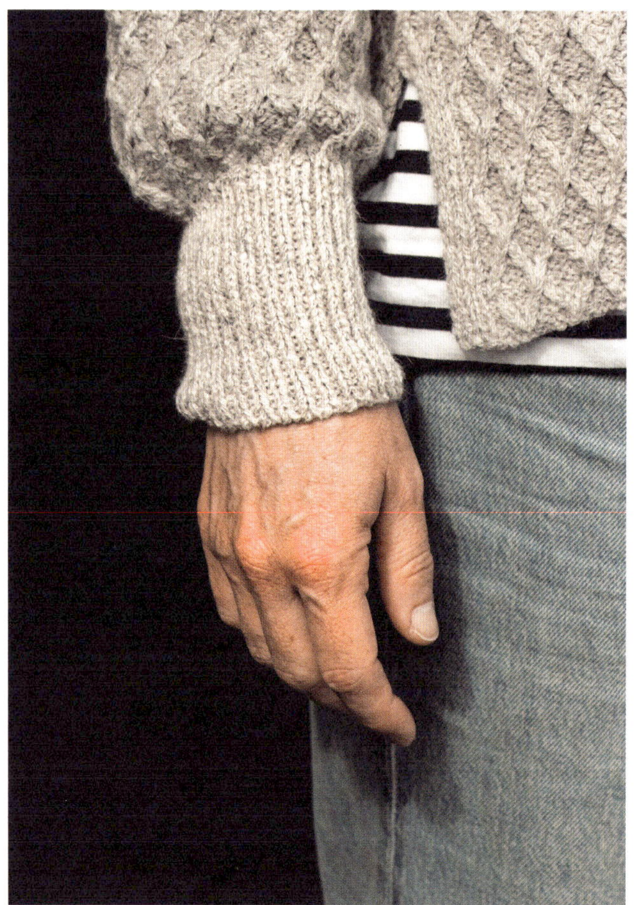

MARTHA

Cardigan with a Texture Pattern

An old maritime tradition is to name ships after women. It has been said that this tradition goes all the way back to the ancient Greeks, who gave ships female names. We were inspired by the ship *Martha* from Helsingør when naming this cardigan.

MARTHA is a long cardigan with wide buttonless front bands. It has high slits at the sides and ribbing on the three-quarter-length sleeves and lower edge of body. The loose-fitting MARTHA was designed with wide shoulders and sewn-on sleeves.

This relaxed cardigan is knit with a soft and pretty 3-ply Peruvian alpaca yarn in a texture pattern.

MARTHA

PATTERN SUITABLE FOR EXPERIENCED KNITTERS

SIZES	S/M (L/XL, 2XL/3XL)
FINISHED MEASUREMENTS	
Chest Circumference	51¼ (59¾, 68½) in / 130 (152, 174) cm
Length	31 (32, 32¾) in / 79 (81, 83) cm
Sleeve Length	10¾ (11½, 12¼) in / 27 (29, 31) cm
GAUGE	22 sts × 30 rows = 4 × 4 in / 10 × 10 cm in texture pattern with 2 strands of yarn held together. Make a gauge swatch before you begin knitting to ensure that you are working at the correct gauge. Adjust needle size if necessary to obtain correct gauge.
MATERIALS	
Yarn	Vilja (formerly Indiecita) by Filcolana (100% alpaca, 175 yd/160 m / 50 g)
Yarn Amounts	20 (24, 26) skeins
Needles	US size 4 / 3.5 mm: 32 in / 80 cm circular and set of 5 dpns if you are not using magic loop
Notions	4 stitch markers

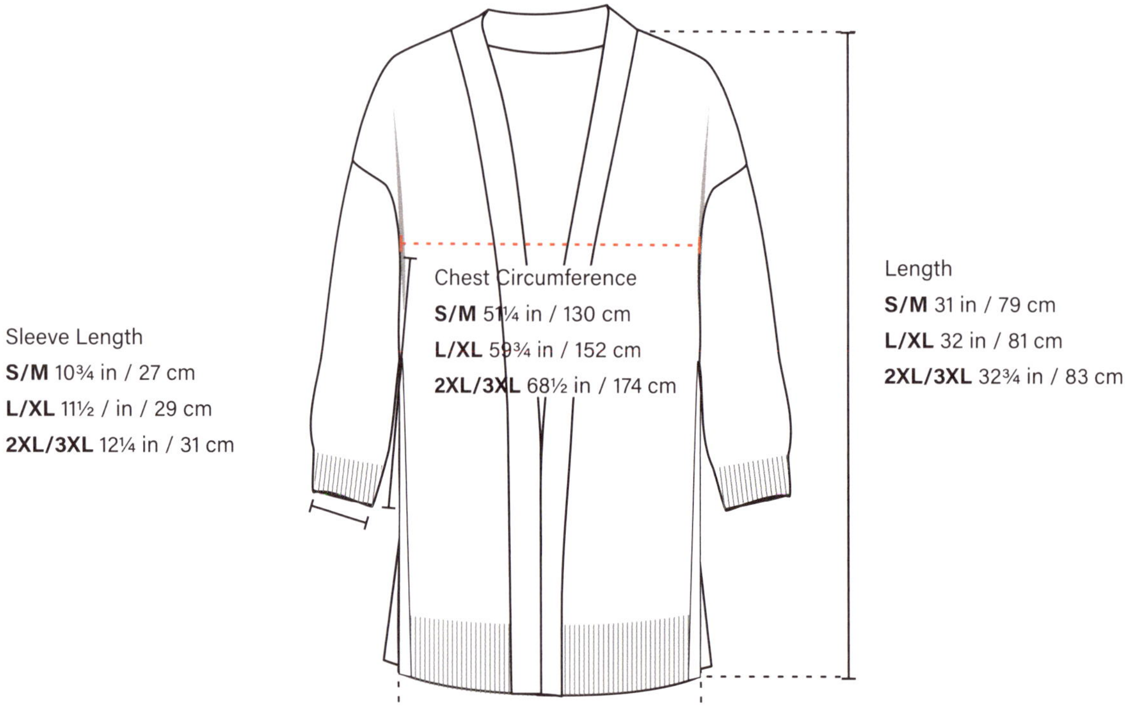

Chest Circumference
S/M 51¼ in / 130 cm
L/XL 59¾ in / 152 cm
2XL/3XL 68½ in / 174 cm

Sleeve Length
S/M 10¾ in / 27 cm
L/XL 11½ / in / 29 cm
2XL/3XL 12¼ in / 31 cm

Length
S/M 31 in / 79 cm
L/XL 32 in / 81 cm
2XL/3XL 32¾ in / 83 cm

Garment Construction

This cardigan is worked from the bottom up with two strands of yarn held together throughout. It begins with a ribbed lower edge for the back and the two front pieces, which are then joined for the body and worked back and forth in pattern. The body is divided at the underarms and then the back and front are worked separately. The sleeves are made last.

Back

With circular needle and two strands of yarn held together, CO 144 (168, 188) sts. Work back and forth in k1, p1 ribbing for 3¼ in / 8 cm. On the next row, increase 12 sts evenly spaced as follows:
Size S/M: K6, M1L, (k12, M1L) 11 times, k6.
Size L/XL: (K14, M1L) 12 times.
Size 2XL/3XL: K6, M1L, (k16, M1L) 11 times, k6.
= 156 (180, 200) sts.

Now begin the texture pattern (see Texture Pattern). Work in pattern until back measures 5½ in / 14 cm. Set back aside.
NOTE: Make sure that the pattern ends on the same row on back and both fronts.

Fronts

With circular needle and two strands of yarn held together, CO 72 (84, 94) sts. Work k1, p1 ribbing for 3¼ in / 8 cm. On the next row, increase 6 sts evenly spaced as follows:
Size S/M: (K12, M1L) 6 times.
Size L/XL: (K14, M1L) 6 times.
Size 2XL/3XL: K2, M1L, (k18, M1L) 5 times, k2.
= 78 (90, 100) sts.

Now begin the texture pattern (see Texture Pattern).
NOTE: Be aware that the pattern ends unevenly on the fronts but the pattern will work out evenly once all the pieces are joined for the body.

Work in pattern until front measures 5½ in / 14 cm. Set piece aside. Make the second front piece as for the first.
NOTE: Make sure that the pattern ends on the same row on back and both fronts.

Body

Arrange back and the two fronts on one circular needle, placing markers at the same time: Slip right front sts to circular needle, pm (right side), place back sts on circular needle, pm (left side), place left front sts on circular needle = 312 (360, 400) sts total. Continue in pattern, and, *at the same time*, increase every 2¼ in / 5.5 cm a total of 6 times. The new sts are *not* included in the pattern but form a Stockinette stitch gusset on each side of the cardigan as follows: Work in pattern to left side marker, place new marker on right needle, M1L, sl left side marker to right needle, CO 1 st using backward loop method, place new marker. Work in pattern to right side marker, place new marker on right needle, M1L, sl right side marker to right needle, M1R, place new marker. Work in pattern to end of row. Continue increasing inside these two markers so a gusset forms on each side of the cardigan. There should now be a total of 336 (384, 424) sts, including the gusset sts.

At the same time, when body measures 15½ in / 39 cm, begin decreasing at neck edge to shape the fronts: *Work 2 sts in pattern, sl 1, k2tog, psso, work to last 5 sts, k3tog, work in pattern to end of row*; rep from * to * on every 12th row a total of 10 (10, 11) times = 20 (20, 22) sts decreased on each front. Continue working patterns and neck shaping as est; *at the same time*, when body measures 23¼ in / 59 cm and then BO 8 sts at each side for underarms (= BO 4 sts at end of one rnd and 4 sts at the beginning of the next, on each side of BOR and side markers) = 280 (328, 364) sts rem or 140 (164, 182) sts each for back and front. Continue to work back and fronts separately, working gussets in Stockinette and *not* in pattern.

MARTHA Chart Symbols for Body

☐	Knit on RS, purl on WS
⊡	Purl on RS, knit on WS

← Read odd-numbered rows from right to left

→ Read even-numbered rows from left to right

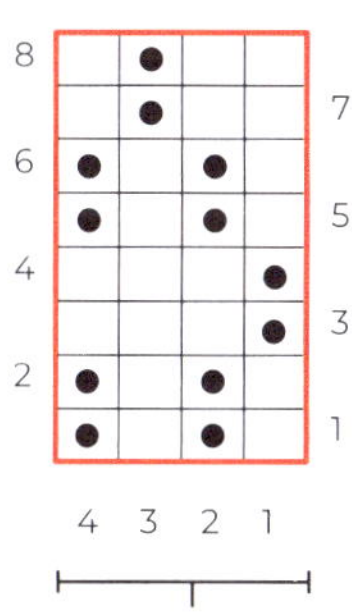

4 st-repeat,
repeat as instructed
in pattern

Texture pattern

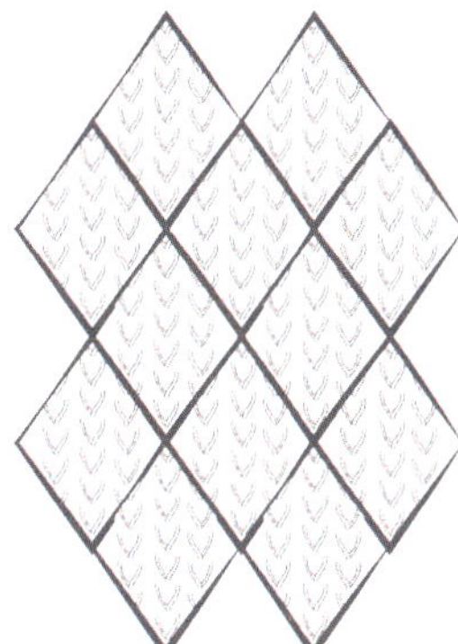

Texture Pattern

Worked over a multiple of 4 sts / 8 rows
Row 1: *K1, p1*; rep from * to *.
Row 2: *K1, p1*; rep from * to *.
Row 3: *P1, k3*; rep from * to *.
Row 4: *P3, k1*; rep from * to *.
Row 5: *K1, p1*; rep from * to *.
Row 6: *K1, p1*; rep from * to *.
Row 7: *K2, p1, k1*; rep from * to *.
Row 8: *P1, k1, p2*; rep from * to.
Rep Rnds 1–8.

Back

Work in pattern until piece measures approx. 30¼ (31, 32) in / 77 (79, 81) cm. BO the center 46 (46, 50) sts as follows:
Size S/M: Work 47 sts, BO 46, work 46 sts.
Size L/XL: Work 59 sts, BO 46, work 58 sts.
Size 2XL/3XL: Work 66 sts, BO 50, work 65 sts.
NOTE: 1 st remains from last bind-off.

Begin working each shoulder separately. Decrease to shape neck at neck edge, *at the same time,* continuing in pattern: BO 2 sts at neck edge once, then 1 st once. Continue until piece measures 31 (32, 32¾) in / 79 (81, 83) cm. Place rem 44 (56, 63) shoulder sts on a holder. Work second shoulder the same way, decreasing at neck edge as above to mirror shaping.

Fronts

Work in pattern until piece measures approx. 31 (32, 32¾) in / 79 (81, 83) cm. Place rem 60 (72, 80) sts on a holder. Work second front to match—reversing neck shaping.

Sleeves

With dpns and two strands of yarn held together, CO 48 (56, 64) sts. Divide sts onto 4 dpns and join to work in the rnd, being careful not to twist cast-on row. Pm for BOR. Work k1, p1 ribbing until cuff measures 1½ in / 4 cm. On next rnd, increase 20 (20, 20) sts evenly spaced as follows:
Size S/M: K5, M1L, (k2, M1L) 19 times, k5.
Size L/XL: K1, M1L, (k3, M1L) 18 times, k1, M1L.
Size 2XL/3XL: K4, M1L, (k3, M1L) 19 times, k3.
= 68 (76, 84) sts.

Pm after first and before last st. Work in pattern (see Texture Pattern—Sleeves). *At the same time*, after ⅜ (⅜, ⅜) in / 1 (1, 1) cm, increase 1 st outside each marker (= M1L after BOR marker and M1R before last marker). Work new sts into pattern. Increase the same way every ⅜ (⅜, ⅜) in / 1 (1, 1) cm a total of 12 (12, 12) times = 92 (100, 108) sts. Continue in pattern until sleeve measures 10¾ (11½, 12¼) in / 27 (29, 31) cm. Loosely BO all sts.

Texture Pattern—Sleeves

Rnd 1: *K1, p1*; rep from * to *.
Rnd 2: *K1, p1*; rep from * to *.
Rnd 3: *P1, k3*; rep from * to *.
Rnd 4: *P1, k3*; rep from * to *.
Rnd 5: *K1, p1*; rep from * to *.
Rnd 6: *K1, p1*; rep from * to *.
Rnd 7: *K2, p1, k1*; rep from * to *.
Rnd 8: *K2, p1, k1*; rep from * to *.
Rep Rnds 1–8.

Cardigan Edging

We recommend working with two dpns. Begin at lower edge of right front. Pick up and knit 1 st at lower right front edge with dpns. Slide st to tip of needle. CO 8 more sts with knitted-on cast-on. *Work in p1, k1 ribbing over 9 sts, pick up and knit 1 st along front edge, turn. K2tog (picked-up st tog with next st on needle), work in pattern to end. Continue in this manner, picking up approx. 3 sts for every 4 rows or sts along right front edge, back neck edge, then left front edge. BO in pattern.

Finishing

Weave in all ends neatly on WS by sewing into the tops of the sts so the yarn won't show on RS.

Seam shoulders with Kitchener st. Attach sleeves.

Wash cardigan following instructions on ball band. Lay sweater on a dry towel, pat it out to finished measurements, and leave until completely dry.

MAREN

Fisherman's Wife's Shawl in Seed Stitch

There used to be a fish market on Gammel Strand in Copenhagen, where fishermen's wives sold the day's catch. The photo shown here is from 1954. One way for the women to keep themselves warm was to wrap a shawl around their shoulders and cross it over the chest, as seen on the granite sculpture behind the merchant. The sculpture, carved by Charles Svejstrup Madsen, is called *The Fisherman's Wife*.

MAREN is an isosceles triangle with a simple seed stitch pattern and finished with I-cord. The Fisherman's Wife's shawl shown here was knit with one strand of 100 percent alpaca held together with one strand of a strong Merino-wool/nylon blend—a mix closely resembling the heathery shades of a sandy beach.

MAREN

PATTERN SUITABLE FOR INTERMEDIATE KNITTERS

SIZES	One size
FINISHED MEASUREMENTS	
Length	19¾ in / 50 cm
Width	94½ in / 240 cm
GAUGE	22 sts × 38 rows = 4 × 4 in / 10 × 10 cm in seed stitch with 1 strand of each yarn held together. Make a gauge swatch before you begin knitting to ensure that you are working at the correct gauge. Adjust needle size if necessary to obtain correct gauge.
MATERIALS	
Yarn	Arwetta by Filcolana (80% Merino wool/20% nylon, 230 yd/210 m / 50 g) Alva by Filcolana (100% alpaca, 191 yd/175 m / 25 g)
Yarn Amounts	Arwetta 250 g Alva 125 g
Needles	US size 6 / 4 mm: 24 in / 60 cm circular and set of 5 dpns

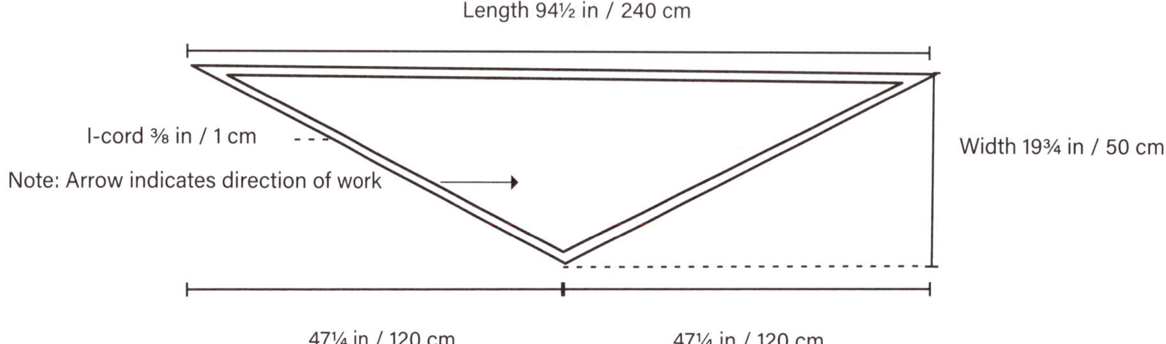

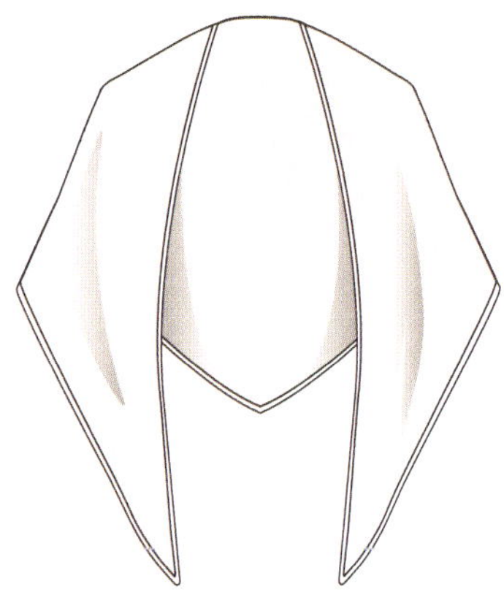

Garment Construction

This shawl is knit as an isosceles triangle in a pretty seed stitch pattern and I-cord edging. It is constructed in two steps: The shawl itself is knit first. It begins at one point of the triangle and increases only along one side. When the shawl is the desired width, the increases are complete and decreases begin on the same side. Finally, an I-cord is worked around the shawl edges.

Shawl

With circular needle and one strand each Alva and Arwetta held together, CO 3 sts.
Row 1 (RS): K3.
Row 2: Sl 1, M1L, k1, p1.
Rows 3–7: Sl 1, work in Seed to st last st, p1.
Row 8 (WS; increase row): Sl 1, M1L, work in pattern as est to last st, p1.
Working new sts into Seed st, work Increase Row every 6th row until shawl measures 8 in / 20 cm and there are 16 sts.
Work Increase Row every 4th row until shawl measures 47¼ in / 120 cm across.

Decrease Row (WS): Sl 1, k2tog tbl, work in seed st until 1 st rem, p1.
Work Decrease Row every 4th row until shawl measures approx. 39½ in / 100 cm from tip and 16 sts remain.
Work Decrease Row every 6th row until shawl measures 47¼ in / 120 cm from tip where the decreases began = 3 sts rem. BO the rem 3 sts.

Seed Stitch

For seed stitch, work knit over purl and purl over knit on every row.
Row 1: *K1, p1*; rep from * to *.
Row 2: *P1, k1*; rep from * to *.
Rep Rows 1 and 2.

I-Cord Edging

We recommend using 2 dpns for the edging. Begin at the lower tip. Pick up and knit 1 st at beginning point of shawl. Slide st to end of dpns. CO 4 sts with knitted-on cast-on. *K3, k2tog tbl. Pick up and knit 1 st from shawl's edge. Slide sts to opposite end of needle*; rep from * to * to a corner; work I-cord corner (see I-Cord Corner). Repeat until the entire shawl is edged with I-cord. BO the 4 rem sts.

I-Cord Corner

K3, k2tog tbl, pick up and knit 1 st from edge of shawl in the corner st. Slide the 5 sts to needle tip. K3, k2tog tbl. Slide the 4 sts on right needle to opposite end of needle without picking up a st. K4, pick up and knit 1 st from shawl edge in the same corner st. Slide the 5 sts to opposite end of needle. K3, k2tog. Slide sts to opposite end of needle.

Finishing

Weave in all ends neatly on WS by sewing into the tops of the sts so the yarn won't show on RS.

Join I-cord with Kitchener st over bound-off sts.

Wash shawl following instructions on ball band. Lay shawl on a dry towel, pat it out to finished measurements, and leave until completely dry.

MAREN Chart Symbols

☐ Knit on RS, purl on WS
⊡ Purl on RS, knit on WS

← Read odd-numbered rows from right to left
→ Read even-numbered rows from left to right

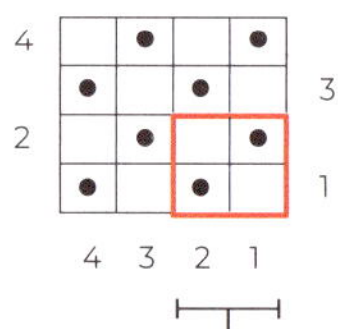

Seed Stitch repeat = 2 sts.
Repeat as instructed in pattern

WELLIES

Baby Socks

A pair of knit socks with a slight whiff of saltwater for the smallest ones. The inspiration for them came, of course, from the high-leg Wellington rubber boots.

WELLIES are knit with a bright yellow 80 percent Merino wool/20 percent nylon yarn that is great for socks that are durable and washable.

A blue contrast color tops the legs of the "rubber boots." The soles, knit at a firm gauge, have a little garter stitch edge.

WELLIES

PATTERN SUITABLE FOR EXPERIENCED KNITTERS

SIZES	0–3 (6, 9) months
FINISHED MEASUREMENTS	
Leg Length	3¼ (3½, 4) in / 8 (9, 10) cm
Foot Length	3½ (4, 4¼) in / 9 (10, 11) cm
GAUGE	22 sts × 38 rows = 4 × 4 in / 10 × 10 cm in Stockinette stitch with larger needles. Make a gauge swatch before you begin knitting to ensure that you are working at the correct gauge. Adjust needle size if necessary to obtain correct gauge.
MATERIALS	
Yarn	Arwetta by Filcolana (80% Merino wool/20% nylon, 230 yd/210 m / 50 g)
Yarn Amounts	MC, yellow: 1 skein for all sizes CC, blue: 1 skein for all sizes
Needles	US sizes 1½ and 2½ / 2.5 and 3 mm: 24 in / 60 cm circulars for magic loop, or sets of 5 dpns
Notions	3 stitch markers

3 months 5½ in / 14 cm
6 months 6 in / 15 cm
9 months 6¼ in / 16 cm

Ribbing length
All Sizes ⅝ in / 1.5 cm

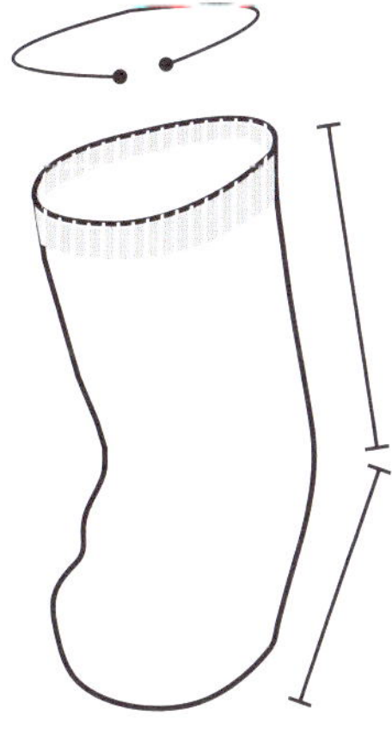

Leg Length
3 months 3¼ in / 8 cm
6 months 3½ in / 9 cm
9 months 4 in / 10 cm

Foot Length
3 months 3½ in / 9 cm
6 months 4 in / 10 cm
9 months 4¼ in / 11 cm

Garment Construction

The WELLIES are knit from the bottom up, beginning with the sole, then the top of the foot, and last, the leg of the sock.

Sole

With smaller-size dpns and MC, CO 5 sts. Working back and forth, knit 1 row. On the next row, increase at both sides:

Row 1 (increase row): K1, M1L, knit until 1 st rem, M1R, k1.
Row 2: Knit without increases.
Rep Rows 1 and 2 a total of 6 (7, 8) times. Continue in garter st until sole measures 2½ (2¾, 3¼) in / 6 (7, 8) cm.

Now decrease on every other row:
Row 1 (decrease row): K1, k2tog, knit to last 3 sts, k2tog, k1.
Row 2: Knit without decreases.
Rep Rows 1 and 2 a total of 6 (7, 8) times. BO rem sts and cut yarn.

Edging on Sole

Beginning at the center of the heel, pick up and knit a total of 64 (70, 76) sts around sole. Join and work k1, p1 ribbing for 1 round and then continue in Fisherman's Rib:

Fisherman's Rib

Worked over a multiple of 2 sts / 2 rnds
Rnd 1: *K1 in st below, p1*; rep from * to *.
Rnd 2: *K1, p1*; rep from * to *.
Rep Rnds 1 and 2 three times. Now work a rnd, placing markers as follows: K16 (19, 20), pm1, k32 (32, 36), pm2, k16 (19, 20) to BOR. Change to larger-size needles and begin decreasing to shape top of sock.

Shape Instep

Rnd 1: K16 (19, 20), slm, *k2tog*; work from * to * a total of 16 (16, 18) times, slm, k16 (19, 20) = 48 (54, 58) sts rem.
Rnd 2: K2tog, knit until 2 sts before marker 1, k2tog, slm, knit to marker 2, slm, k2tog, knit until 2 sts before BOR, k2tog = 44 (50, 54) sts rem.
Rnd 3: Knit.
Rnd 4: Knit to marker 1, slm, *k2tog*; work from * to * a total of 8 (8, 8) times, k0 (0, 2), slm, knit to BOR marker = 36 (42, 46) sts rem.
Rnd 5: Knit.
Rnd 6: Knit until 2 sts before marker 1, k2tog, slm, knit to marker 2, slm, k2tog, knit to BOR = 34 (40, 44) sts rem.
Rnd 7: Knit.
Rnd 8: Knit until 2 sts before marker 1, k2tog, slm, knit to marker 2, slm, k2tog, knit to BOR = 32 (38, 42) sts rem.

Continue in Stockinette until leg measures 2½ (3, 3¼) in / 6.5 (7.5, 8.5) cm. Change to smaller-size dpns and CC (Blue). Work k1, p1 ribbing for ⅝ (⅝, ⅝) in / 1.5 (1.5, 1.5) cm. BO in ribbing.
Make the second sock the same way.

Finishing

Weave in all ends neatly on WS by sewing into the tops of the sts so the yarn won't show on RS.

Wash socks following instructions on ball band. Lay socks on a dry towel, pat out to finished measurements, and leave until completely dry.

BUBBLE AND TEXTURED KNITS

INSPIRATION

Bubble Pattern
Texture Mix
Horizontal Panels
Single-Color Sweaters
Zipper and Button Closures

SNEKKERSTEN

Sweater with Bubble Pattern and a Zipped Neck Opening

SNEKKERSTEN was inspired by a photo of fisherman Jørgen Børgesen from Snekkersten, who sat and repaired his nets while wearing a bubble-pattern sweater and a captain's hat.

The traditional bubble pattern goes back to the nineteenth century, when sweaters such as Jørgen's were worn as part of fishermen's and mariners' work outfits. The iconic panels of bubbles are still a favorite both in contemporary hand knitting and in general for today's styles. Timeless, functional designs—a modern classic.

This sweater was knit with a 3-ply organic wool yarn that lends itself well to textured knitting.

SNEKKERSTEN has a bubble variation on the top of the body, a ribbed finish on the body, and ribbing on the cuffs. The sweater also has a zipper at the neck ribbing, making it easily adjustable to suit the whims of the weather.

SNEKKERSTEN

PATTERN SUITABLE FOR EXPERIENCED KNITTERS

SIZES	S (M, L, XL, 2XL)
FINISHED MEASUREMENTS	
Chest Circumference	37¾ (39½, 42½, 44, 47¼) in / 96 (100, 108, 112, 120) cm
Length	26½ (27¼, 28, 28¾, 29½) in / 67 (69, 71, 73, 75) cm
Sleeve Length	21¾ (22, 22, 22½, 22¾) in / 55 (56, 56, 57, 58) cm
GAUGE	24 sts × 36 rows = 4 × 4 in / 10 × 10 cm in Stockinette. Make a gauge swatch before you begin knitting to ensure that you are working at the correct gauge. Adjust needle size if necessary to obtain correct gauge.
MATERIALS	
Yarn	Jensen by Isager (100% Merino wool, 137 yd/125 m / 50 g)
Yarn Amounts	11 (12, 13, 13, 14) hanks
Needles	US size 2½ / 3 mm: 32 in / 80 cm circular and set of 5 dpns if you are not using magic loop
Notions	4 stitch markers; zipper to fit from base of neck to top of collar; matching sewing thread for sewing in zipper

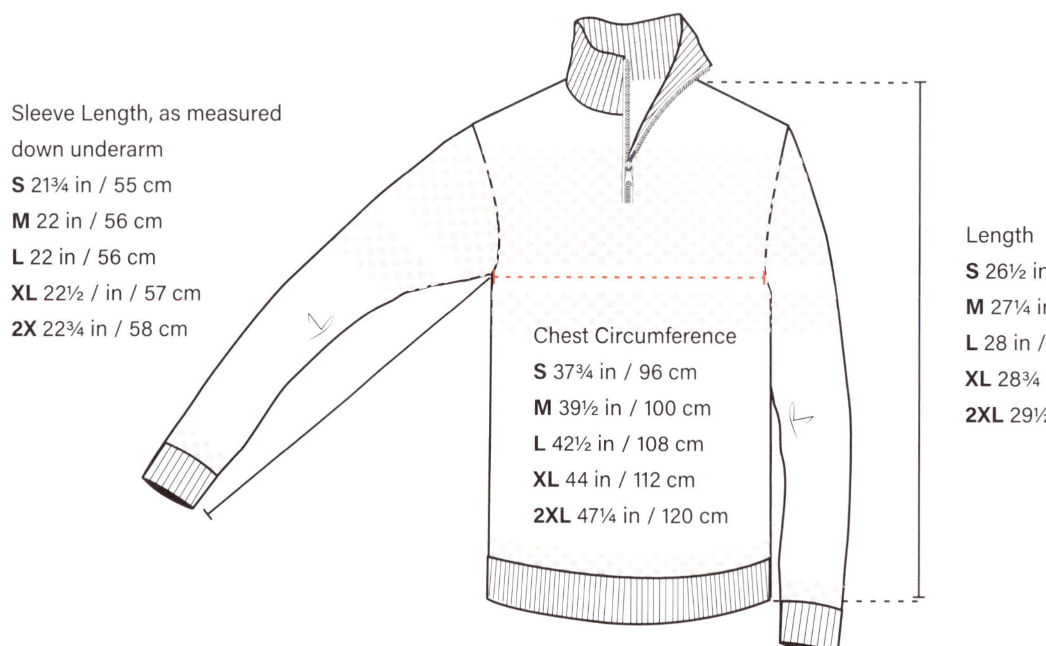

Garment Construction

SNEKKERSTEN is worked from the bottom up. The body is knit first and then the sleeves. The body divides at the underarms and then the front and back are worked separately. The front divides for the zipper from the top of the yoke up to the top end of the collar. Finally, you'll pick up stitches for the collar, knit the collar, and finish with edges for setting in the zipper.

Body

With circular needle, CO 208 (224, 240, 256, 272) sts. Join to work in the rnd, being careful not to twist cast-on row. Work the ribbed lower edge, and, *at the same time,* place markers: Pm (BOR and right side), work k1, p1 ribbing for 104 (112, 120, 128, 136) sts, pm (left side), work k1, p1 ribbing to end. Continue in ribbing as est for 2½ in / 6 cm. Knit 1 rnd and then begin pattern (see Bubble Pattern—In the Round).

Bubble Pattern (in the Round)

Worked over a multiple of 4 sts / 12 rnds.
Rnds 1–5: Knit.
Rnd 6: *K3, bubble, tighten yarn*; rep from * to *.
Rnds 7–11: Knit.
Rnd 12: K1, bubble, tighten yarn, *K3, bubble, tighten yarn*; rep from * to * to last 2 sts, k2.
Rep Rnds 1–12 for pattern.

Bubble Stitch

Count down 4 rnds from the first st on left needle. Insert right needle into st, knit the new st through that st. Slip st off left needle and let the old st, behind the new st, run down to the last rnd where the new st has been made. Tighten yarn.

Work Rnds 1–12 of Bubble Pattern once, then work Rnds 1–6 once more; this section measures approx. 2 in / 5 cm. Continue in Stockinette, *at the same time,* increasing for the body silhouette as follows: *K1, M1L, knit until 1 st before left side marker, M1R, k2, M1L, knit until 1 st before right side marker, M1R, k1*. Work from * to * a total of 4 times with 1½ in / 4 cm between increase rnds = a total of 224 (240, 256, 272, 288) sts.

When body measures 15 (15½, 15¾, 16¼, 16½) in / 38 (39, 40, 41, 42) cm, work Rnds 1–12 of Bubble Pattern twice, then work Rnds 1–6 once more; piece should measure approx. 17 (17¼, 17¾, 18¼, 18½) in / 43 (44, 45, 46, 47) cm. Knit 1 rnd. Divide body for front and back with 112 (120, 128, 136, 144) sts for each; begin working back and forth.

Back

Begin decreasing to shape armholes while continuing in Stockinette: On every RS row: *K2tog, work to last 2 sts, k2tog*; work from * to * a total of 5 (6, 6, 7, 7) times = 102 (108, 116, 122, 130) sts rem. When the Stockinette section measures 1¼ in / 3 cm from end of last Bubble Pattern, ending with a WS row; change to Bubble Pattern (Flat) (see page 144).

NOTE: Continue bubble pattern so it aligns with previous bubbles on body as much as possible. The bubbles are worked on RS.

SNEKKERSTEN Chart Symbols

☐	Knit on RS, purl on WS
	Work Rnds/Rows 1-5 or 7-11 in Stockinette (beginning with a purl row if working flat). On Rnd/Row 6 or 12, Bubble Stitch: Insert right needle into st 4 sts down from st on left needle. Knit new st; drop st on left needle and let it run down to loop.

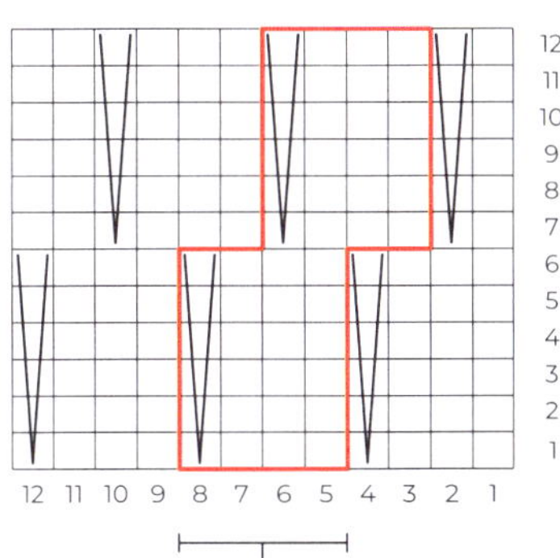

Bubble Pattern (in the Round)
4-st repeat
work as instructed in pattern

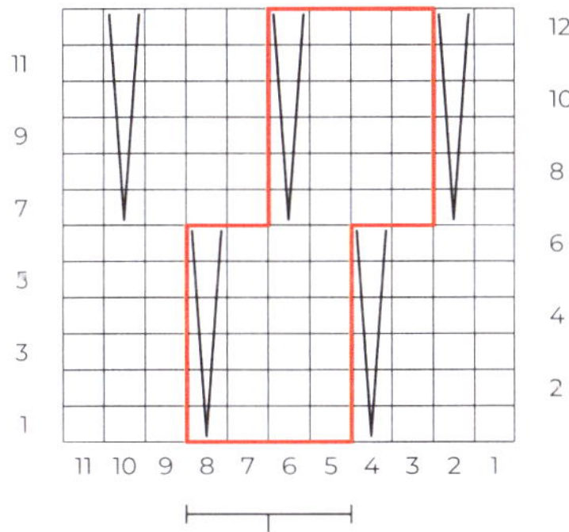

Bubble Pattern (Flat)
4-st repeat
work as instructed in pattern

Note: Chart begins with a WS row. Work Row 1 from left to right.

SNEKKERSTEN Chart Symbols

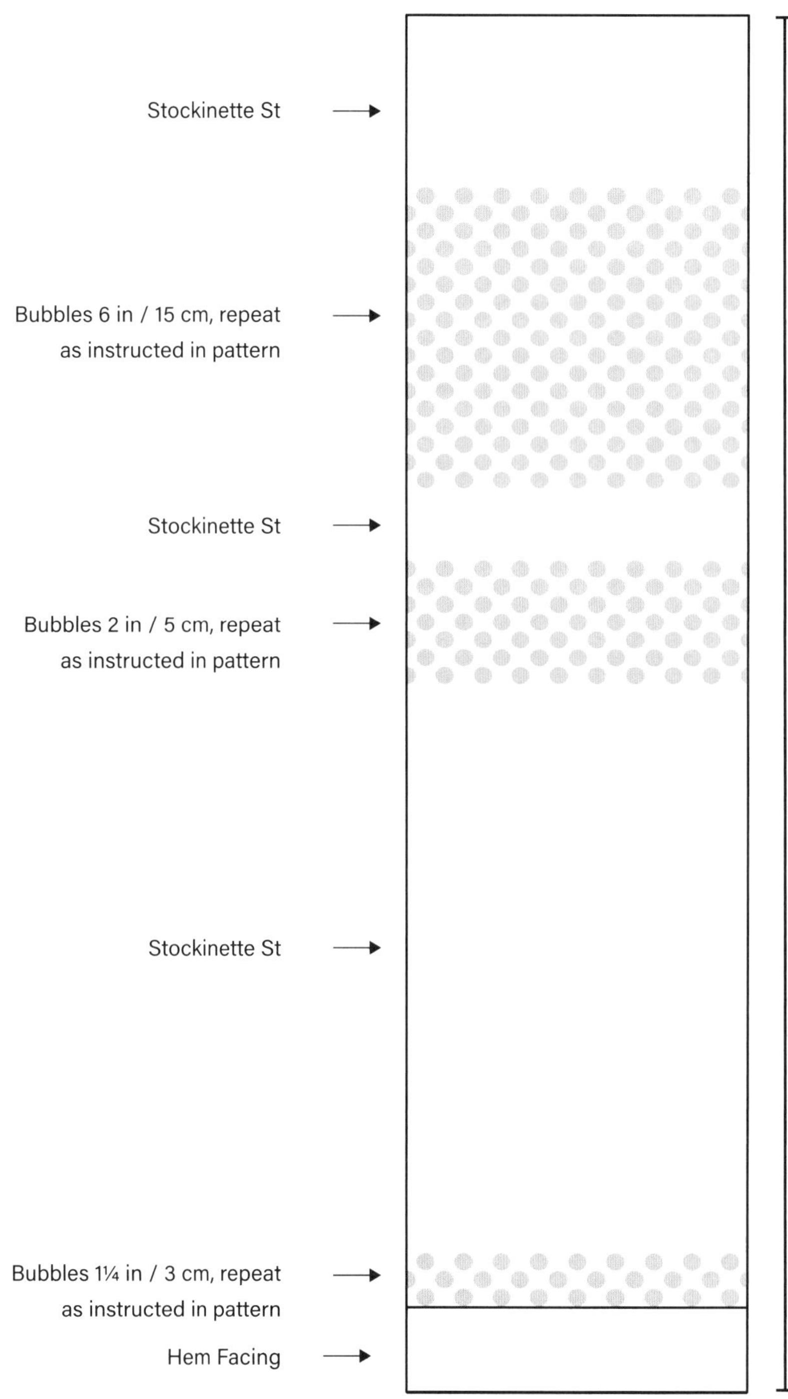

Bubble Pattern (Flat)

Worked over a multiple of 4 sts + 3 / 12 rows
Rows 1–5: Work in Stockinette st (knit on RS, purl on WS).
Row 6 (RS): *K3, bubble, tighten yarn*; rep from * to * to last 3 sts, k3.
Rows 7–11: Work in Stockinette st.
Row 12: K1, bubble, tighten yarn, *k3, bubble, tighten yarn*; rep from * to * to last st, k1.
Rep Rows 1–12 until pattern measures 6 in / 15 cm. Work in Stockinette until work measures 25½ (26½, 27¼, 28, 28¾) in / 65 (67, 69, 71, 73) cm. BO the center 34 (34, 42, 44, 52) sts as follows:
Size S: K37, BO 28, k36.
Size M: K40, BO 28, k39.
Size L: K40, BO 36 k39.
Size XL: K42, BO 38, k41.
Size 2XL: K42, BO 46, k41.
NOTE: 1 st remains from last bind-off.
= 31 (34, 34, 36, 36) sts per shoulder.

Work each shoulder separately. Continuing in Stockinette, shape shoulder starting on next row: BO 2 sts at neck edge twice, then 1 st twice. Continue straight until body measures 26½ (27¼, 28, 28¾, 29½) in / 67 (69, 71, 73, 75) cm. Place rem 31 (34, 34, 36, 36) shoulder sts on a holder. Make the second shoulder the same way, binding off at neck edge as above to mirror shaping.

Front

The front is worked back and forth. Begin decreasing to shape armholes; *at the same time*, continuing in Stockinette as follows: *K2tog, knit to last 2 sts, k2tog*; work from * to * a total of 5 (6, 6, 7, 7) times = a total of 102 (108, 116, 122, 130) sts rem.

When the Stockinette section measures approx. 1¼ in / 3 cm from end of last Bubble Pattern, ending with a WS row, change to Bubble Pattern (Flat) and work in pattern until pattern measures approx. 3¼ in / 8.5 cm = approx. 7 bubble rows.

Now divide the front for the zipper. Begin by placing a marker at center front (cf): Work in pattern as est until 4 sts before cf marker, BO 8 sts, continue in pattern to end of row = 47 (50, 54, 57, 61) sts rem for each shoulder. Work each shoulder separately, continuing bubble pattern as est. When bubble pattern measures approx. 6 in / 15 cm, change to Stockinette. Work in Stockinette until work measures 24½ (25¼, 25¼, 26¾, 27½) in / 62 (64, 64, 68, 70) cm. BO 7 (7, 11, 12, 16) sts at neck edge = 40 (43, 43, 45, 45) sts rem for each shoulder.

Begin decreasing for neckline and shoulder while continuing in Stockinette, as follows: BO 2 sts at neck edge once, then 1 st 4 times and, at the same time, BO 2 sts at armhole edge once, then 1 st once. Work until body measures 26½ (27¼, 28, 28¾, 29½) in / 67 (69, 71, 73, 75) cm. Place rem 31 (34, 34, 36, 36) shoulder sts on a holder. Make opposite shoulder the same way, binding off at shoulder and neck edges as above to mirror shaping.

Sleeves

With dpns, CO 44 (48, 48, 52, 52) sts. Divide sts onto 4 dpns and join to work in the rnd, being careful not to twist cast-on row. Pm for BOR after first and before last st. Work k1, p1 ribbing for 2½ in / 6 cm. Knit 1 rnd. Work Rnds 1–12 of Bubble Pattern in the Round once, then Rnds 1-6 once. Change to Stockinette, *at the same time*, increasing 1 st at each side of marked sts with M1 (= increase after first st and before last st). Increase the same way every ⅜ in / 1 cm a total of 22 (22, 24, 26, 26) times = 88 (92, 96, 104, 104) sts. Continue in Stockinette until sleeve measures 19¾ (20, 20, 20½, 21) in / 50 (51, 51, 52, 53) cm from previous bubble pattern and then work in bubble pattern for 2 in / 5 cm; knit 1 rnd. The sleeve should now be 21¾ (22, 22, 22½, 22¾) in / 55 (56, 56, 57, 58) cm long.

Now bind off to shape underarm: BO 10 (12, 12, 14, 14) sts centered on underarm [= BO 5 (6, 6, 7, 7) sts at end of one round and beginning of the next, on each side of BOR marker] = 78 (80, 84, 90, 90) sts rem. Work sleeve back and forth, decreasing for the sleeve top while continuing in pattern. Begin with 1¼ in / 3 cm in Stockinette and then approx. 6 in / 15 cm bubble pattern. Decrease sleeve top on RS rows (= every other row): K2tog tbl at beginning of row and k2tog at end of row. Purl back. Decrease the same way 21 (21, 23, 23, 24) times = 36 (38, 38, 44, 42) sts rem. Continuing in Stockinette, for all sizes, BO 2 sts at beginning of following 2 rows, then 3 sts at beginning of following 2 rows, then 4 sts at beginning of following 2 rows. Loosely BO rem 18 (20, 20, 26, 24) sts. Set sleeve aside while you make second sleeve the same way.

Neck Edging

Join left and right shoulders with Kitchener st. Attach sleeves to body. The neck edge is doubled. With circular needle and RS facing, pick up and knit approx. 96 (100, 100, 106, 106) sts around neck. Work back and forth in k1, p1 ribbing until neckband measures 6¼ in / 16 cm. BO all sts in pattern. Fold neck down to WS and sew BO edge to pick-up edge, beginning and ending 4 sts in from the front edges, which will be used for the zipper.

Zipper

A zipper casing has 2 sides—a front and a back. Begin with the front on the left side of the sweater. Knit a Stockinette edging along the zipper edge on the neckline as follows. Begin at base of neck on left side. We recommend using two dpns for this: Pick up and knit 1 st on neckline, slide st to needle tip, CO 3 new sts with knitted-on cast-on. Work *k2, k2tog, pick up and knit 1 st from sweater edge with yarn on left side of work; turn and work the 4 sts in Stockinette to beginning of row*; rep from * to * until an edging has been worked from the base of neck to the top of the collar. Make an edging along opposite side the same way.

Now pick up and knit sts on the back of left side, at base of neck on back. Pick up and knit 5 sts and work edging until it measures 9½ in / 24 cm, from the base of neck to folded neck edge. Make the right side to match. Using an overhand stitich, sew the edges of the back facing together with the sweater, so there is an opening at outer edge for the zipper to sit in. Place the zipper between the front and back pieces, using pins to mark neck for beginning and end of the zipper placement. Open the zipper completely. Pin zipper along both sides. Use a matching sewing thread to sew in zipper firmly with overhand st along both sides of zipper. Make sure to pull the knitted edge so the zipper sits smoothy, because the knitted piece is more elastic than the zipper. Sew the zipper edges together at base of neck.

Finishing

Weave in all ends neatly on WS by sewing into the tops of the sts so the yarn won't show on RS.

Wash sweater following instructions on ball band. Lay sweater on a dry towel, pat it out to finished measurements, and leave until completely dry.

To ensure that the bubbles show well and so each will not flatten, it is important to make sure that the dropped stitch runs all the way down to the stitch where you inserted the needle before knitting the loop stitch.

So that the zipper will lay smoothly, it is important to pull the knitted edge so it aligns smoothly with the zipper, because the knitted front is more elastic than the zipper.

Snekkersten

STORM

Textured Sweater for Children and Adults

A harsh life where wind, waves, and rain show their teeth is an everyday reality for those who go to sea. The expression "with a seat on the water's surface" paints a picture of being at sea—a changing, unpredictable experience. When one finds oneself in stormy weather, the situation can also be quite challenging, so the expression is just right for this design.

Texture patterns on sweaters have historically been found in England, Ireland, Scotland, and the Netherlands, where they were given the names of specific local patterns and motif arrangements. That way, it was possible to identify where a mariner came from. Each of the five different motifs in this design have nautical names. We call them Hail, Waves, Fishing Net, Fishing Huts, and Tidewater.

STORM is a round-neck textured sweater with a wide raglan and ribbed edges on cuffs and the lower body. It was knit with a 100 percent Norwegian Merino wool yarn. The yarn is soft, not superwash, and perfect for emphasizing the textured motifs.

STORM is a comfortable pullover, suitable for all ages and genders.

STORM, ADULT VERSION

PATTERN SUITABLE FOR INTERMEDIATE KNITTERS

SIZES	S (M, L, XL, 2XL)
FINISHED MEASUREMENTS	
Chest Circumference	41 (42½, 44, 45¾, 47¼) in / 104 (108, 112, 116, 120) cm
Length	25¼ (26, 26¾, 27½, 28¼) in / 64 (66, 68, 70, 72) cm
Sleeve Length	21¾ (22, 22, 22½, 22¾) in / 55 (56, 56, 57, 58) cm
GAUGE	23 sts × 33 rows = 4 × 4 in / 10 × 10 cm in Stockinette with larger-size needles. Make a gauge swatch before you begin knitting to ensure that you are working at the correct gauge. Adjust needle size if necessary to obtain correct gauge.
MATERIALS	
Yarn	Double Sunday by Sandnes Garn (100% Norwegian Merino wool, 137 yd/108 m / 50 g)
Yarn Amounts	12 (13, 15, 16, 17) skeins
Needles	US sizes 2½ and 6 / 3 and 4 mm: 24 in / 60 cm circulars and sets of 5 dpns if you are not using magic loop
Notions	8 stitch markers; blunt tapestry needle

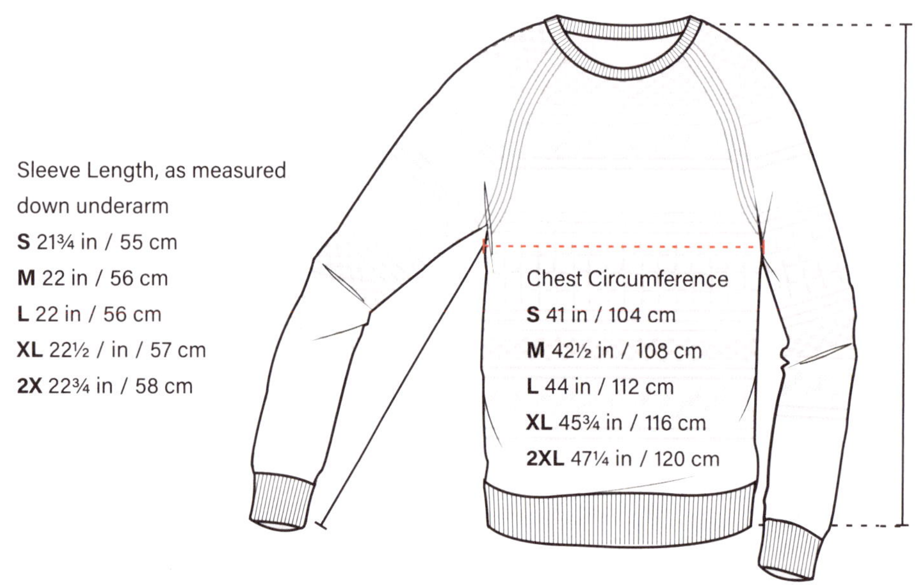

Garment Construction

STORM is worked from the bottom up. The body is knit first and then the sleeves. The body and sleeves are then joined on a circular needle for the yoke worked in the round. The body and sleeves are worked with the same sequence of motifs.

Body

With circular needle, CO 216 (240, 264, 288, 312) sts. Join to work in the rnd, being careful not to twist cast-on row. Pm as you set up ribbing: Pm (BOR), work k2, p2 ribbing for 108 (120, 132, 144, 156) sts, pm, continue ribbing to end of rnd. Continue in ribbing for 2½ in / 6 cm and then begin texture pattern. Work each motif in order as written below.

Texture Motif Patterns—Body

Hail (worked over a multiple of 4 sts / 8 rnds)
Rnds 1–3: Knit.
Rnd 4: *P1, k3*; rep from * to *.
Rnds 5–7: Knit.
Rnd 8: *K2, p1, k1*; rep from * to * to last 2 sts, p1, k1.
Rep Rnds 1–8 until panel measures approx. 3 (3½, 4¼, 4¼, 4½) in / 7.5 (9, 11, 11, 11.5) cm. Work 3 rnds in Stockinette.

Waves
Rnd 1: Knit.
Rnd 2: Purl.
Rnd 3: Knit.
Rnd 4: Purl.
Rnd 5: Knit.

Tidewater (worked over a multiple of 12 sts / 12 rnds)
Rnd 1: *P6, k6*; rep from * to *.
Rnd 2: *P5, k6, p1*; rep from * to *.
Rnd 3: *P4, k6, p2*; rep from * to *.
Rnd 4: *P3, k6, p3*; rep from * to *.
Rnd 5: *P2, k6, p4*; rep from * to *.
Rnd 6: *P1, k6, p5*; rep from * to *.
Rnd 7: *K6, p6*; rep from * to *.
Rnd 8: *K5, p6, k1*; rep from * to *.
Rnd 9: *K4, p6, k2*; rep from * to *.
Rnd 10: *K3, p6, k3*; rep from * to *.
Rnd 11: *K2, p6, k4*; rep from * to *.
Rnd 12: *K1, p6, k5*; rep from * to *.
Rep Rnds 1–12 until panel measures approx. 2½ (2½, 2¾, 2¾, 3¼) in / 6 (6, 7, 7, 8) cm.

Waves
Rnd 1: Knit.
Rnd 2: Purl.
Rnd 3: Knit.
Rnd 4: Purl.
Rnd 5: Knit.

Fishing Net (worked over a multiple of 4 sts / 4 rnds)
Rnd 1: *K2, p2*; rep from * to *.
Rnd 2: Work as for Rnd 1.
Rnd 3: *P2, k2*; rep from * to *.
Rnd 4: Work as for Rnd 3.
Rep Rnds 1–4 until panel measures approx. 2 in / 5 cm.

Waves
Rnd 1: Knit.
Rnd 2: Purl.
Rnd 3: Knit.
Rep Rnds 2 and 3 three more times.

Fishing Huts (worked over a multiple of 8 sts / 16 rnds)
Rnds 1–8: *K4, p4*; rep from * to *.
Rnds 9–16: *P4, k4*; rep from * to *.
Rep Rnds 1–16 until piece measures approx. 13½ (14¼, 14½, 15½, 15½) in / 34 (36, 37, 39, 39) cm from CE edge.

Shape underarm as follows: Begin at BOR, BO 4 sts, work 100 (112, 124, 136, 148) sts, BO 8 sts, work to last 4 sts, BO 4 sts = 200 (224, 248, 272, 296) sts rem. Make note of last rnd worked in texture pattern. Set body aside while you make sleeves.

Sleeves

With dpns, CO 50 (54, 56, 62, 64) sts. Divide sts onto 4 dpns and join to work in the round, being careful not to twist cast-on row. Pm for BOR. Work k2, p2 ribbing for 2½ in / 6 cm. Pm after first st and before last st. Begin working sleeve shaping as follows: increase 1 st outside each marker with M1 (= K1, slm, M1R, knit to marker, M1L, slm, k1). Work new sts into pattern. Increase the same way every ¾ in / 2 cm a total of 17 (17, 18, 18, 19) times = 84 (88, 92, 98, 102) sts. *At the same time*, work the texture pattern. Work each motif in order as written below for sleeves until sleeve measures 21¾ (22, 22, 22½, 22¾) in 55 (56, 56, 57, 58) cm.

Texture Motif Patterns—Sleeves

Hail (worked over a multiple of 4 sts / 8 rnds)
Rnds 1–3: Knit.
Rnd 4: *P1, k3*; rep from * to *.
Rnds 5–7: Knit.
Rnd 8: *K2, p1, k1*; rep from * to *.
Rep Rnds 1–8 until panel measures approx. 3 (3½, 4¼, 4¼, 4½) in / 7.5 (9, 11, 11, 11.5) cm. Work 3 rnds in Stockinette.

Waves
Rnd 1: Knit.
Rnd 2: Purl.
Rnd 3: Knit.
Rnd 4: Purl.
Rnd 5: Knit.

Tidewater (worked over a multiple of 12 sts / 10 rnds)
Rnd 1: *P6, k6*; rep from * to *.
Rnd 2: *P5, k6, p1*; rep from * to *.
Rnd 3: *P4, k6, p2*; rep from * to *.
Rnd 4: *P3, k6, p3*; rep from * to *.
Rnd 5: *P2, k6, p4*; rep from * to *.
Rnd 6: *P1, k6, p5*; rep from * to *.
Rnd 7: *K6, p6*; rep from * to *.
Rnd 8: *K5, p6, k1*; rep from * to *.
Rnd 9: *K4, p6, k2*; rep from * to *.
Rnd 10: *K3, p6, k3*; rep from * to *.
Rnd 11: *K2, p6, k4*; rep from * to *.
Rnd 12: *K1, p6, k5*; rep from * to *.
Rep Rnds 1–12 until panel measures approx. 3½ in / 9 cm.

Waves
Rnd 1: Knit.
Rnd 2: Purl.
Rnd 3: Knit.
Rnd 4: Purl.
Rnd 5: Knit.

Fishing Net (worked over a multiple of 4 sts / 4 rnds)
Rnds 1–2: *K2, p2*; rep from * to *.
Rnds 3–4: *P2, k2*; rep from * to *.
Rep Rnds 1–4 until panel measures approx. 3½ in / 9 cm.

Waves
Rnd 1: Knit.
Rnd 2: Purl.
Rnd 3: Knit.
Rep Rnds 2–3, three more times.

Fishing Huts (worked over a multiple of 8 sts / 16 rnds)
Rnds 1–8: *K4, p4*; rep from * to *.
Rnds 9–16: *P4, k4*; rep from * to *.
Rep Rnds 1–16 until piece measures approx. 13½ (14¼, 14½, 15½, 15½) in / 34 (36, 37, 39, 39) cm, ending on same row of pattern that you did for body before underarm BO.

STORM Chart Symbols

- ☐ Knit on RS, purl on WS
- ⊡ Purl on RS, knit on WS

Texture Motif Patterns—Body

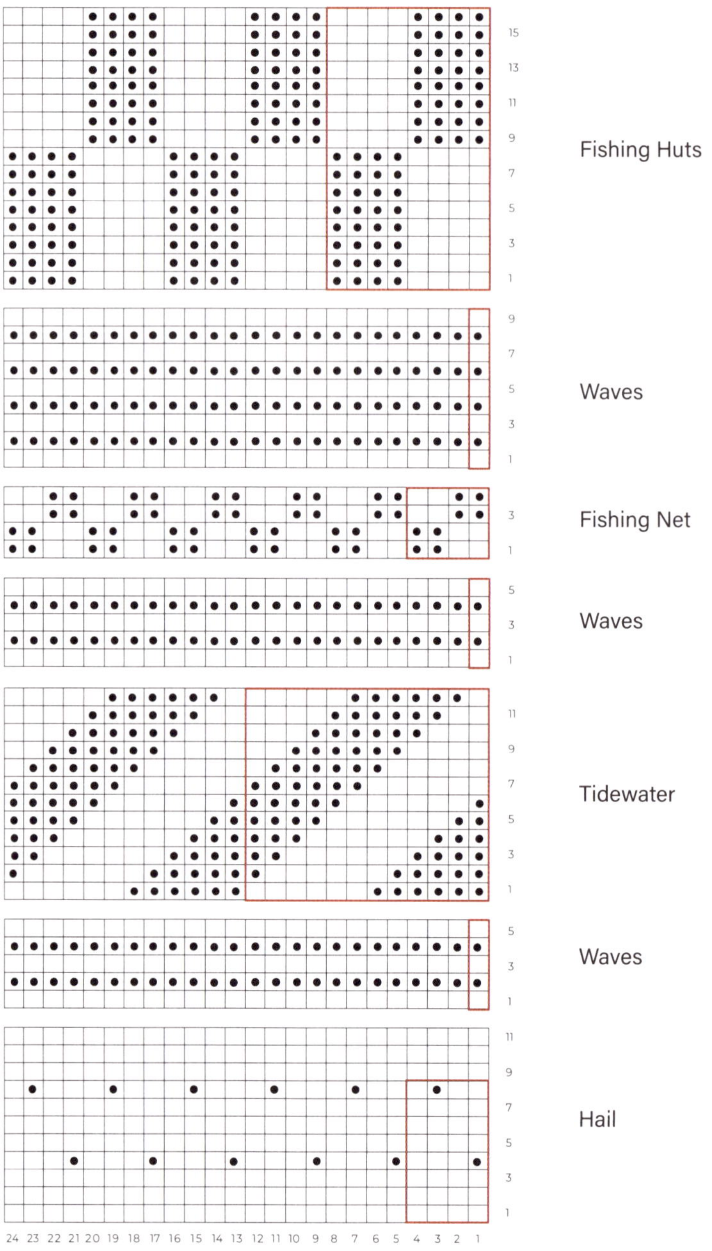

Fishing Huts

Waves

Fishing Net

Waves

Tidewater

Waves

Hail

Texture Motif Patterns—Yoke

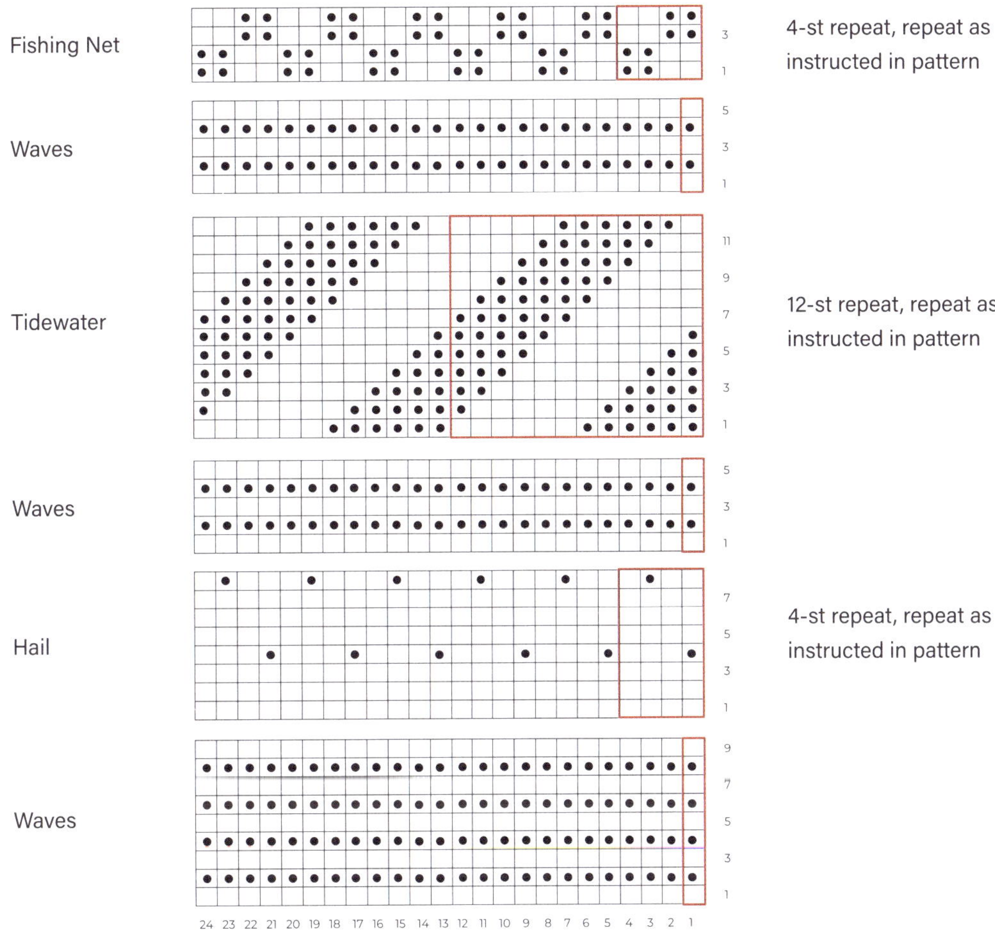

Now shape underarm by binding off 8 sts centered on underarm: BO 4 sts outside of each marker (= after BOR marker and before last marker) = 76 (80, 84, 90, 94) sts rem. Set sleeve aside while you work second sleeve the same way.

Join Body and Sleeves

Arrange the sleeves on circular needle with body, matching underarms. The pattern panels on body and sleeves should align. Begin by placing 8 markers. The round begins at left shoulder on back of sweater, beginning with the left sleeve.

Marker 1: K1, pm, work until 1 st before next piece intersection.
Marker 2: Pm, k1, yo, k1.
Marker 3: Pm, work until 1 st before next piece intersection.
Marker 4: Pm, k1, yo, k1.
Marker 5: Pm, work until 1 st before next piece intersection.
Marker 6: Pm, k1, yo, k1.
Marker 7: Pm, work until 1 st before next piece intersection.
Marker 8: Pm, k1, yo.

The yoke now has 356 (388, 420, 456, 488) sts, including the yos. On the next rnd, work each yo as k1tbl.

Raglan Decreases

Begin decreasing at each marker on every 3rd rnd: Work until 2 sts before marker. Sl 1, k1, psso, slm, k3, slm, k2tog = 8 sts decreased. Continuing to work in texture pattern as est and working the 3 raglan sts between markers in Stockinette st, rep the raglan decreases on every third rnd a total of 30 (34, 35, 36, 37) times. At the same time, after 22 (26, 27, 27, 28) decrease rnds [= 180 (180, 204, 240, 264) sts rem], begin neck shaping; work back and forth while continuing raglan shaping and texture pattern sequence.

NOTE: Once you are working back and forth, the raglan decreases are worked in reverse on WS so they will look the same on RS: P2tog, p3 (raglan sts), p2tog tbl.

Neckline

Shape neckline by binding off on a row without raglan decreases: Work to marker 3, BO the center 32 (34, 34, 36, 36) sts for front neck and continue in pattern to end of rnd. Cut yarn. Rejoin yarn to left neck edge with WS facing. BO 2 sts at each neck edge once, then 1 st 5 times. Continue working raglan decreases until they are complete, then BO rem sts in pattern.

Texture Motif Patterns—Yoke

Continue Fishing Huts until panel measures approx. 2¾ (3¼, 3½, 3½, 3½) in / 7 (8, 9, 9, 9) cm.

Waves
Rnd 1: Knit.
Rnd 2: Purl.
Rnd 3: Knit.
Rep Rnds 2–3, three times more.

Hail (worked over a multiple of 4 sts / 8 rnds)
Rnds 1–3: Knit.
Rnd 4: *P1, k3*; rep from * to *.
Rnds 5–7: Knit.
Rnd 8: *K2, p1, k1*; rep from * to *.
Rep Rnds 1–8 until panel measures approx. 2½ in / 6 cm.
Work 3 rnds in Stockinette.

Waves
Rnd 1: Knit.
Rnd 2: Purl.
Rnd 3: Knit.
Rnd 4: Purl.
Rnd 5: Knit.

Tidewater (worked over a multiple of 12 sts / 12 rnds)
Rnd 1: *P6, k6*; rep from * to *.
Rnd 2: *P5, k6, p1*; rep from * to *.
Rnd 3: *P4, k6, p2*; rep from * to *.
Rnd 4: *P3, k6, p3*; rep from * to *.
Rnd 5: *P2, k6, p4*; rep from * to *.
Rnd 6: *P1, k6, p5*; rep from * to *.
Rnd 7: *K6, p6*; rep from * to *.
Rnd 8: *K5, p6, k1*; rep from * to *.
Rnd 9: *K4, p6, k2*; rep from * to *.
Rnd 10: *K3, p6, k3*; rep from * to *.
Rnd 11: *K2, p6, k4*; rep from * to *.
Rnd 12: *K1, p6, k5*; rep from * to *.
Rep Rnds 1–12 until panel measures approx. 2 in / 5 cm.

Waves
Rnd 1: Knit.
Rnd 2: Purl.
Rnd 3: Knit.
Rnd 4: Purl.
Rnd 5: Knit.

Fishing Net (worked over a multiple of 4 sts / 4 rnds)
Rnds 1–2: *K2, p2*; rep from * to *.
Rnds 3–4: *P2, k2*; rep from * to *.
Rep Rnds 1–4 for remainder of piece.

Neckband

The neckband is doubled. With smaller-size circular needle and RS facing, pick up and knit approx. 104 (104, 112, 116, 120) sts around neck. Join to work in the round and work k2, p2 ribbing until band measures 2 in / 5 cm. Fold neckband to WS and with RS facing, *lift 1 st from base of neckband onto left needle and k2tog, joining the neckband to itself*; rep from * to *, being careful to align sts on base of neckband with live sts. Alternatively, bind off neckband, fold and sew down on WS.

Finishing

Weave in all ends neatly on WS by sewing into the tops of the sts so the yarn won't show on RS.

Wash sweater following instructions on ball band. Lay sweater on a dry towel, pat it out to finished measurements, and leave until completely dry.

STORM, Child Version

PATTERN SUITABLE FOR INTERMEDIATE KNITTERS

SIZES	4 (6, 8, 10, 12) years
FINISHED MEASUREMENTS	
Chest Circumference	23¾ (26¾, 30, 33, 36¼) in / 60 (68, 76, 84, 92) cm
Length	15¾ (17¼, 19, 20½, 22) in / 40 (44, 48, 52, 56) cm
Sleeve Length	12¼ (13½, 14½, 15¾, 17) in / 31 (34, 37, 40, 43) cm
GAUGE	23 sts × 33 rows = 4 × 4 in / 10 × 10 cm in Stockinette with larger-size needles. Make a gauge swatch before you begin knitting to ensure that you are working at the correct gauge. Adjust needle size if necessary to obtain correct gauge.
MATERIALS	
Yarn	Double Sunday by Sandnes Garn (100% Norwegian Merino wool, 137 yd/108 m / 50 g)
Yarn Amounts	5 (6, 7, 9, 10) skeins
Needles	US sizes 2½ and 6 / 3 and 4 mm: 24 in / 60 cm circulars and sets of 5 dpns if you are not using magic loop
Notions	8 stitch markers, blunt tapestry needle

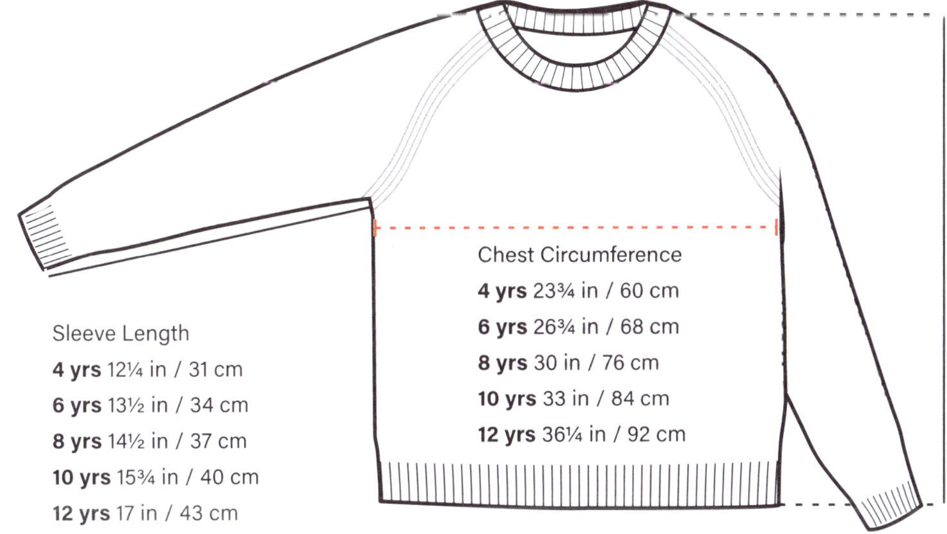

Garment Construction

STORM is worked from the bottom up. The body is knit first and then the sleeves. The body and sleeves are then joined on a circular needle for the yoke worked in the round. The body and sleeves are worked with the same sequence of motifs.

Body

With larger circular needle, CO 120 (144, 168, 192, 216) sts. Join to work in the rnd, being careful not to twist cast-on row. Pm as you set up ribbing: Pm (BOR), work k2, p2 ribbing for 60 (72, 84, 96, 108) sts, pm, work ribbing to end of rnd. Continue in ribbing for 1¼ in / 3 cm and then begin texture pattern. Work each motif in order as written below.

Texture Motif Patterns—Body

Hail (worked over a multiple of 4 sts / 8 rnds)
Rnds 1–3: Knit.
Rnd 4: *P1, k3*; rep from * to *.
Rnds 5–7: Knit.
Rnd 8: *K2, p1, k1*; rep from * to * until 2 st rem, p1, k1.
Rep Rnds 1–8 until panel measures approx. 1¼ (2, 2½, 3¼, 4) in / 3 (5, 6, 8, 10) cm.
Work 3 rnds in Stockinette.

Waves
Rnd 1: Knit.
Rnd 2: Purl.
Rnd 3: Knit.
Rnd 4: Purl.
Rnd 5: Knit.
Tidewater (worked over a multiple of 12 sts / 12 rnds)
Rnd 1: *P6, k6*; rep from * to *.
Rnd 2: *P5, k6, p1*; rep from * to *.
Rnd 3: *P4, k6, p2*; rep from * to *.
Rnd 4: *P3, k6, p3*; rep from * to *.
Rnd 5: *P2, k6, p4*; rep from * to *.
Rnd 6: *P1, k6, p5*; rep from * to *.
Rnd 7: *K6, p6*; rep from * to *.
Rnd 8: *K5, p6, k1*; rep from * to *.
Rnd 9: *K4, p6, k2*; rep from * to *.
Rnd 10: *K3, p6, k3*; rep from * to *.
Rnd 11: *K2, p6, k4*; rep from * to *.
Rnd 12: *K1, p6, k5*; rep from * to *.
Rep Rnds 1–12 until panel measures approx. 2 in / 5 cm.

Waves
Rnd 1: Knit.
Rnd 2: Purl.
Rnd 3: Knit.
Rnd 4: Purl.
Rnd 5: Knit.

Fishing Net (worked over a multiple of 4 sts / 4 rnds)
Rnds 1–2: *K2, p2*; rep from * to *.
Rnds 3–4: *P2, k2*; rep from * to *.
Rep Rnds 1–4 until panel measures approx. 1⅜ in / 3.5 cm.

Waves
Rnd 1: Knit.
Rnd 2: Purl.
Rnd 3: Knit.
Rep Rnds 2 and 3 three more times.

Fishing Huts (worked over a multiple of 8 sts / 16 rnds)
Rnds 1–8: *K4, p4*; rep from * to *.
Rnds 9–16: *P4, k4*; rep from * to *.
Rep Rnds 1–16 until body measures approx. 9 (10¼, 11½, 11¾, 12¼) in / 23 (26, 29, 30, 31) cm. Shape underarm as follows: Begin at BOR, BO 4 sts, work 52 (64, 76, 88, 100) sts, BO 8 sts, work to last 4 sts, BO 4 sts. Cut yarn. A total of 104 (128, 152, 176, 200) sts rem. Make note of last rnd worked in Texture Pattern Sequence. Set body aside while you make sleeves.

Sleeves

With larger-size dpns, CO 36 (36, 40, 44, 44) sts. Divide sts onto 4 dpns and join to work in the round, being careful not to twist cast-on row. Work k2, p2 ribbing for 1¼ in / 3 cm. Pm after first st and before last st. Begin working sleeve shaping as follows: increase 1 st outside each marked st with M1 (= K1, slm, M1R, knit to marker, M1L, slm, k1). Work new sts into pattern. Increase the same way every ¾ in / 2 cm a total of 11 (12, 13, 14, 16) times = 58 (60, 66, 72, 76) sts. *At the same time*, work the texture pattern as follows:

Texture Motif Patterns—Sleeves

Hail (worked over a multiple of 4 sts / 8 rnds)
Rnds 1-3: Knit.
Rnd 4: *P1, k3*; rep from * to *.
Rnds 5-7: Knit.
Rnd 8: *K2, p1, k1*; rep from * to *.
Rep Rnds 1–8 until panel measures approx. 1½ (3, 4, 5¼, 6¼) in / 4 (7, 10, 13, 16) cm.
Work 3 rnds in Stockinette.

Waves
Rnd 1: Knit.
Rnd 2: Purl.
Rnd 3: Knit.
Rnd 4: Purl.
Rnd 5: Knit.

Tidewater (worked over a multiple of 12 sts / 12 rnds)
Rnd 1: *P6, k6*; rep from * to *.
Rnd 2: *P5, k6, p1*; rep from * to *.
Rnd 3: *P4, k6, p2*; rep from * to *.
Rnd 4: *P3, k6, p3*; rep from * to *.
Rnd 5: *P2, k6, p4*; rep from * to *.
Rnd 6: *P1, k6, p5*; rep from * to *.
Rnd 7: *K6, p6*; rep from * to *.
Rnd 8: *K5, p6, k1*; rep from * to *.
Rnd 9: *K4, p6, k2*; rep from * to *.
Rnd 10: *K3, p6, k3*; rep from * to *.
Rnd 11: *K2, p6, k4*; rep from * to *.
Rnd 12: *K1, p6, k5*; rep from * to *.
Rep Rnds 1–12 until panel measures approx. 2 in / 5 cm.

Waves
Rnd 1: Knit.
Rnd 2: Purl.
Rnd 3: Knit.
Rnd 4: Purl.
Rnd 5: Knit.

Fishing Net (worked over a multiple of 4 sts / 4 rnds)
Rnds 1-2: *K2, p2*; rep from * to *.
Rnds 3-4: *P2, k2*; rep from * to *.
Rep Rnds 1–4 until panel measures approx. 1⅜ in / 3.5 cm.

Waves
Rnd 1: Knit.
Rnd 2: Purl.
Rnd 3: Knit.
Rep Rnds 2 and 3 three more times.

Fishing Huts (worked over a multiple of 8 sts / 16 rnds)
Rnds 1-8: *K4, p4*; rep from * to *.
Rnds 9-16: *P4, k4*; rep from * to *.
Rep Rnds 1–16 until panel measures approx. 2½ in / 6.5 cm.

Now, shape underarm by binding off 8 sts centered on underarm: BO 4 sts outside of each marker = 50 (52, 58, 64, 68) sts rem. Set sleeve aside while you work second sleeve the same way.

STORM Chart Symbols

☐ Knit on RS, purl on WS

⊡ Purl on RS, knit on WS

Texture Motif Patterns—Body

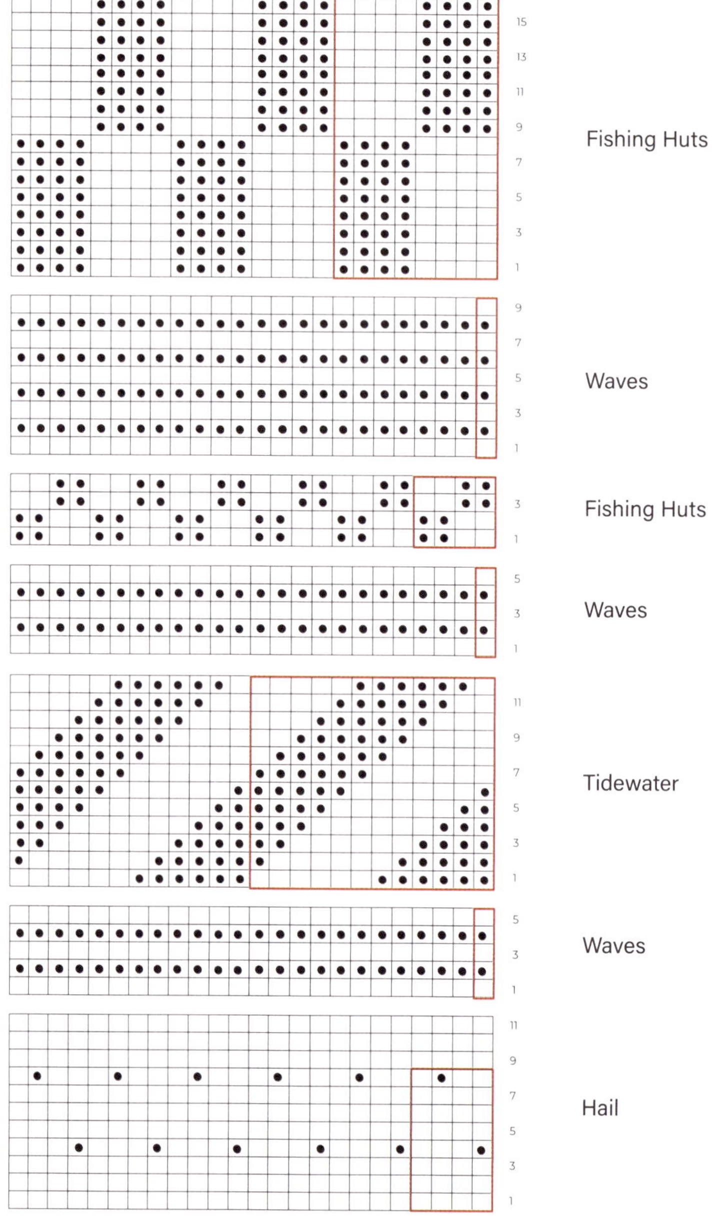

Texture Motif Patterns—Yoke

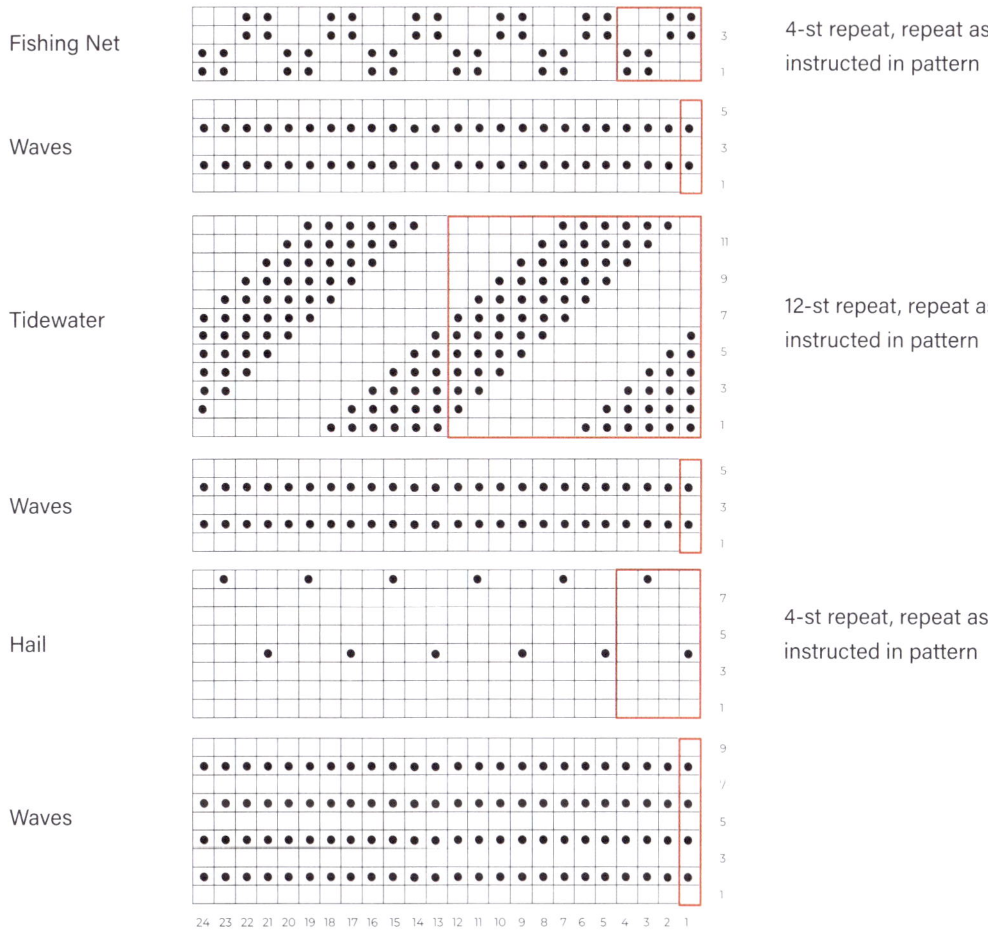

Now, shape underarm by binding off 8 sts centered on underarm: BO 4 sts outside of each marker = 50 (52, 58, 64, 68) sts rem. Set sleeve aside while you work second sleeve the same way.

Join Body and Sleeves

Arrange the sleeves on circular needle with body, matching underarms. The pattern panels on body and sleeves should align. Begin by placing 8 markers. The round begins at left shoulder on back of sweater, beginning with the left sleeve.

Marker 1: K1, pm, work until 1 st before next piece intersection.
Marker 2: Pm, k1, yo, k1.
Marker 3: Pm, work until 1 st before next piece intersection.
Marker 4: Pm, k1, yo, k1.
Marker 5: Pm, work until 1 st before next piece intersection.
Marker 6: Pm, k1, yo, k1.
Marker 7: Pm, work until 1 st before next piece intersection.
Marker 8: Pm, k1, yo.

The yoke now has 208 (236, 272, 308, 340) sts, including the yarnovers. On the next rnd, work each yarnover as k1tbl.

Raglan Decreases

Begin decreasing at each marker on every 3rd rnd: Work until 2 sts before marker. Sl 1, k1, psso, slm, k3, slm, k2tog = 8 sts decreased. Continuing to work in texture pattern as est and working the 3 raglan sts between markers in Stockinette st, rep the raglan decreases on every third rnd a total of 14 (17, 21, 24, 27) times. At the same time, after 10 (12, 16, 19, 22) decrease rnds [= 128 (140, 144, 156, 164) sts rem], begin neck shaping; work back and forth while continuing raglan shaping and texture pattern sequence.

NOTE: Once you are working back and forth, the raglan decreases are worked in reverse on WS so they will look the same on RS: P2tog, p3 (raglan sts), p2tog tbl.

Neckline

Shape neckline by binding off on a row without raglan decreases: Work to marker 3, BO the center 16 (18, 19, 20, 20) sts for front neck and continue in pattern to end of rnd. Cut yarn. Rejoin yarn to left neck edge with WS facing. BO 2 sts at each neck edge once, then 1 st 5 times. Continue working raglan decreases until they are complete, then BO rem sts in pattern.

Texture Motif Patterns—Yoke

Waves
Rnd 1: Knit.
Rnd 2: Purl.
Rnd 3: Knit.
Rep Rnds 2–3, three more times.

Hail (worked over a multiple of 4 sts / 8 rnds)
Rnds 1–3: Knit.
Rnd 4: *P1, k3*; rep from * to *.
Rnds 5–7: Knit.
Rnd 8: *K2, p1, k1*; rep from * to *.
Rep Rnds 1–8 until Hail panel measures approx. 1¾ in / 4.5 cm. Work 3 rnds in Stockinette.

Waves
Rnd 1: Knit.
Rnd 2: Purl.
Rnd 3: Knit.
Rnd 4: Purl.
Rnd 5: Knit.

Tidewater (worked over a multiple of 12 sts / 12 rnds)
Rnd 1: *P6, k6*; rep from * to *.
Rnd 2: *P5, k6, p1*; rep from * to *.
Rnd 3: *P4, k6, p2*; rep from * to *.
Rnd 4: *P3, k6, p3*; rep from * to *.
Rnd 5: *P2, k6, p4*; rep from * to *.
Rnd 6: *P1, k6, p5*; rep from * to *.
Rnd 7: *K6, p6*; rep from * to *.
Rnd 8: *K5, p6, k1*; rep from * to *.
Rnd 9: *K4, p6, k2*; rep from * to *.
Rnd 10: *K3, p6, k3*; rep from * to *.
Rnd 11: *K2, p6, k4*; rep from * to *.
Rnd 12: *K1, p6, k5*; rep from * to *.
Rep Rnds 1–12 until panel measures approx. 1¼ in / 3 cm.

Waves
Rnd 1: Knit.
Rnd 2: Purl.
Rnd 3: Knit.
Rnd 4: Purl.
Rnd 5: Knit.

Fishing Net (worked over a multiple of 4 sts / 4 rnds)
Rnds 1–2: *K2, p2*; rep from * to *.
Rnds 3–4: *P2, k2*; rep from * to *.
Rep Rnds 1–4 until panel measures approx. 2 (2¼, 3, 3¾, 4½) in / 5 (5.5, 7.5, 9.5, 11.5) cm.

Neckband

The neckband is doubled. With smaller-size circular needle and RS facing, pick up and knit approx. 96 (96, 104, 104, 104) sts around neck. Join to work in the round and work k2, p2 ribbing until band measures 1½ in / 4 cm. Fold neckband to WS and with RS facing, *lift 1 st from base of neckband onto left needle and k2tog, joining the neckband to itself*; rep from * to *, being careful to align sts on base of neckband with live sts. Alternatively, bind off neckband, fold neckband and sew down on WS.

Finishing

Weave in all ends neatly on WS by sewing into the tops of the sts so the yarn won't show on RS.

Wash sweater following instructions on ball band. Lay sweater on a dry towel, pat it out to finished measurements, and leave until completely dry.

RUTH

Textured Vest

The design for RUTH was inspired by a young woman, whom we named Ruth, who was photographed while waiting in line. She and her friends stand near the stairs for a DFDS cruise liner—probably sometime in the 1960s—ready to board.

The RUTH vest has a repeating texture pattern on front and back. The lower edge of the body is worked in Stockinette. The soft RUTH vest is knit with a strand of mohair held together with a strand of wool. The effect of using two different yarns together adds a heathered look, and the yarns' differences create a fine depth of color.

The vest features narrow ribbed edges around the armholes and neck, a contrast to a rolled edge on the hem.

RUTH

PATTERN SUITABLE FOR INTERMEDIATE KNITTERS

SIZES	S (M, L, XL, 2XL)
FINISHED MEASUREMENTS	
Chest Circumference	36¼ (39½, 42½, 45¾, 52¾) in / 92 (100, 108, 116, 134) cm
Length	21¼ (22, 22¾, 25¼, 26¾) in / 54 (56, 58, 64, 68) cm
GAUGE	25 sts × 32 rows/rnds = 4 × 4 in / 10 × 10 cm in Stockinette with 1 strand of each yarn held together with larger-size needles. Make a gauge swatch before you begin knitting to ensure that you are working at the correct gauge. Adjust needle size if necessary to obtain correct gauge.
MATERIALS	
Yarn	Organic Wool 1 by Krea Deluxe (100% wool, 159 yd/145 m / 50 g) Deluxe Silk Mohair by Krea Deluxe (45% silk, 33% mohair, 22% alpaca, 262 yd/240 m / 20 g)
Yarn Amounts	Organic Wool 1: 4 (5, 6, 7, 8) balls Deluxe Silk Mohair: 4 (5, 5, 6, 6) balls
Needles	US sizes 2½ and 6 / 3 and 4 mm: 32 in / 80 cm circulars and sets of 5 dpns if you are not using magic loop
Notions	2 stitch markers; blunt tapestry needles

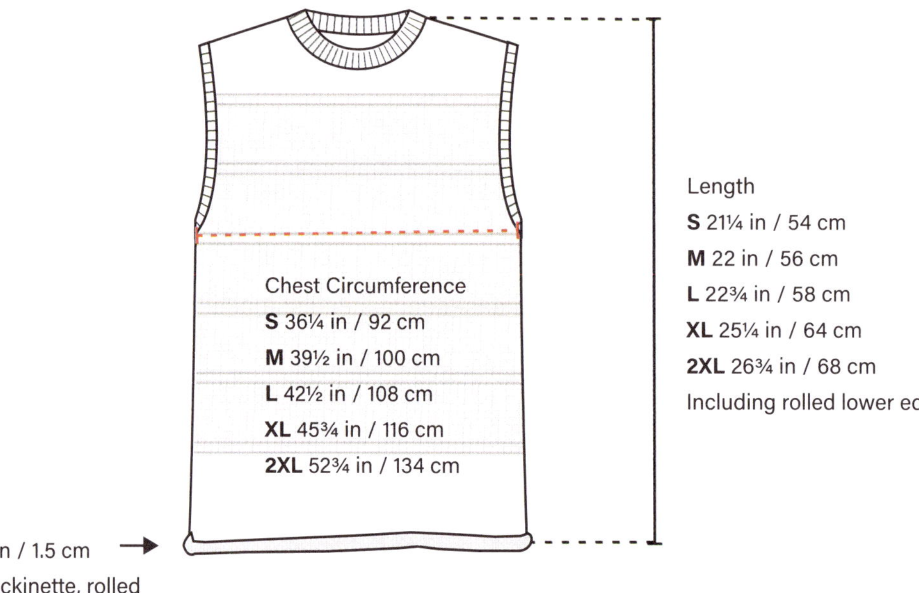

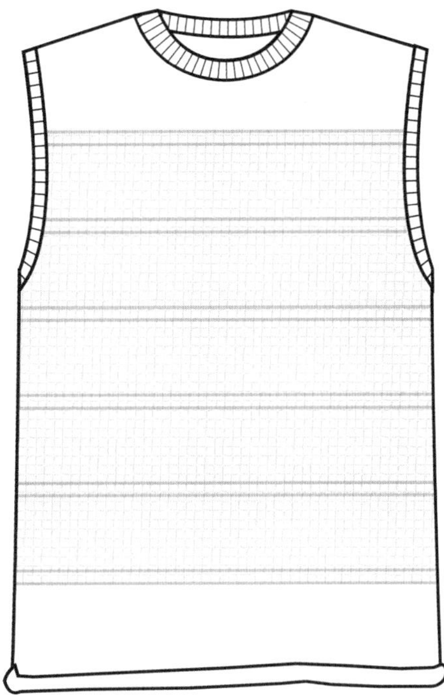

Garment Construction

RUTH is worked from the bottom up, beginning with a rolled edge. The body is worked around to the underarms in Stockinette and knit-purl texture patterns. It is divided at the underarms for back and front, which are then worked separately.

Body

With larger-size circular needle and one strand each Wool 1 and Deluxe Silk Mohair held together, CO 200 (216, 232, 248, 264) sts. Join to work in the rnd, being careful not to twist cast-on row. Pm at same time as beginning rolled edge: Pm (BOR), k100 (108, 116, 124, 132), pm, knit to end of rnd. Continue in Stockinette until body measures 6 (6¼, 6¾, 8¾, 9¾) in / 15 (16, 17, 22, 25) cm. Now begin working texture motifs (see Knit-Purl Motifs) in the round as follows: Work Waves, then Fishing Net 4 (4, 4, 4, 4) times. Work one more Waves panel. Continue in Stockinette after texture motifs are complete.

At the same time, when body measures 11½ (11¾, 12¼, 14¼, 15½) in / 29 (30, 31, 36, 39) cm, BO to shape underarms: BO 4 sts, work in pattern to 4 sts before side marker, BO 8 sts, work in pattern until 4 sts before BOR marker, BO 4 sts = 184 (200, 216, 232, 248) sts rem. Front and back each have 92 (100, 108, 116, 124) sts.

Knit-Purl Motifs

Waves
Rnd 1: Knit.
Rnd 2: Purl.
Rnd 3: Knit.
Rnd 4: Purl.
Rnd 5: Knit.

Fishing Net (worked over a multiple of 4 sts / 4 rnds)
Rnds 1–2: *K2, p2*; rep from * to *.
Rnds 3–4: *P2, k2*; rep from * to *.
Rep Rnds 1–4 five times for 20 rnds total.

Front

Work back and forth, continuing in pattern as est. Shape armholes as follows: BO 2 sts at beginning of next 2 rows, then 1 st at beginning of next 8 rows = 80 (88, 96, 104, 112) sts rem.

Neck shaping

Continue in pattern until armhole depth measures 8 (7½, 7½, 8, 8¼) in / 18 (19, 19, 20, 21) cm. BO the center 42 (46, 48, 52, 54) sts for front neck as follows:
Size S: Work 19 sts, BO 42, work 18 sts.
Size M: Work 21 sts, BO 46, work 20 sts.
Size L: Work 24, sts BO 48, work 23 sts.
Size XL: Work 26 sts, BO 52, work 25 sts.
Size 2XL: Work 29 sts, BO 54, work 28 sts.
NOTE: 1 st remains from last bind-off.
= 19 (21, 24, 26, 29) sts rem for each shoulder. Work each shoulder separately.

BO 2 sts at neck edge once, then 1 (1, 2, 2, 2) st(s) once = 16 (18, 20, 22, 25) sts rem.
Continue in Stockinette until body measures 21¼ (22, 22¾, 25¼, 26¾) in / 54 (56, 58, 64, 68) cm. Place rem sts on a holder. Work opposite shoulder the same way, binding off at neck edge as above to mirror shaping.

Back

Work back as for front through end of armhole shaping = 80 (88, 96, 104, 112) sts rem.

Neck Shaping

When armhole depth measures 9 (9½, 9¾, 10¼, 10¾) in / 23 (24, 25, 26, 27) cm, BO the center 42 (46, 48, 52, 54) sts for back neck as for front. Work each shoulder separately.

BO 2 sts at neck edge once, then 1 (1, 2, 2, 2) st(s) once = 16 (18, 20, 22, 25) sts rem.
Continue in Stockinette until body measures 21¼ (22, 22¾, 25¼, 26¾) in / 54 (56, 58, 64, 68) cm. Place rem 16 (18, 20, 22, 25) sts on a holder. Work opposite shoulder the same way, binding off at neck edge as above to mirror shaping.

Shoulders

Join each shoulder as follows: Turn work to WS. With left hand, hold the two needles so that RS of shoulders are together. Join with three-needle bind-off.

Armhole Edgings

Now work an edging around each armhole: With smaller-size circular needle, beginning at center of underarm, pick up and knit a multiple of 4 sts around armhole. Work k2, p2 ribbing for ⅝ in / 1.5 cm. BO loosely in ribbing. Work second armhole edging the same way.

Neckband

With smaller-size circular needle, beginning at left shoulder, pick up and knit approx. 92 (96, 104, 108, 108) sts (a multiple of 4 sts) around neck. Work k2, p2 ribbing for 1½ in / 4 cm. BO loosely in ribbing.

Finishing

Weave in all ends neatly on WS by sewing into the tops of the sts so the yarn won't show on RS.

Wash vest following instructions on ball band. Lay vest on a dry towel, pat it out to finished measurements, and leave until completely dry.

RUTH Chart Symbols

☐ Knit on RS, purl on WS

⊡ Purl on RS, knit on WS

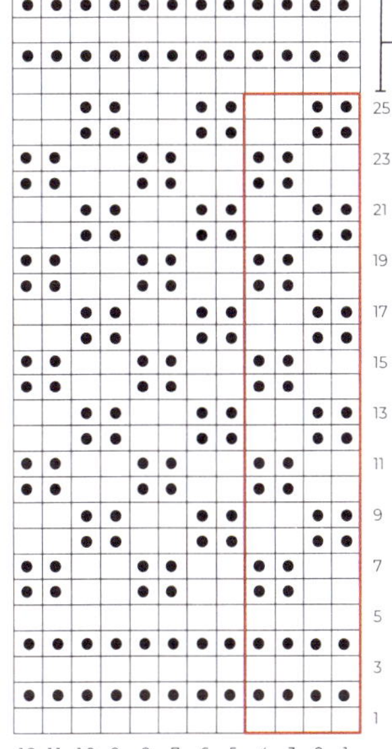

End of pattern work

Combined repeat with Waves and Fishing Net = 25 rounds. Repeat as instructed in pattern

WILLOW

Hooded Onesie with Bubble Pattern

The name for this onesie pattern, WILLOW, was inspired by an approximately 150-year-old willow tree on Skotterup beach.

Willow branches were used by fishermen to make eel traps on the steep Skotterup site. A fisherman's wife, Maren Andersdatter (1768–1852), found a hardy willow species and experimented to see if it would set roots despite saltwater spray over the beach in harsh weather. It did, and although the tree is now almost lying on the ground and seems to be taking a nap, there is still life in the old lady.

The WILLOW onesie was knit with a soft, pure new wool yarn. The yarn is worsted-spun for a round, regular yarn structure that makes the bubbles pop distinctly. The bubble structure creates small, isolated pockets of air for warmth, protecting the wearer against cold. Time for us to turn in for a nap.

WILLOW

PATTERN SUITABLE FOR EXPERIENCED KNITTERS

SIZES	3 (6, 9) months
FINISHED MEASUREMENTS	
Chest Circumference	25¼ (27½, 30) in / 64 (70, 76) cm
Total Length	22¾ (25¼, 26) in / 58 (64, 66) cm
Sleeve Length, with Cuff Folded	7½ (8¼, 9½) in / 19 (21, 24) cm
Sleeve Length, with Cuff Unfolded	9½ (11, 12¾) in / 24 (28, 32) cm
GAUGE	20 sts × 32 rows/rnds = 4 × 4 in / 10 × 10 cm in Stockinette with larger-size needles. Make a gauge swatch before you begin knitting to ensure that you are working at the correct gauge. Adjust needle size if necessary to obtain correct gauge.
MATERIALS	
Yarn	Peruvian by Filcolana (100% wool, 109 yd/100 m / 50 g)
Yarn Amounts	7 (8, 8) skeins
Needles	US sizes 2½ and 6 / 3 and 4 mm: 32 in / 80 cm circulars and set of 5 dpns if you are not using magic loop
Notions	6 stitch markers; 5 (5, 6) buttons; sewing needle and thread to match buttons; crochet hook, US size D-3 / 3 mm, if desired for picking up and knitting sts along front

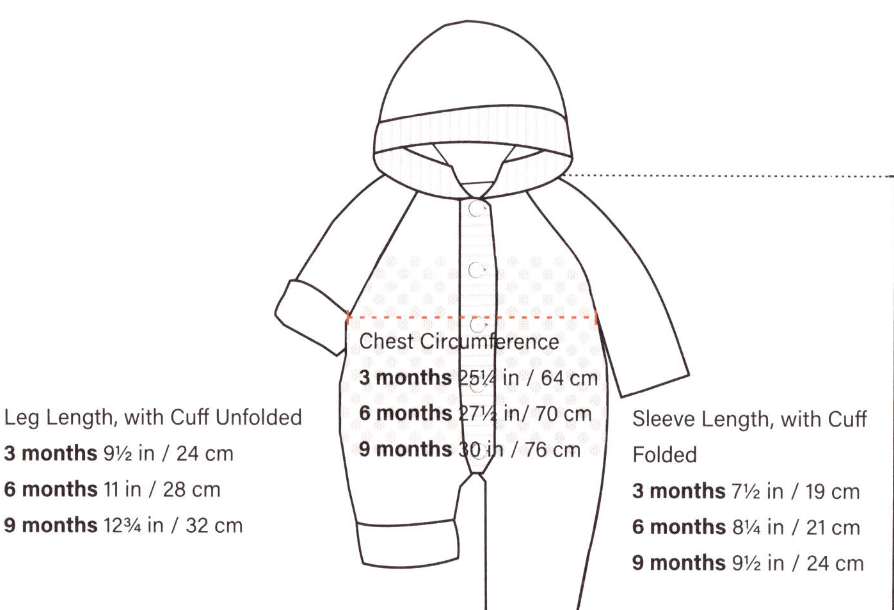

Garment Construction

The WILLOW hooded onesie is worked from the bottom up. The two legs are each worked first and then joined on a circular needle, then the body is worked. The sleeves are knit separately and joined to the body, and then the yoke is worked. The piece finishes with a hood before the ribbed edging along front edges and hood is added.

Legs

With smaller-size dpns, CO 38 (38, 42) sts. Divide the sts onto 4 dpns and join to work in the round, being careful not to twist cast-on row. Pm for BOR. Begin with the folded hem: knit in Stockinette for 2½ in / 6 cm. On next rnd, increase 6 (7, 9) sts evenly spaced as follows:
Size 3 months: (K6, M1L) 6 times, k2.
Size 6 months: (K5, M1L) 7 times, k3.
Size 9 months: (K4, M1L) 9 times, k6.
= 44 (45, 51) sts.

Place markers after first st and before last st. Change to larger-size dpns. Knit in Stockinette for 2½ in / 6 cm.

Begin shaping leg with increases: At inner side of leg, M1 on outer side of each marker (= K1, slm, M1R, knit to marker, M1L, slm, k1). Increase the same way every ¾ in / 2 cm a total of 9 (10, 11) times = 62 (65, 73) sts. Continue in Stockinette until leg measures 9½ (11, 12¾) in / 24 (28, 32) cm long or desired length.

Set first leg aside while you make second leg the same way.

Body

Arrange both legs on larger-size circular needle, starting at center front: CO 8 sts, knit sts of right leg, CO 7 (9, 9) sts [the middle st is center back (cb)], knit left leg sts = a total of 139 (147, 163) sts. Continue in Stockinette, placing markers at same time: Pm for BOR, k4, pm (cf), k35 (36, 40), pm (right side), k34 (37, 41), place 2 markers around next st for cb [the middle st of the 7 (9, 9) cast-on sts], k34 (37, 41), pm for left side, knit to end of rnd. Knit 4 rnds. BO 8 sts at center front for buttoned opening = a total of 131 (139, 155) sts rem. From now on, work back and forth, beginning with a WS row.

Bubble Pattern

Worked over a multiple of 4 sts +3 / 12 rows
Rows 1–5: K1, work in Stockinette to last st, k1.
Row 6 (RS): K1, bubble, tighten yarn, *k3, bubble, tighten yarn*; rep from * to * to last st, k1.
Rows 7–11: K1, work in Stockinette to last st, k1.
Row 12: *K3, bubble, tighten yarn*; rep from * to * to last 3 sts, k3.
Rep Rows 1–12 for pattern.

Bubble Stitch
Count down 4 rows from the first st on left needle. Insert right needle into st, knit the new st through that st. Slip st off left needle and let the old st, behind the new st, run down to the last row where the new st has been made. Tighten yarn.

Work in Bubble-Pattern until piece measures 9 (9½, 9¾) in / 23 (24, 25) cm from edge of crotch. BO 6 sts for each underarm as follows: *Work until 3 sts before first side marker, BO 3 sts, remove marker, BO 3 sts*; rep from * to * at opposite side = 119 (127, 143) sts rem. Set piece aside.
When picking up sts for front bands, be careful that the bubble pattern aligns on each side of the button bands—make sure that they lie straight over each other, so they won't looked skewed.

Sleeves

With smaller-size dpns, CO 36 (38, 38) sts. Divide sts onto dpns and join to work in the round, being careful not to twist cast-on row. Pm for BOR. Begin with the folded cuff: knit in Stockinette for 2½ in / 6 cm. On next rnd, increase 4 sts evenly spaced as follows: (K9, M1L) 4 times, k0 (2, 2) = 40 (42, 42) sts.

Change to larger-size dpns. Now begin increasing on each side of BOR marker with M1 (M1L after marker and M1R before marker). Increase the same way every ¾ in / 2 cm 6 (7, 8) times = 52 (56, 58) sts.

Continue until sleeve measures 7½ (8¼, 9½) in / 19 (21, 24) cm long or desired length. BO 6 sts for underarm as follows: Work until 3 sts before BOR, BO 3 sts, remove marker, BO 3 sts = 46 (50, 52) sts rem.

Set first sleeve aside while you make second sleeve the same way.

Join Body and Sleeves

Arrange the sleeves on circular needle with body, matching underarms = 211 (227, 247) sts total. Pm at each junction of body and sleeve = 4 markers. Yoke is worked in Stockinette. Work 1 row in Stockinette. Begin raglan shaping at each marker. Always decrease on RS at each marker as follows, removing the marker and replacing it after the decrease: *Knit until 1 st before marker, sl 2 sts to right needle as if to knit tog, k1, psso*; rep from * to * of end of row = 8 sts decreased. Decrease the same way on every RS row 15 (17, 19) times = 91 (91, 95) sts rem. BO loosely on WS.

Hood

With larger-size circular needle, beginning at front, pick up and knit 80 (80, 86) sts around neckline. The hood is worked back and forth in Stockinette. Begin by placing marker as follows: work 40 (40, 43) sts in Stockinette, pm, work in Stockinette to end of row. Continue in Stockinette until hood measures 7 (7¾, 8¼) in / 18 (19.5, 21) cm. Now, on every other row, decrease to shape hood: *Work until 3 sts before marker, k2tog tbl, k1, slm, k1, k2tog, knit to end of row*; work from * to * 3 (3, 5) times total = 74 (74, 76) sts rem.

Fold hood in half across, with 37 (37, 38) sts on each side. Join the two sides with Kitchener st.

Front Bands

The edging is worked back and forth all in one piece along front edges and around hood. Decide whether you want the buttonholes on the left or right front.

Button Band

The band begins at lower edge at crotch on right front. With smaller-size circular needle, using crochet hook US D-3 / 3.25 mm if necessary, with RS facing, pick up and knit 1 st in each edge st. Pick up 3 sts for every 4 rows along right front, front of hood, then left front. Make sure you pick up sts straight along edge and you have a multiple of 4+2 sts in the end. Work 4 rows in k2, p2 ribbing.

On the left or right front, make 5 (5, 6) buttonholes spaced about 2½ in / 6 cm apart as follows: Beginning on WS, work to first marker, *k2tog, yo twice, tighten yarn, work in ribbing as est to next buttonhole*; rep from * to * for a total of 5 (5, 6) buttonholes. On next row, k1 into double yarnover and tighten. Continue in ribbing until band measures 1¼ in / 3 cm. BO in pattern.

Finishing

Weave in all ends neatly on WS by sewing into the tops of the sts so the yarn won't show on RS.

Sew buttonhole end of front band to BO crotch sts, using mattress st over the bound-off sts. Sew button end behind buttonhole end.
Sew on 5 (5, 6) buttons to match buttonholes.

Wash onesie following instructions on ball band. Lay onesie on a dry towel, pat it out to finished measurements, and leave until completely dry.

So the raglan decreases will look correct, slip the 2 sts at the same time as if to knit together. If you don't slip the stitches this way, the decrease will look twisted.

WILLOW Chart Symbols

(blank square)	Kn t on RS, purl on WS
•	Purl on RS, kn t on WS
(bubble stitch)	Work Rnds/Rows 1-5 or 7-11 in Stockinette (beginning with a purl row if working flat). On Rnd/Row 6 or 12, Bubble Stitch: Insert right needle into st 4 sts down from st on left needle. Knit new st; drop st on left needle and let it run down to loop.

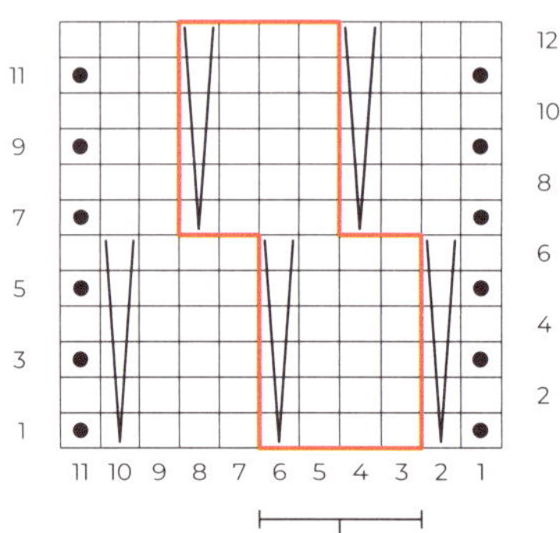

Bubble Pattern
4-st repeat
work as instructed in pattern

Note: Chart begins with a WS row. Work Row 1 from left to right.

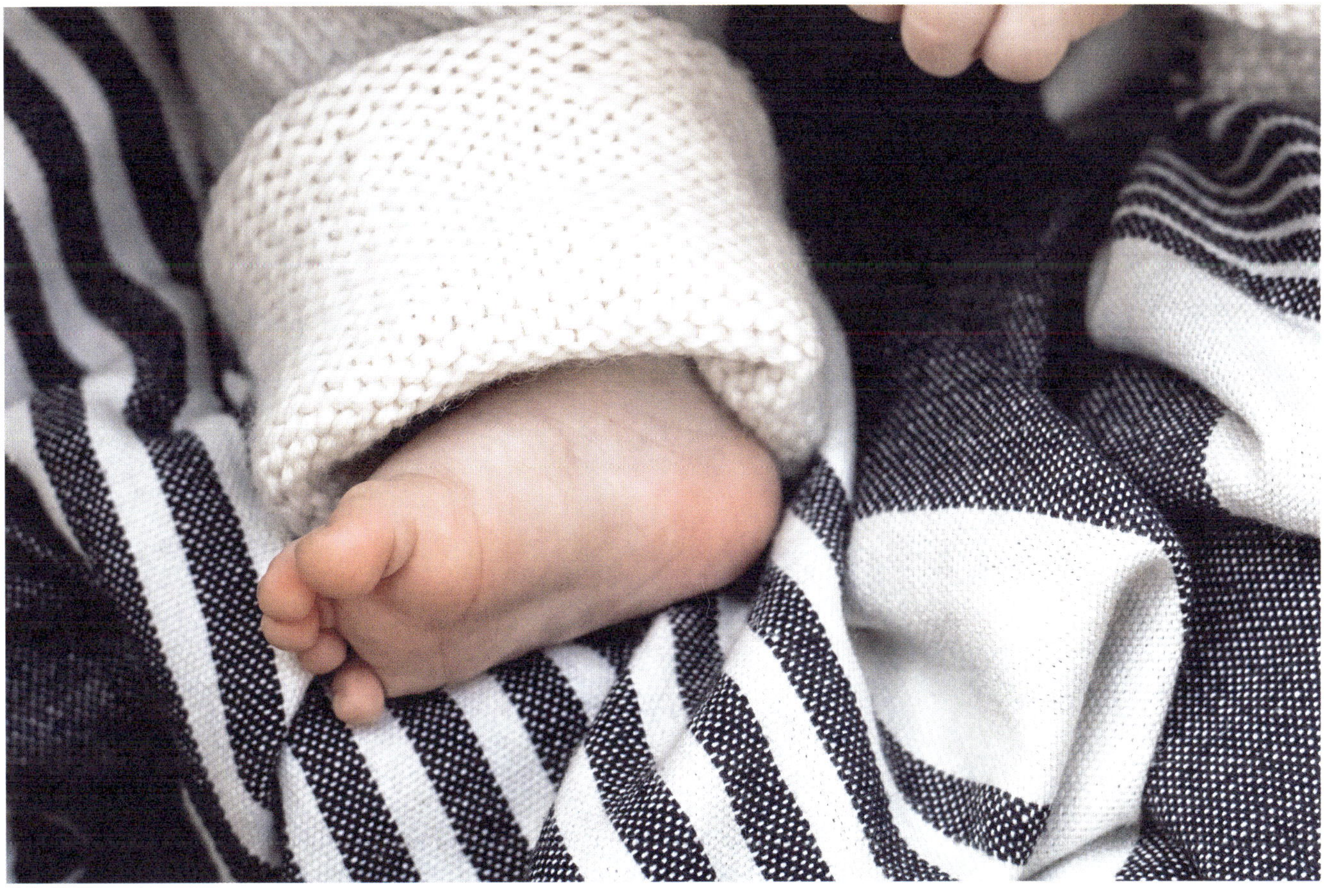

SAIL

Blanket with Bubble Pattern

SAIL takes its name from the maritime expression "Set all sails," meaning to move ahead with full power toward something. If one has done that, one has earned a little rest with a warm blanket.

This blanket is covered with an all-over bubble pattern and finished with a seed stitch edging.

SAIL is a warm and soft blanket, knit with a high-quality, natural white organic Merino yarn. The yarn is perfect for making all the bubbles pop on the surface.

SAIL

PATTERN SUITABLE FOR EXPERIENCED KNITTERS

FINISHED MEASUREMENTS

Finished Measurements	27½ × 35½ in / 70 × 90 cm

GAUGE

28 sts × 40 rows = 4 × 4 in / 10 × 10 cm in Bubble Pattern.
Make a gauge swatch before you begin knitting to ensure that you are working at the correct gauge. Adjust needle size if necessary to obtain correct gauge.

MATERIALS

Yarn	Organic Wool 1 by Krea Deluxe (100% wool, 159 yd/145 m / 50 g)
Yarn Amounts	16 balls
Needles	US size 2½ / 3 mm: 32 in / 80 cm circular
Notions	2 stitch markers

Blanket Construction

The blanket features an allover bubble pattern edged with seed stitch. The edging goes all the way around the blanket, which is worked from the bottom up. It begins with a seed stitch panel at lower edge. The bubble section is framed by seed stitch panels at each side. The blanket is finished with seed stitch across the top.

Blanket

CO 197 sts. The first row = WS. Work back and forth in seed st (see Patterns), placing markers to separate seed and bubble sections as follows: *Work 14 seed sts, pm, continue in seed st to last 14 sts, pm, work in seed st to end of row. Continue in seed st until piece measures 2 in / 5 cm, ending with a RS row.

Now set up Bubble Pattern as follows: Work seed st to marker, slm, work Row 1 in Bubble Pattern, work seed st to end.

Continue in patterns as est with seed and bubble patterns until piece measures approx. 33½ in / 85 cm.

Finish blanket with 2 in / 5 cm seed st. BO loosely in seed st.

Patterns

Seed Stitch (worked over a multiple of 2 sts / 2 rows)
Work first row alternating knit and purl sts. On next row, work knit over purl and purl over knit:
Row 1: *K1, p1*; rep from * to *.
Row 2: *P1, k1*; rep from * to *.
Rep Rows 1 and 2 for pattern.

Bubble Pattern (worked over a multiple of 4 sts + 1 / 12 rows)
Rows 1–5: Beginning with a purl row, work in Stockinette.
Row 6 (RS): Bubble, tighten yarn, *k3, bubble, tighten yarn*; rep from * to * to end of row.
Rows 7–11: Work in Stockinette.
Row 12: K2, bubble, tighten yarn, *k3, bubble, tighten yarn*; rep from * to * until 2 sts before marker, k2.
Rep Rows 1–12.

Bubble Stitch
Count down 4 rnds from the first st on left needle. Insert right needle into st, knit the new st through that st. Slip st off left needle and let the old st, behind the new st, run down to the last rnd where the new st has been made. Tighten yarn.

Finishing

Weave in all ends neatly on WS by sewing into the tops of the sts so the yarn won't show on RS.

Wash blanket following instructions on ball band. Lay blanket on a dry towel, pat it out to finished measurements, and leave until completely dry.

SAIL Chart Symbols

Knit on RS, purl on WS

Purl on RS, knit on WS

Bubble Stitch

Count down 4 rnds from the first st on left needle. Insert right needle into st, knit the new st through that st. Slip st off left needle and let the old st, behind the new st, run down to the last rnd where the new st has been made. Tighten yarn.

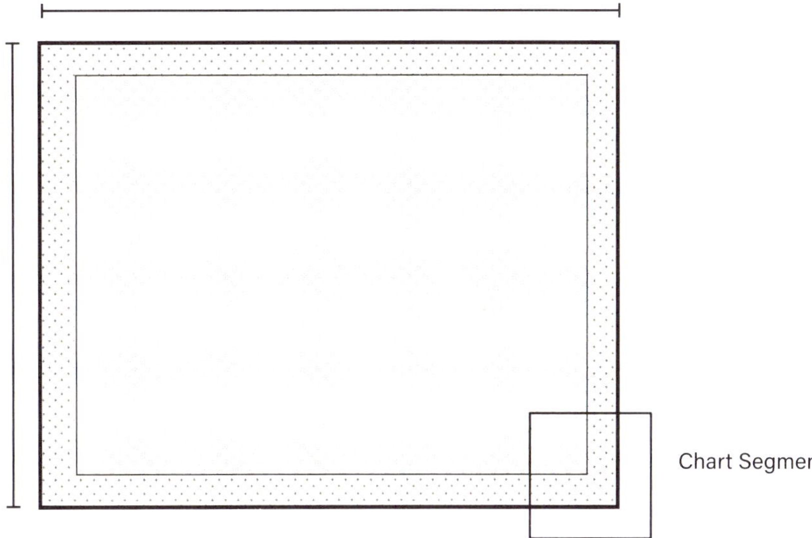

Kn t on RS, purl on WS

Purl on RS, kn t on WS

Work Rnds/Rows 1-5 or 7-11 in Stockinette (beginning with a purl row if working flat). On Rnd/Row 6 or 12, Bubble Stitch: Insert right needle into st 4 sts down from st on left needle. Knit new st; drop st on left needle and let it run down to loop.

Bubble Pattern
4-st repeat
work as instructed in pattern

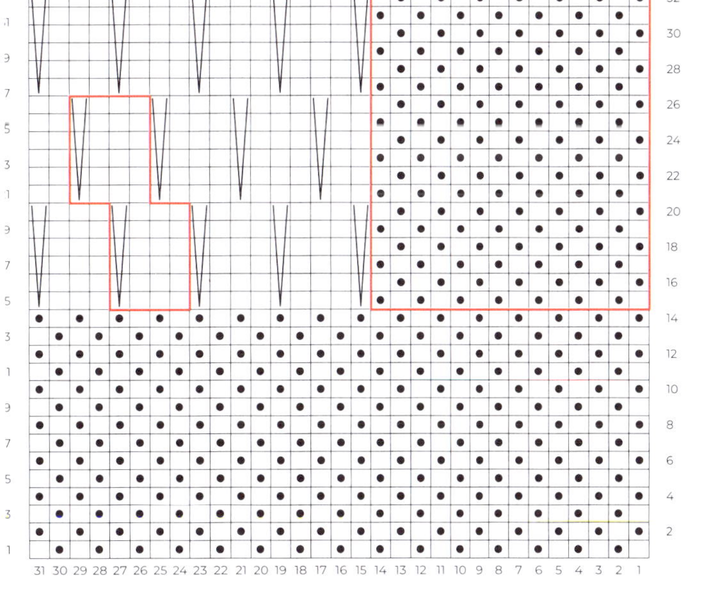

Note: Patterns begin with a WS row.

CLASSIC STRIPED KNITS

INSPIRATION

Iconic Breton
Two-Color Stripes
Stockinette
Shoulder Buttons
Classic Anchor Motif

SAILOR

Striped Sailor's Pullover

Striped pullovers are practically synonymous with sailor's sweaters. The iconic ecru and blue striped Breton top (from Brittany, hence the name) goes back to the nineteenth century and the French navy. The stripes have since been used in fashion designs and immortalized by designers such as Coco Chanel and Jean Paul Gaultier and, since then, have been interpreted by numerous mainstream brands. The Marinière, the original sailor's shirt from the French navy, inspired the various versions of SAILOR sweaters in this book.

SAILOR is a striped sweater buttoned on the shoulder, with ribbing around the neckline and sleeve cuffs, as well as running down the body, for an open/loose finish. It is made with a rolled edge on the body for the child's size, and for adults, we have regular and oversize versions. It's truly a modern classic.

We used a 4-ply worsted-spun wool yarn for the SAILOR Child and SAILOR Oversize sweaters. The yarn is round and very regular, which lends itself well to stitch definition and two-color knitting. For the SAILOR Adult sweater, we used a 3-ply firm and round wool yarn, recommended for outdoor and leisurewear sweaters.

SAILOR, Oversize Version

PATTERN SUITABLE FOR EXPERIENCED KNITTERS

SIZES	S (M, L, XL, 2XL)
FINISHED MEASUREMENTS	
Chest Circumference	41 (44, 47¼, 50½, 53½) in / 104 (112, 120, 128, 136) cm
Length	22½ (23¼, 24, 24¾, 25½) in / 57 (59, 61, 63, 65) cm
Sleeve Length	14¼ (15, 15¾, 16½, 17¼) in / 36 (38, 40, 42, 44) cm
GAUGE	19 sts × 28 rnds = 4 × 4 in / 10 × 10 cm in Stockinette with larger-size needles. Make a gauge swatch before you begin knitting to ensure that you are working at the correct gauge. Adjust needle size if necessary to obtain correct gauge.
MATERIALS	
Yarn	Peruvian by Filcolana (100% wool, 109 yd/100 m / 50 g)
Yarn Amounts	Main color: 203 Camel: 9 (10, 11, 12, 13) skeins Stripes (CC): 101 Natural White: 3 (4, 4, 4, 5) skeins
Needles	US size 6 / 4 mm: 32 in / 80 cm circular and set of 5 dpns if you are not using magic loop; US 2½ / 3 mm short circular for neckband only
Notions	4 stitch markers; 4 buttons, ¾ in / 20 mm in diameter; sewing needle and thread to match buttons

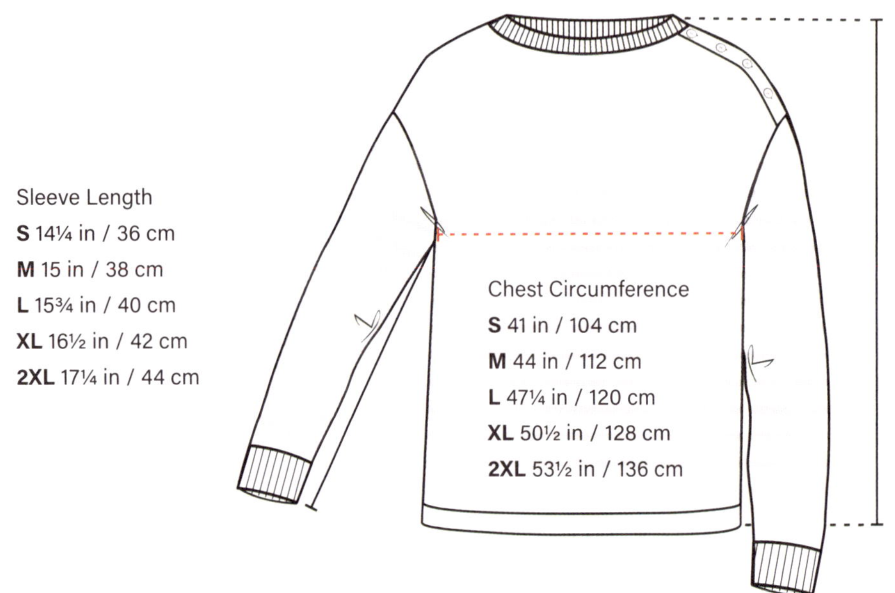

Garment Construction

SAILOR is worked from the bottom up, with a folded hem edging the body. The body is divided at the underarms and the front and back are then worked separately. The sleeves are worked from the cuff up. The sweater finishes with a button band along one shoulder and ribbing around the neckline.

Body

With larger-size circular needle and MC, CO 198 (214, 228, 244, 260) sts. Join to work in the rnd, being careful not to twist cast-on row. Begin working folded hem while placing markers: Pm (BOR), k99 (107, 114, 122, 130), pm, knit to end of rnd. Knit for 1⅜ in / 3.5 cm. Purl 1 rnd (fold line) and knit for another 1⅜ in / 3.5 cm. Fold hem to WS at purl rnd and join live sts to cast-on row: *With RS facing, lift a st from cast-on row and place it on left needle, k2tog, joining cast-on and live st*; rep from * to *. Make sure that you align each cast-on st with its live st on needle so hem won't skew. From this point on, take measurements from purl foldline.

Next Rnd: Increase 12 (16, 16, 16, 16) sts evenly spaced as follows:
Size S: (K16, M1L, k17, M1L) 6 times.
Size M: (K13, M1L) 16 times, k6.
Size L: (K14, M1L) 16 times, k4.
Size XL: (K15, M1L) 16 times, k4.
Size 2XL: (K16, M1L) 16 times, k4.
= 210 (230, 244, 260, 276) sts.

Knit for 4 in / 10 cm.

Stripe Pattern

Begin Stripe Pattern as follows: *Change to stripe color (CC), knit 3 rnds, change to MC, knit 6 rnds*; work from * to * a total of 9 (10, 10, 11, 12) times. When body measures 14¼ (14½, 15, 15½, 15¾) in / 36 (37, 38, 39, 40) cm, BO 2 sts on each side of BOR and side markers for center of each underarm = 202 (222, 236, 252, 268) sts rem. Divide body for front and back with 101 (111, 118, 126, 134) sts for each. Work each piece back and forth in Stockinette, continuing stripe pattern as est to total number of repeats as specified above. After completing stripe pattern, continue with MC only.

Back

Shape armholes as you continue stripe pattern. At underarm, BO 2 sts each at beginning of next 2 (2, 2, 4, 4) rows = 97 (107, 114, 118, 126) sts rem. Continue without further decreasing until body measures 21¾ (22½, 23¼, 24, 24¾) in / 55 (57, 59, 61, 63) cm. BO the center 45 (53, 56, 60, 66) sts for back neck as follows:
Size S: K26, BO 45 sts, k25.
Size M: K27, BO 53 sts, k26.
Size L: K29, BO 56 sts, k28.
Size XL: K29, BO 60 sts, k28.
Size 2XL: K30, BO 66 sts, k29.
NOTE: 1 st remains from last bind-off.

Work each shoulder separately. Work neck shaping at neck edge: BO 2 sts and then BO 1 st = 23 (24, 26, 26, 27) sts rem. Continue until body measures 22½ (23¼, 24, 24¾, 25½) in / 57 (59, 61, 63, 65) cm. BO shoulder sts. Make other shoulder the same way, binding off at neck edge as above to mirror shaping.

Front

Shape armholes at beginning of each row as you continue stripe pattern. BO 2 sts at beginning of next 2 (2, 2, 4, 4) rows = 97 (107, 114, 118, 126) sts rem. Continue without further decreasing until body measures 22 (22¾, 23¾, 24½, 25¼) in / 56 (58, 60, 62, 64) cm. BO the center 43 (51, 52, 56, 62) sts for front neck as follows:
Size S: K27, BO 43 sts, k26.
Size M: K28, BO 51 sts, k27.
Size L: K31, BO 52 sts, k30.
Size XL: K31, BO 56 sts, k30.
Size 2XL: K32, BO 62 sts, k31.
NOTE: 1 st remains from last bind-off.

Stripe Colors

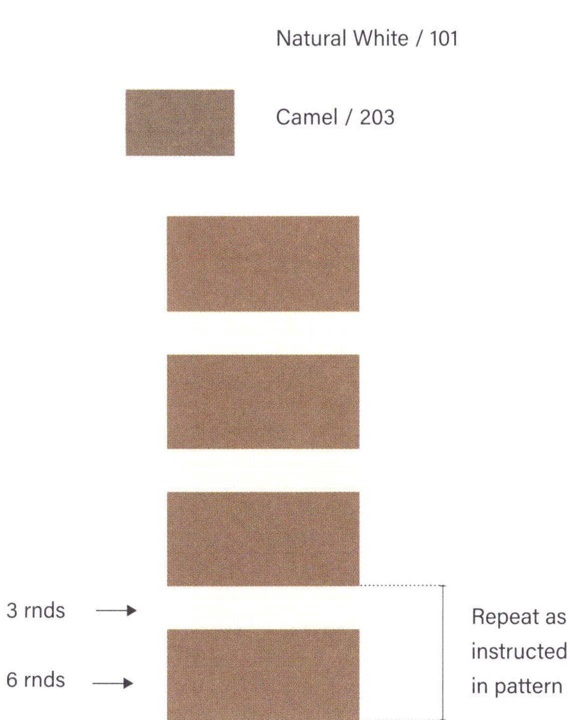

Work each shoulder separately. Work neck shaping at neck edge: BO 2 sts. BO 1 st 2 (2, 3, 3, 3) times = 23 (24, 26, 26, 27) sts rem. Continue until body measures 24½ (25¼, 26, 26¾, 27½) in / 62 (64, 66, 68, 70) cm. Loosely BO shoulder sts. Make other shoulder the same way, binding off at neck edge as above to mirror shaping.

Sleeves

With dpns and MC, CO 32 (32, 36, 36, 38) sts. Divide sts onto 4 dpns and join to work in the round, being careful not to twist cast-on row. Pm for BOR. Work k1, p1 ribbing for 2½ in / 6 cm. Pm after first and before last st. On next rnd, knit, increasing 8 sts evenly spaced as follows:
Sizes S and M: (K4, M1L) 8 times.
Sizes L and XL: (K4, M1L, k5, M1L) 4 times.
Size 2XL: (K4, M1L, k5, M1L) 4 times, k2.
= 40 (40, 44, 44, 46) sts.

Knit for 4 in / 10 cm and then begin stripe pattern (see Stripe Pattern—Sleeves). *At the same time*, begin shaping sleeve: Increase with M1 outside each marker (= K1, slm, M1R, knit to marker, M1L, slm, k1). Increase the same way on every 6th rnd a total of 17 (18, 18, 20, 21) times = 74 (76, 80, 84, 88) sts. Continue in stripes.

Stripe Pattern—Sleeves

Change to stripe color (CC), knit 3 rnds, change to MC, knit 6 rnds; work from * to * a total of 7 (8, 8, 9, 10) times. Make sure sleeve and body stripes align. Change to MC and work only with MC for rest of sleeve.

When sleeve measures 14¼ (15, 15¾, 16½, 17¼) in / 36 (38, 40, 42, 44) cm long, BO 4 sts centered at underarm (= BO 2 sts on each side of BOR marker). Now work back and forth in Stockinette over rem 70 (72, 76, 80, 84) sts. With RS facing, shape sleeve cap: (On every row, BO 1 st each at beginning of next 2 rows) 3 times. Then BO 2 sts at beginning of next 2 rows; BO 3 sts at beginning of next 2 rows; BO 4 sts at beginning of next 2 rows. BO rem 46 (48, 52, 56, 60) sts. Set sleeve aside while you make second sleeve the same way.

Shoulder Bands

Join either right or left shoulder with Kitchener st. This shoulder will not have the buttons.

With RS of body aligned with RS of sleeve, attach sleeve to side with seamed shoulder by sewing from WS along armhole.

Work buttonhole band on open front shoulder: With smaller-size circular needle, MC, and RS facing, pick up and knit approx. 26 (26, 28, 28, 30) sts with 1 st in each st across front shoulder, bringing yarn through from WS. Work 3 rows back and forth in Stockinette. Then make 3 buttonholes approx. 1¼ in / 3 cm apart as follows: Yo, k2tog for each buttonhole.

Work 2 rows in Stockinette. Loosely BO on next (WS) row.

Now make button band on back shoulder. With smaller-size circular needle and RS facing, pick up and knit approx. 26 (26, 28, 28, 30) sts with 1 st in each st across back, bringing yarn through from WS. BO on next (WS) row.

Neckband

The neckband is doubled. With smaller-size circular needle and RS facing and beginning at one edge of button band, pick up and knit an even number of sts along neck opening, including the button bands.

Work back and forth in k1, p1 ribbing for 3 rows. On next row, on front side of neckband, make a buttonhole on 3rd st from edge and another after 6 rows. Continue in ribbing as est until band measures 1½ in / 4 cm. BO in ribbing. Fold neckband and sew down on WS. Sew edges of two neckband buttonholes together to form one doubled buttonhole. Attach sleeve.

Finishing

Weave in all ends neatly on WS by sewing into the tops of the sts so the yarn won't show on RS.

Sew on buttons to back shoulder band.

Wash sweater following instructions on ball band. Lay sweater on a dry towel, pat it out to finished measurements, and leave until completely dry.

SAILOR, Adult Version

PATTERN SUITABLE FOR EXPERIENCED KNITTERS

SIZES	S (M, L, XL, 2XL)
FINISHED MEASUREMENTS	
Chest Circumference	37¾ (39½, 42½, 44, 47¼) in / 96 (100, 108, 112, 120) cm
Length	24½ (25¼, 26¾, 27½, 29¼) in / 62 (64, 66, 68, 70) cm
Sleeve Length	21¾ (22, 22, 22½, 22¾) in / 55 (56, 56, 57, 58) cm
GAUGE	22 sts × 28 rnds = 4 × 4 in / 10 × 10 cm in Stockinette with larger-size needles. Make a gauge swatch before you begin knitting to ensure that you are working at the correct gauge. Adjust needle size if necessary to obtain correct gauge.
MATERIALS	
Yarn	Jensen Yarn by Isager (100% wool, 137 yd/125 m / 50 g)
Yarn Amounts	Main color (MC), 100 Navy: 7 (8, 9, 10, 11) hanks Stripes (CC), 0 White: 3 (4, 4, 4, 5) hanks
Needles	US size 4 / 3.5 mm: 32 in / 80 cm circular and set of 5 dpns if you are not using magic loop; US 2½ / 3 mm short circular for neckband only
Notions	4 stitch markers; 4 buttons, ¾ in / 20 mm in diameter; sewing needle and thread to match buttons

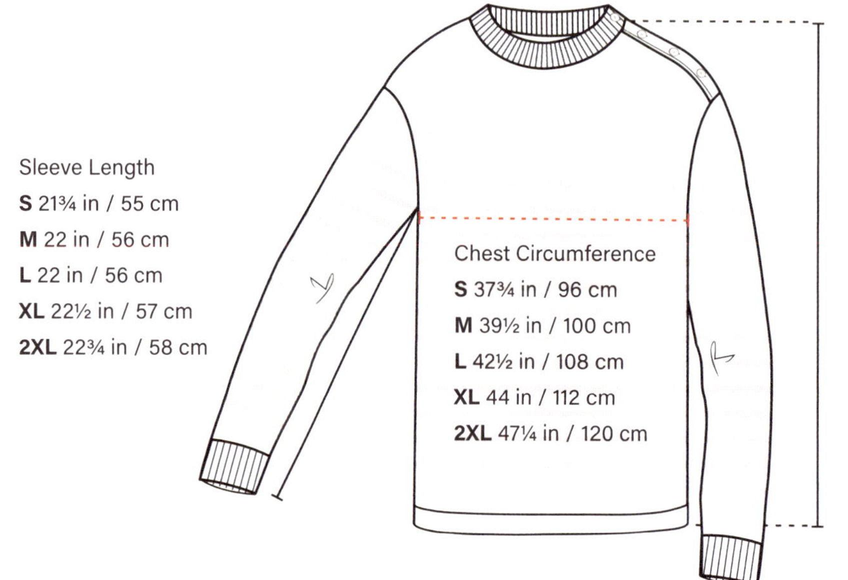

Garment Construction

SAILOR is worked from the bottom up, with a folded hem edging the body. The body is divided at the underarms and the front and back are then worked separately. The sleeves are worked from the cuff up. The sweater finishes with a button band along one shoulder and ribbing around the neckline.

Body

With larger-size circular needle and MC, CO 198 (206, 224, 232, 250) sts. Join to work in the rnd, being careful not to twist cast-on row. Begin working folded hem while placing markers: Pm (BOR), k99 (103, 112, 116, 125), pm, knit to end of rnd. Knit for 1⅜ in / 3.5 cm. Purl 1 rnd (fold line) and knit for another 1⅜ in / 3.5 cm. Fold hem to WS at purl rnd and join live sts to cast-on row: *With RS facing, lift a st from cast-on row and place it on left needle, k2tog, joining cast-on and live st*; rep from * to *. Make sure that you align each cast-on st with its live st on needle so hem won't skew. From this point on, take measurements from purl foldline.

Next Rnd: Increase 14 (14, 14, 14, 14) sts evenly spaced as follows:
Size S: (K14, M1L) 14 times, k2.
Size M: (K14, M1L) 14 times, k10.
Size L: (K16, M1L) 14 times.
Size XL: (K16, M1L) 14 times, k8.
Size 2XL: (K17, M1L) 14 times, k12.
= 212 (220, 238, 246, 264) sts.

Knit for 4 in / 10 cm.

Stripe Pattern

Begin Stripe Pattern as follows: *Change to stripe color (CC), knit 3 rnds, change to MC, knit 6 rnds*; work from * to * a total of 10 (10, 11, 12, 13) times. When body measures 14¼ (15, 15¾, 16½, 17¼) in / 36 (38, 40, 42, 44) cm, BO 1 (1, 1, 2, 2) sts on each side of BOR and side markers for center of each underarm = 208 (216, 234, 238, 256) sts rem. Divide body for front and back with 104 (108, 117, 119, 128) sts for each. Work each piece back and forth in Stockinette, continuing stripe pattern as est to total number of repeats as specified above. After completing stripe pattern, continue with MC only.

Back

Shape armholes as you continue stripe pattern. At underarm, BO 2 sts each at beginning of next 2 rows and then BO 1 (1, 1, 2, 2) st(s) each at beginning of next 2 rows = 102 (106, 115, 115, 124) sts rem. Continue in stripe pattern until piece measures 23¾ (24½, 25¼, 26, 26¾) in / 60 (62, 64, 66, 68) cm. BO the center 38 (38, 45, 43, 50) sts for back neck as follows:
Size S: 32, BO 38 sts, k31.
Size M: K34, BO 38 sts, k33.
Size L: K35, BO 45 sts, k34.
Size XL: K36, BO 43 sts, k35.
Size 2XL: K37, BO 50 sts, k36.
NOTE: 1 st remains from last bind-off.

Work each shoulder separately = 32 (34, 35, 36, 37) sts rem for each shoulder. Work neck shaping at neck edge: BO 2 sts at beginning of row, then BO 1 st = 29 (31, 32, 33, 34) sts rem. Continue until body measures 24½ (25¼, 26, 26¾, 27½) in / 62 (64, 66, 68, 70) cm. Loosely BO shoulder sts. Make other shoulder the same way, binding off at neck edge as above to mirror shaping.

Front

Shape armholes at beginning of each row as you continue stripe pattern. BO 2 sts at beginning of next 2 rows, and then BO 1 (1, 1, 2, 2) st(s) at beginning of next 2 rows = 102 (106, 115, 115, 124) sts rem. Continue in stripe pattern until piece measures 22 (22¾, 23¾, 24½, 25¼) in / 56 (58, 60, 62, 64) cm. BO the center 36 (36, 41, 39, 46) sts for front neck as follows:
Size S: 33, BO 36 sts, k32.
Size M: K35, BO 36 sts, k34.
Size L: K37, BO 41 sts, k36.

Size XL: K38, BO 39 sts, k37.
Size 2XL: K39, BO 46 sts, k38.
NOTE: 1 st remains from last bind-off.
= 33 (35, 37, 38, 39) sts rem for each shoulder

Work each shoulder separately. Work neck shaping at neck edge: BO 2 sts at neck edge once, then 1 st 2 (2, 3, 3, 3) times = 29 (31, 32, 33, 34) sts rem. Continue until body measures 24½ (25¼, 26, 26¾, 27½) in / 62 (64, 66, 68, 70) cm. Loosely BO shoulder sts. Make other shoulder the same way, binding off at neck edge as above to mirror shaping.

Sleeves

With dpns and MC, CO 40 (44, 44, 48, 54) sts. Divide sts onto 4 dpns and join to work in the round, being careful not to twist cast-on row. Pm for BOR. Work k1, p1 ribbing for 2½ in / 6 cm. Pm after first and before last st. On next rnd, knit, increasing 8 sts evenly spaced as follows:
Size S: (K5, M1L) 8 times.
Sizes M and L: (K5, M1L, k6, M1L) 4 times.
Size XL: (K6, M1L) 8 times.
Size 2XL: (K6, M1L, k7, M1L) 4 times, k2.
= 48 (52, 52, 56, 62) sts.

Knit for 4 in / 10 cm and then begin stripe pattern (see Stripe Pattern—Sleeves). *At the same time*, begin shaping sleeve: Increase with M1 outside each marker (= K1, slm, M1R, knit to marker, M1L, slm, k1). Increase the same way every ¾ in / 2 cm a total of 20 (22, 22, 25, 26) times = 88 (96, 96, 106, 114) sts. Continue in stripes.

Stripe Pattern—Sleeves

Change to stripe color (CC), knit 3 rnds, change to MC, knit 6 rnds; work from * to * a total of 12 (13, 14, 14, 15) times. Make sure sleeve and body stripes align. Change to MC and work only with MC for rest of sleeve.

When sleeve measures 21¾ (22, 22, 22½, 22¾) in / 55 (56, 56, 57, 58) cm long, BO 4 (4, 4, 8, 8) sts centered on underarm [= BO 2 (2, 2, 4, 4) sts on each side of BOR marker). Now work back and forth in Stockinette over rem 84 (92, 92, 98, 106) sts. With RS facing, shape sleeve cap: (BO 1 st each at beginning of next 2 rows) 3 times = 78 (86, 86, 92, 100) sts rem. Next, BO 2 sts at beginning of next 2 rows; BO 3 sts at beginning of next 2 rows; BO 4 sts at beginning of next 2 rows. Loosely BO rem 60 (68, 68, 74, 82) sts. Set sleeve aside while you make second sleeve the same way.

Shoulder Bands

Join either right or left shoulder with Kitchener st. With RS of body aligned with RS of sleeve, attach sleeve to side with seamed shoulder by sewing from WS along armhole. Make sure stripes on sleeves and body align as you attach each sleeve.

Work buttonhole band on open front shoulder: With smaller-size circular needle, MC, and RS facing, pick up and knit approx. 29 (31, 32, 33, 34) sts with 1 st in each st across front shoulder, bringing yarn through from WS. Work 3 rows back and forth in Stockinette. Then make 3 buttonholes approx. 1¼ in / 3 cm apart as follows: Yo, k2tog for each buttonhole.

Work 3 rows in Stockinette, purl 1 row on RS (fold line). Work 3 rows in Stockinette. Then, make 3 (3, 3, 3, 3) buttonholes approx. 1¼ in / 3 cm apart. Work 2 rows in Stockinette, then BO loosely on next (WS) row.

Stripe Colors

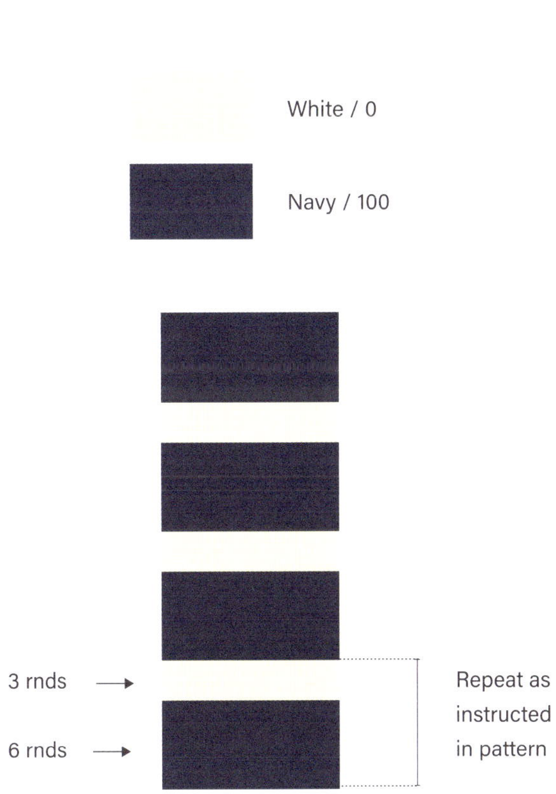

Now make button band on back shoulder. With smaller-size circular needle, MC, and RS facing, pick up and knit approx. 29 (31, 32, 33, 34) sts with 1 st in each st across back, bringing yarn through from WS. BO on next (WS) row.

Neckband

The neckband is doubled. With smaller-size circular needle, MC, and RS facing and beginning at one edge of button band, pick up and knit an even number of sts along neck opening, including the button bands.

Work back and forth in k1, p1 ribbing for 3 rows. On next row, on front side of neckband, make a buttonhole on 3rd st from edge and another after 6 rows. Continue in ribbing as est until band measures 1½ in / 4 cm. BO in ribbing. Fold neckband and sew down on WS. Seam outer edge of left shoulder. Sew edges of two neckband buttonholes together to form the doubled buttonhole. Attach left sleeve.

Finishing

Weave in all ends neatly on WS by sewing into the tops of the sts so the yarn won't show on RS.

Sew on buttons to left back shoulder band.

Wash sweater following instructions on ball band. Lay sweater on a dry towel, pat it out to finished measurements, and leave until completely dry.

SAILOR, Child Version

PATTERN SUITABLE FOR EXPERIENCED KNITTERS

SIZES	4 (6, 8, 10, 12) years
FINISHED MEASUREMENTS	
Chest Circumference	26¾ (30, 33, 36¼, 39½) in / 68 (76, 84, 92, 100) cm
Length	17 (18¼, 19¼, 20½, 22½) in / 43 (46, 49, 52, 57) cm
Sleeve Length	10¼ (11½, 12¾, 13¾, 15) in / 26 (29, 32, 35, 38) cm
GAUGE	19 sts × 32 rnds = 4 × 4 in / 10 × 10 cm in Stockinette with larger-size needles. Make a gauge swatch before you begin knitting to ensure that you are working at the correct gauge. Adjust needle size if necessary to obtain correct gauge.
MATERIALS	
Yarn	Peruvian by Filcolana (100% wool, 109 yd/100 m / 50 g)
Yarn Amounts	Main color (MC), Natural White 101: 4 (4, 5, 5, 6) skeins Stripes (CC), Cobalt Blue 249 100: 2 (2, 2, 2, 2) skeins
Needles	US sizes 2½ and 6 / 3 and 4 mm: 32 in / 80 cm circulars and sets of 5 dpns if you are not using magic loop
Notions	4 stitch markers; 4 buttons, ¾ in / 20 mm in diameter; sewing needle and thread to match buttons

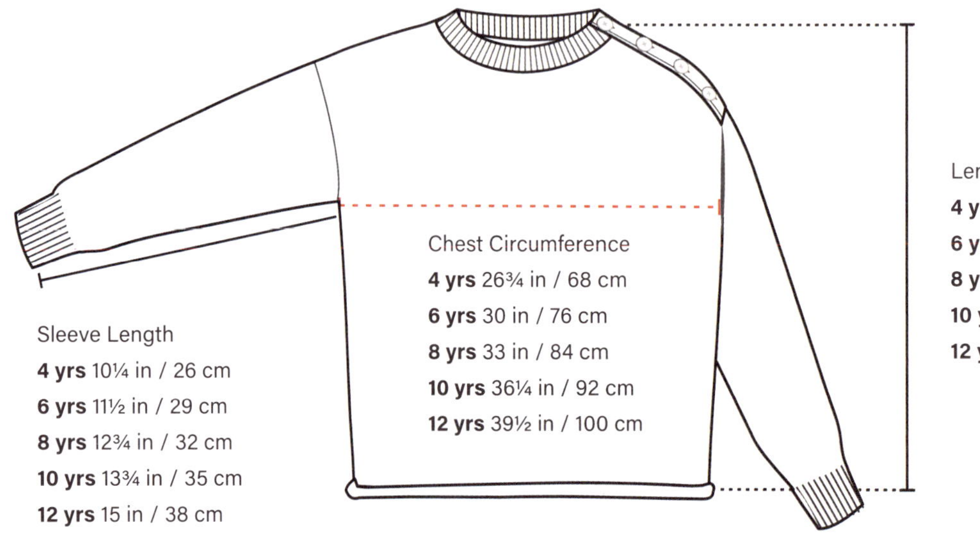

Garment Construction

SAILOR is worked from the bottom up, beginning with a rolled hem on the body. The body is divided at the underarms and the front and back are then worked separately. The sleeves are picked up and worked from the top down. The sweater finishes with a button band on one shoulder and ribbing around the neckline.

Body

With larger-size circular needle and MC, CO 114 (130, 142, 160, 174) sts. Join to work in the rnd, being careful not to twist cast-on row. Begin working the rolled hem in Stockinette: Knit for 1½ in / 4 cm while placing markers on first rnd: Pm (BOR), k57 (65, 71, 80, 87), pm, knit to end of rnd.

Begin shaping body as you also begin stripe pattern (see Stripe Pattern). Shape body as follows: *K1, M1R, knit until 1 st before marker at side, M1L, k1, slm, k1, M1R, knit until 1 st before marker for right side, M1L, k1*. Work from * to * a total of 4 times, with 1½ in / 4 cm between increase rnds = a total of 130 (146, 158, 176, 190) sts.

Stripe Pattern

Begin Stripe Pattern as follows: *Change to stripe color (CC), knit 3 rnds, change to MC, knit 6 rnds*; rep from * to * until body measures approx. 11 (12¼ (13½, 13¾, 14¼) in / 28 (31, 34, 35, 36) cm.

Shape armholes at each side: BO 2 sts centered at each side for underarms [= BO 1 st on each side of BOR and side markers] = 126 (142, 154, 172, 186) sts rem.

Divide body for front and back with 63 (71, 77, 86, 93) sts for each. Work each piece back and forth in Stockinette, continuing stripe pattern as est. After completing stripe pattern, continue with MC only.

Front

Continue as est until front measures 3½ (4, 4¼, 4¾, 5¼) in / 9 (10, 11, 12, 13) cm above underarms or entire body length is approx. 14½ (15¾, 17, 18¼, 20) in / 37 (40, 43, 46, 51) cm. BO the center 21 (23, 25, 28, 31) sts for front neck as follows: K21 (24, 26, 29, 31) (left shoulder), bind off 21 (23, 25, 28, 31) sts for neck, knit to end of row (right shoulder) = 21 (24, 26, 29, 31) sts rem for each shoulder. Now work each shoulder separately.

Continue shaping neck: BO 2 sts at neck edge once, then 1 st 1 (1, 1, 2, 2) time(s) = 18 (21, 23, 25, 27) sts rem on shoulder. Continue straight without shaping until piece measures 17 (18¼, 19¼, 20½, 22½) in / 43 (46, 49, 52, 57) cm. BO rem sts. Make opposite shoulder the same way, binding off at neck edge as above to mirror shaping.

Back

Continue as est until back measures approx. 16¼ (17¼, 18½, 19¼, 21¼) in / 41 (44, 47, 49, 54) cm. BO the center 21 (23, 25, 28, 31) sts for back neck as follows: K21 (24, 26, 29, 31) (right shoulder), BO 21 (23, 25, 28, 31) sts for neck, knit to end of row (left shoulder) = 21 (24, 26, 29, 31) sts rem for each shoulder. Work each shoulder separately. Continue shaping at neck edge: BO 2 sts at neck edge once, then 1 st 1 (1, 1, 2, 2) time(s) = 18 (21, 23, 25, 27) sts rem for shoulder. Work without further shaping until piece measures 17 (18¼, 19¼, 20½, 22½) in / 43 (46, 49, 52, 57) cm. BO rem sts. Make opposite shoulder the same way, decreasing at neck edge as above to mirror shaping.

When changing colors, smooth the transition between the new and old colors: After a color change, at beginning of next round, grab the first stitch of previous round (below the one on the needle), place it on the left-hand needle, and knit it together with first stitch on next round.

Stripe Colors

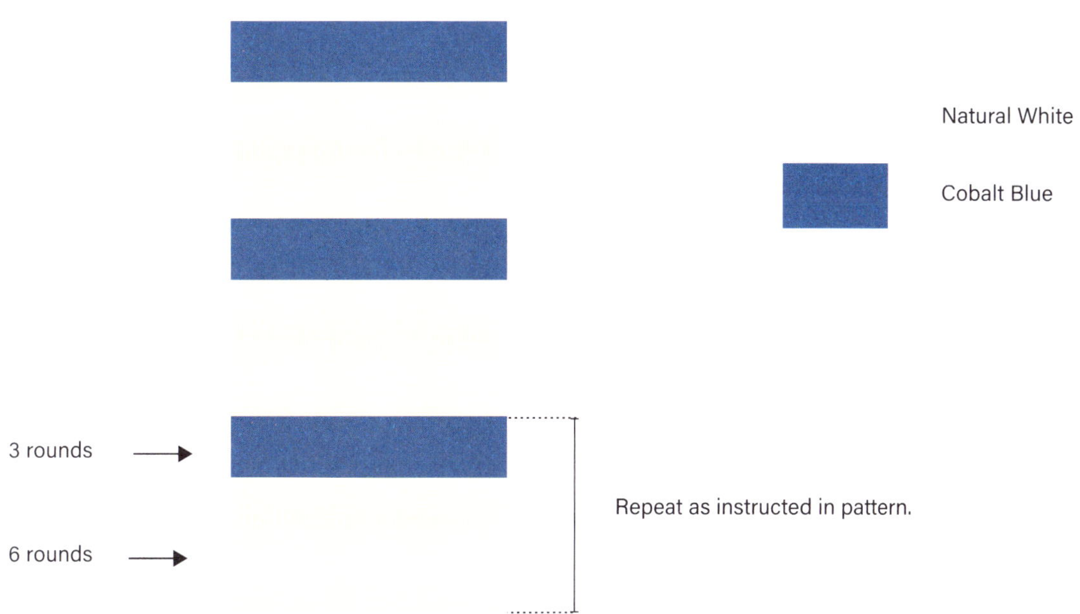

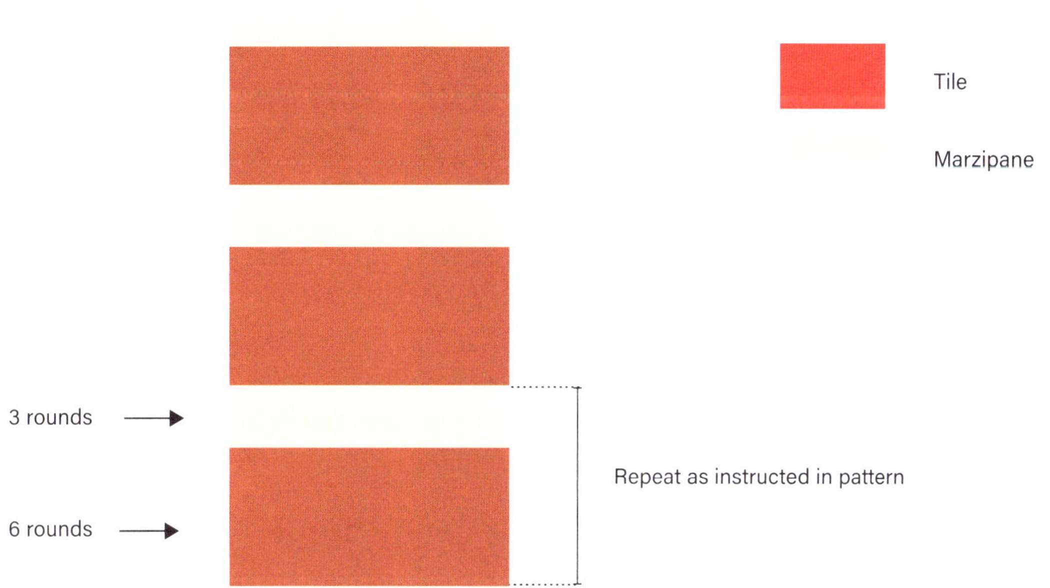

Shoulders

Seam right or left shoulder with Kitchener st.

Sleeves

Begin with sleeve opposite seamed shoulder. The sleeves are worked from the top down with short row shaping (see German Short Rows, at right). Join bottom of armhole by sewing first 2 sts at armhole with Kitchener st, before you pick up and knit sts for sleeve. Begin at front, with MC, starting after first stripe lowest on armhole, pick up and knit approx. 24 (28, 28, 30, 32) sts to top of armhole, pm at top, pick up and knit another approx. 24 (28, 28, 30, 32) sts after marker to stripe lowest on armhole. Purl until 5 sts past top marker; sl and turn. Knit until 5 sts past top marker; sl and turn. *Purl until 5 sts past previous turn; sl and turn. Knit until 5 sts past previous turn; sl and turn*; rep from * to * until you've turned a total of 4 (5, 5, 6, 6) times on each side of top marker. You should now be on WS; cut yarn.

Continue on RS of sleeve. With MC, work 2 rows Stockinette, change to CC and begin Stripe Pattern (see Stripe Pattern). Pick up and knit 2 sts along armhole in stripe, knit to end, pick up and knit 2 sts. Work 1 row Stockinette and then begin working in the round: pick up and knit 1 st in first stripe of armhole, knit, pick up and knit 1 st in last stripe lowest on armhole = 54 (62, 62, 66, 70) sts. Pm between the last 2 sts picked up at base of sleeve (BOR). The sleeve shaping will be on each side of this marker. Knit for about ¾ in / 2 cm, then begin decreasing to shape sleeve every ¾ in / 2 cm a total of 10 (11, 11, 12, 14) times as follows: K1, k2tog, knit until 3 sts before BOR marker, k2tog tbl, k1 = 34 (40, 40, 42, 42) sts rem. Continue as est until sleeve measures 9 (10¼, 11½, 12¾, 13¾) in / 23 (26, 29, 32, 35) cm long or desired length. On next rnd, decrease 6 (8, 8, 6, 6) sts evenly spaced as follows:
Size 4: (K3, k2tog) 6 times, k4.
Sizes 6 and 8: (K3, k2tog) 8 times.
Sizes 10 and 12: (K5, k2tog) 6 times.
= 28 (32, 32, 36, 36) sts rem.

With MC, work k2, p2 ribbing for 1¼ in / 3 cm. BO using your favorite stretchy BO method.

Shoulder

Now make buttonhole band on front shoulder opposite seamed shoulder. With smaller-size circular needle and RS facing, pick up and knit approx. 18 (21, 23, 26, 28) sts along edge (= about 1 st in each st). Work 3 rows in Stockinette and then make 3 buttonholes spaced about ¾ (1, 1¼, 1½, 1½) in / 2 (2.5, 3, 4, 4) cm apart. For each buttonhole: Yo, k2tog. Work 3 rows in Stockinette. Purl 1 row (fold line). Work 3 rows in Stockinette then make 3 buttonholes spaced about ¾ (1, 1¼, 1½, 1½) in / 2 (2.5, 3, 4, 4) cm apart. Work 3 rows in Stockinette. BO loosely on WS.

Make button band on back: With smaller-size circular needle and WS facing, pick up and knit approx. 18 (21, 23, 26, 28) sts along back shoulder. Purl 1 row. BO loosely on WS.

Make second sleeve the same as the first, picking up through both layers of buttonhole band.

Neckband

The neckband is doubled. With smaller-size circular needle, beginning at edge of shoulder band, pick up and knit a multiple of 4+2 sts along neck. Work back and forth in k2, p2 ribbing for 3 rows.

On next row, on front side of neckband, make a buttonhole on 3rd st from edge and another after another 6 rows. Continue in ribbing as est until band measures 1½ in / 4 cm. Fold neckband and sew down on WS. Sew edges of two neckband buttonholes together to form one doubled buttonhole.

German Short Rows

Work up to the st where you will turn and work it. Sl st just worked st and turn work—the st is now on the right needle together with sts not worked. Hold working yarn over the right needle and pull up until the "knot" lies centered on the right needle. The yarn should now lie over the right needle. Work back over the sts that were already worked on previous row. The slipped st now has two legs which sit together like a type of knot on the needle. When that st is worked later on, work the two legs together as one st.

Finishing

Weave in all ends neatly on WS by sewing into the tops of the sts so the yarn won't show on RS.

Sew 4 buttons on button band.

Wash sweater following instructions on ball band. Lay sweater on a dry towel, pat it out to finished measurements, and leave until completely dry.

KING JENS

Cardigan with Zipper

The photo above shows Jens Kongerslev, also called King Jens, a proud model builder from Hirtshalsprammen. Jens stands in front of his house in a sweater knit in a marled yarn (two-color yarn with a characteristic speckled look). King Jens inspired both the name and design of this striped cardigan, the perfect sweater for an active youngster on adventures—so much on the go.

KING JENS is a wool cardigan with a full-length zipper. It features a navy-blue collar, ribbing, and simple single-color stripes on the chest and back. The body and sleeves are worked with a mouliné (marled) yarn. One strand of navy-blue organic silk/mohair is held together with a hand-dyed multicolor organic wool yarn. The ribbing is worked with a solid navy-blue silk/mohair yarn held together with a strand of organic wool yarn.

KING JENS

PATTERN SUITABLE FOR EXPERIENCED KNITTERS

SIZES	4 (6, 8, 10, 12) years
FINISHED MEASUREMENTS	
Chest Circumference	22¾ (26, 29¼, 32¼, 35½) in / 58 (66, 74, 82, 90) cm
Length	16¼ (17¼, 18½, 19¾, 21) in / 41 (44, 47, 50, 53) cm
Sleeve Length	11¾ (13, 14¼, 15½, 16½) in / 30 (33, 36, 39, 42) cm
GAUGE	26 sts × 32 rows/rnds = 4 × 4 in / 10 × 10 cm in Stockinette with 1 strand each of A and B held together. Make a gauge swatch before you begin knitting to ensure that you are working at the correct gauge. Adjust needle size if necessary to obtain correct gauge.
MATERIALS	
Yarn	Multicolor Organic Wool 1 by Krea Deluxe (100% wool, 328 yd/300 m / 100 g) Organic Wool 1 by Krea Deluxe (100% wool, 159 yd/145 m / 50 g) Deluxe Silk Mohair by Krea Deluxe (45% silk, 33% mohair, 22% alpaca, 262 yd/240 m / 20 g)
Yarn Amounts	Color A: 04 Spotted Blue, Multicolor Organic Wool 1: 5 (5, 5, 6, 6) skeins Color B: 27 Navy Blue Deluxe Silk Mohair: 4 (4, 5, 5, 6) balls Color C: 27 Navy Blue Organic Wool 1: 2 (2, 3, 3, 4) hanks
Needles	US size 2½ / 3 mm: 24 in / 60 cm circular and set of 5 dpns if you are not using magic loop
Notions	4 stitch markers; separating zipper to fit length from lower edge to top of collar; matching sewing thread for sewing in zipper

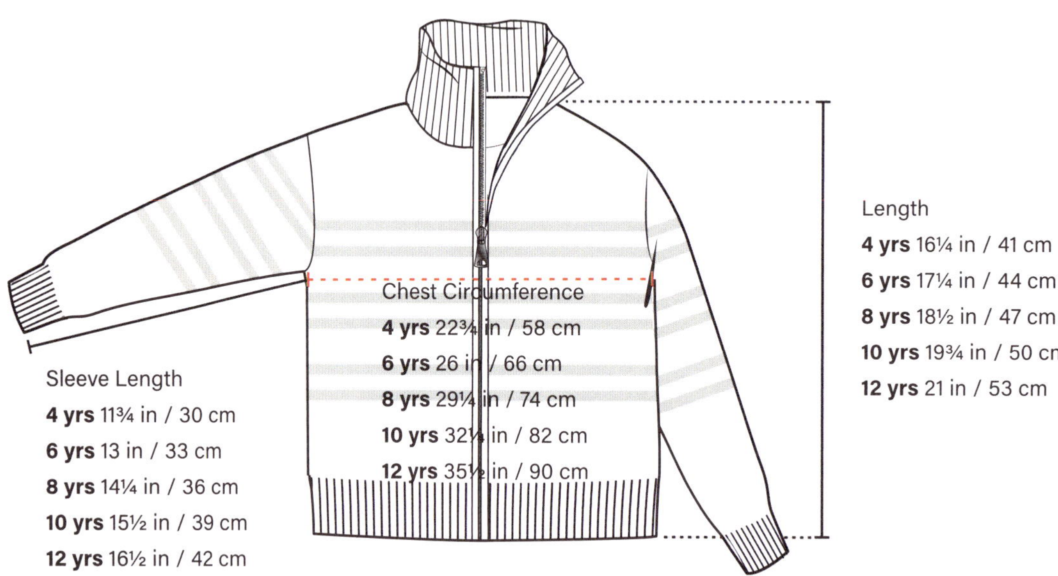

Garment Construction

This cardigan is worked from the bottom up in Stockinette stitch. The body is worked first and then stitches are picked up for the set-in sleeves. Finally, the body is edged with a doubled band for the zipper. Note that the cardigan is knit with two yarns held together (Wool 1 and Deluxe Silk Mohair.) Deluxe Silk Mohair is used throughout and alternately held with the main and stripe colors.

Body

With circular needle and one strand each of color C and color B, CO 148 (172, 192, 212, 232) sts. Work back and forth. *At the same time* as beginning ribbing, place markers: Work k2, p2 ribbing for 37 (43, 48, 53, 58) sts (first front), pm, work ribbing for 74 (86, 96, 106, 116) sts (back), pm, work ribbing for 37 (43, 48, 53, 58) sts (second front).

Continue until ribbing measures 1½ in / 4 cm. Change to Stockinette and colors A and B. Work in Stockinette until body (including ribbing) measures approx. 4¼ (5¼, 6, 6¾, 7½) in / 11 (13, 15, 17, 19) cm. *Change to colors B and C Work in Stockinette for ⅜ in / 1 cm (= 4 rows). Change to colors A and B and work in Stockinette for ⅝ in / 1.5 cm (= 6 rows). Change to colors B and C. Work in Stockinette for ⅜ in / 1 cm (= 4 rows). Change to colors A and B and work in Stockinette for 1⅜ in / 3.5 cm (= 14 rows).* Rep from * to * a total of 3 times.

When body measures approx. 9½ (10¼, 11, 11¾, 12¾) in / 24 (26, 28, 30, 32) cm, shape underarms: Knit until 3 (3, 3, 4, 4) sts before marker, BO 6 (6, 6, 8, 8) sts, removing marker, knit until 3 (3, 3, 4, 4) sts before marker, BO 6 (6, 6, 8, 8) sts, removing marker, knit to end of row = 136 (160, 180, 196, 216) sts rem. Body is now divided for back = 68 (80, 90, 98, 108) sts, and each front = 34 (40, 45, 49, 54) sts. Cut yarn and rejoin to back sts, ready to work a WS row.

Back

Work back and forth, continuing in pattern as est, until piece measures 14 (14¾, 15¾, 16¾, 17¾) in / 35.5 (37.5, 40, 42.5, 45) cm. BO the center 20 (26, 30, 32, 36) sts for back neck as follows:
Size 4: K24, BO 20 sts, k23.
Size 6: K27, BO 26 sts, k26.
Size 8: K30, BO 30 sts, k29.
Size 10: K33, BO 32 sts, k32.
Size 12: K36, BO 36 sts, k35.
NOTE: 1 st remains from last bind-off.

Work each shoulder separately = 24 (27, 30, 33, 36) sts rem for each shoulder. Shape neck by binding off at neck edge as follows: BO 2 sts at each neck edge once, then 1 st once = 21 (24, 27, 30, 33) sts rem for each shoulder.

Shoulder Shaping

The shoulders are shaped separately to slant in toward the neckline so the sweater will fit better. The shaping is achieved through German Short Rows (see opposite), in which you work part of a row, turn, and work back. Begin on WS of right shoulder and on RS on left shoulder as follows:
Row 1 (WS): Purl toward armhole edge to last 3 sts; sl and turn.
Row 2 (RS): Knit to neck edge.
Row 3 (WS): Purl toward armhole edge to last 6 sts; sl and turn.
Rep Rows 2 and 3, with 2 fewer sts before each turn, to last 3 sts. Place shoulder sts on a holder. Make the left shoulder the same way, reversing shaping to match as follows:

Begin on RS of left shoulder:
Purl 1 row.
Row 1 (RS): Knit toward armhole edge to last 3 sts; sl and turn.
Row 2 (WS): Purl to neck.
Row 3 (RS): Knit toward armhole edge to last 6 sts; sl and turn.
Rep Rows 2 and 3, with 2 fewer sts before each turn, to last 3 sts. Place shoulder sts on a holder.

German Short Rows

Work up to the st where you will turn and work it. Sl st just worked and turn work—the st is now on the right needle together with sts not worked. Hold working yarn over the right needle and pull up until the "knot" lies centered on the right needle. The yarn should now lie over the right needle. Work back over the sts that were already worked on previous row. The slipped st now has two legs that sit together like a type of knot on the needle. When that st is worked later on, work the two legs together as one st.

Fronts

Continue pattern as est until each front measures 13 (13¾, 14¾, 15¾, 16¾) in / 33 (35, 37.5, 40, 42.5) cm.

At beginning of RS rows for right front and WS for left front, shape neck: BO 7 (10, 12, 13, 15) sts once, 2 sts once, then 1 st 5 times = 21 (24, 27, 30, 33) sts rem for shoulder.

Shape shoulders same as for back.

Join Shoulders

Join each shoulder as follows: Turn work to WS. With left hand, hold the two needles so that RS of the shoulders are together. Join with three-needle bind-off.

Sleeves

The sleeve caps are shaped with German Short Rows.

With RS facing, using circular needle and picking up in color to match the stripe you are picking up from, pick up and knit 68 (68, 74, 74, 78) sts around armhole, picking up 4 sts along stripes in A and 3 sts along stripes in stripe color, making sure you have the same number of sts on each side of the shoulder seam. Pm at top of shoulder and center of underarm (BOR marker). Shape sleeve top with short rows: Beginning at top marker, k4; sl and turn. You should now be on WS. P7; sl and turn. On next row, work 3 sts past last slipped st. Continue the same way, with 3 more sts after each turn. Work back and forth in Stockinette while working short rows to first stripe. Now continue in stripe pattern (see Sleeve Pattern). So the stripes will look nice as body and sleeve stripes meet, work as follows: *Slip st from left to right needle; turn, sl st to left needle and work with stripe color.* Work next st in stripe, where it is to be turned; rep from * to * until pattern is complete. The last part of sleeve top is worked in the round, be sure the number of rounds on the sleeve matches the number of rounds on body. Now knit sleeve in the round, continuing pattern as est and shaping sleeve as described in Sleeve Pattern.

Sleeve Pattern

The sleeve pattern begins with the first stripe in colors B and C on the yoke: *Change to colors B and C, knit for ⅜ in / 1 cm (= 4 rnds). Change to colors A and B, knit for ⅝ in / 1.5 cm (= 6 rnds). Change to colors B and C, knit for ⅜ in / 1 cm (= 4 rnds). Change to colors A and B, knit for 1⅜ in / 3.5 cm (= 14 rnds)*; work from * to * 3 (3, 3, 3, 3) times.

So that the joins between stripes will look nice, when picking up and knitting stitches around the armholes, it is important to pick up fewer stitches across a stripe than the width of the stripe.

At the same time, work sleeve shaping: The rnd begins at center of underarm. Work for ⅝ in / 1.5 cm and then begin decreasing to shape sleeve: *K2tog, knit until 2 sts before marker, k2tog tbl*; work from * to * every ⅝ inch / 1.5 cm a total of 18 (18, 19, 19, 20) times = 36 (36, 38, 38, 40) sts rem and sleeve should be approx. 10¼ (11½, 12¾, 13¾, 15) in / 26 (29, 32, 35, 38) cm long. Change to colors B and C and knit 1 rnd. Begin k2, p2 ribbing and work until cuff measures 1½ in / 4 cm. BO with your favorite stretchy BO method. Work second sleeve the same way.

Neckband

The neckband is doubled. With circular needle, colors B and C held together and RS facing, pick up and knit approx. 96 (96, 96, 104, 104) sts around neckline. Work k2, p2 ribbing until neckband measures 6¼ in / 16 cm (all sizes). Fold neckband to WS and with RS facing, lift 1 st from base of neckband onto left needle and k2tog, joining the neckband to itself*; rep from * to *, being careful to align sts on base of neckband with live sts. Alternatively, bind off neckband, fold neckband and sew down on WS.

Marled

One strand 04 Spotted Blue, Multicolor Organic Wool 1 (A) + one strand 27 Navy Blue Deluxe Silk Mohair (B)

Single color

Stripes + Ribbing
One strand 27 Navy Blue Organic Wool 1 + (C)
One strand 27 Navy Blue Deluxe Silk Mohair (B)

Zipper

Now pick up and knit sts along each front edge for the casing band for the zipper on WS of each front. The band runs from lower edge of cardigan to top of doubled neckband. Begin with left front at lower edge of sweater on WS of front. Work back and forth as follows: With circular needle and colors B and C held together, pick up and knit 6 sts along bottom of front edge. Work in Stockinette over the 6 sts until band measures approx. 19¼ (20½, 21¾, 22¾, 24) in / 49 (52, 55, 58, 61) cm. BO. Make right front band to match.

Now sew the inner edge of the band to the cardigan with an overcast stitch so there is an opening on outer side in which the zipper will be placed. Place zipper between front and back bands of the casing. Use pins to mark zipper placement, beginning at neckband and at desired end point. Open the zipper completely. Pin the zipper down on both sides. Use matching sewing thread to sew the zipper on with an overcast stitch along both sides of zipper. Make sure to pull the knitted edge so the zipper fits in smoothly, because the knitted edge is more elastic than the zipper.

Finishing

Weave in all ends neatly on WS by sewing into the tops of the sts so the yarn won't show on RS.

Seam underarms.

Wash sweater following instructions on ball band. Lay sweater on a dry towel, pat it out to finished measurements, and leave until completely dry.

KING JENS Stripe Pattern

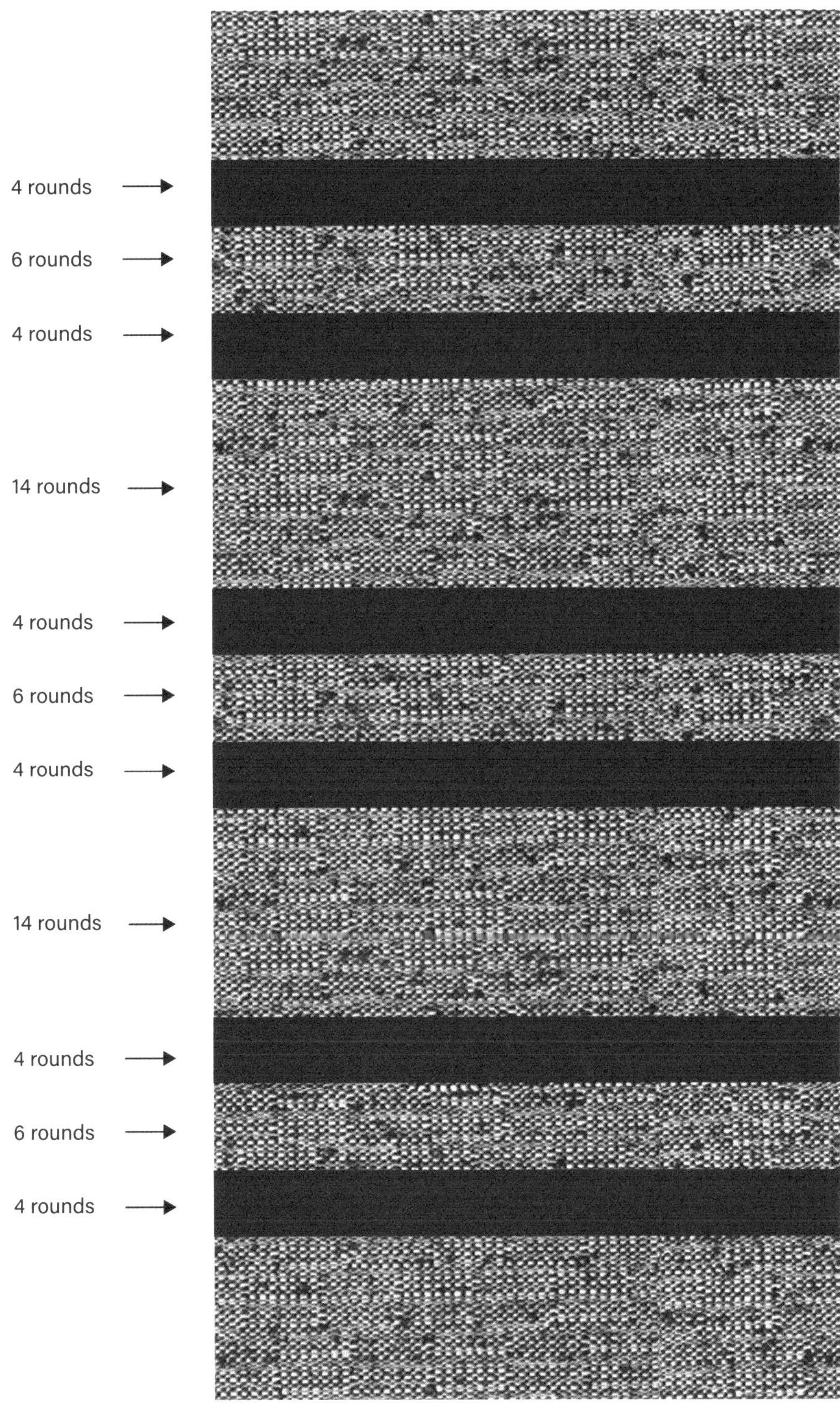

CAPTAIN

Striped Pullover with an Anchor, for the Little Captain

The anchor is a synonym for sailing and sea journeys as well as an iconic symbol in the maritime world. It signifies both a physical use and also a recognizable graphic element in embellishment and decoration. An anchor tattoo represents honor, loyalty, and hope.

The gray anchor on this blue-and-white-striped CAPTAIN sweater sits on the chest of the little captain scouting out new horizons.

CAPTAIN is a striped pullover buttoned on the left shoulder, with an embroidered or an intarsia knitted-in anchor on the chest. Ribbing edges the sleeves and neckline while the lower edge of the body is rolled for a loose fit. The yarn used is worsted-spun 100 percent pure new wool.

CAPTAIN

PATTERN SUITABLE FOR EXPERIENCED KNITTERS

SIZES	2 (4, 6, 8) years
FINISHED MEASUREMENTS	
Chest	23¾ (26¾, 30, 33) in / 60 (68, 76, 84) cm
Length	14½ (17, 18¼, 19¼) in / 37 (43, 46, 49) cm
Sleeve Length	9½ (10¼, 11½, 12¾) in / 24 (26, 29, 32) cm
GAUGE	19 sts × 32 rnds = 4 × 4 in / 10 × 10 cm in Stockinette with larger-size needles. Make a gauge swatch before you begin knitting to ensure that you are working at the correct gauge. Adjust needle size if necessary to obtain correct gauge.
MATERIALS	
Yarn	Peruvian by Filcolana (100% wool, 109 yd/100 m / 50 g)
Yarn Amounts	Main color (MC), 145 Navy Blue: 3 (4, 5, 6) skeins Stripe color (CC), 101 Natural White: 2 (2, 2, 2) skeins Anchor, 954 Light Grey (heather): 1 (1, 1, 1) skein
Needles	US size 6 / 4 mm: 24 in / 60 cm circular and US size 2½ and 6 / 3 and 4 mm: sets of 5 dpns if you are not using magic loop
Notions	3 (4, 4, 4) buttons, ¾ in / 20 mm in diameter; 4 stitch markers

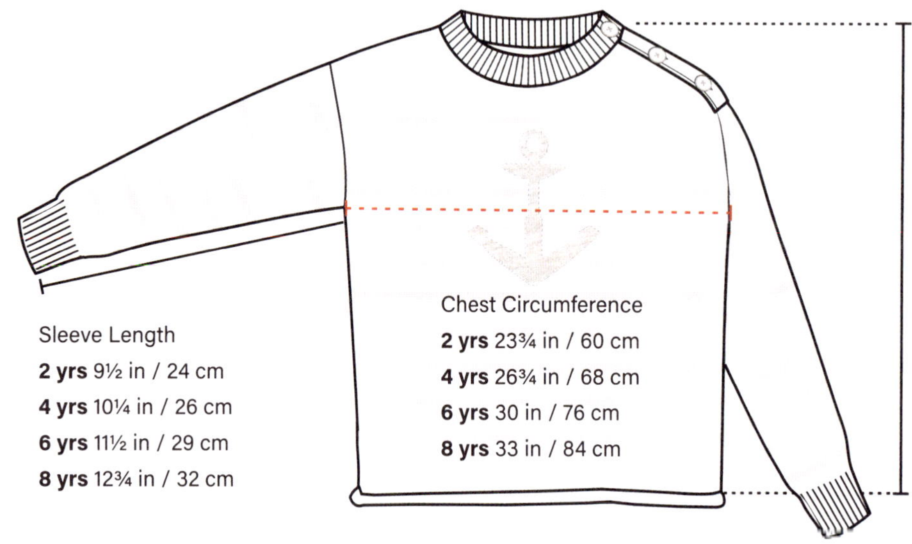

Garment Construction

This pullover is worked from the bottom up. The body is worked first and then the sleeves are picked up and worked top down. Button/buttonhole bands are worked on one shoulder before the neckband. The anchor can be knit in as part of the sweater or embroidered on after the sweater is finished.

Body

With larger-size circular needle and MC, CO 114 (130, 146, 158) sts. Join to work in the rnd, being careful not to twist cast-on row. Knit (for rolled edge) for 1½ in / 4 cm. *At the same time*, on first rnd, pm for front and back: Pm (BOR), k57 (65, 73, 79), pm, knit to end of rnd. After rolled edge, begin stripe pattern.

Stripe Pattern

The stripe pattern is worked 9 (10, 11, 12) times on the body as follows: *Change to CC (stripe color), knit 3 rnds, change to MC, knit 6 rnds*; rep from * to *. After completing stripe pattern, continue with MC only.

When changing colors, smooth the transition between new and old colors: After a color change, at beginning of next round, slip the first stitch of previous round and knit it together with first stitch of new round.

So you won't have so many ends to weave in when working back and forth, work from 2 balls of yarn—one on each side.

If you want to knit the anchor into the front, after working stripe pattern 3 (4, 5, 6) times [= approx. 5 (6 ¼, 7, 8) in / 12.5 (15.5, 18, 20.5) cm], begin knitting the anchor (see Knitted Anchor below).

If you prefer to embroider the anchor, continue in stripe pattern until body measures approx. 9¾ (11, 12¼, 13½) in / 25 (28, 31, 34) cm. BO 2 sts for armhole (1 st on each side of marker) = 110 (126, 142, 154) sts rem. Now work back and front separately in Stockinette = 55 (63, 71, 77) sts for each. *At the same time*, continue stripe pattern for a total of 9 (10, 11, 12) times on sweater. After completing stripe pattern, work only in MC.

Knitted Anchor

Divide the sweater into front and back with 57 (65, 73, 79) sts for each. Now work back and forth in Stockinette on the front. Begin by placing markers to indicate placement of anchor on front: K1, M1R, k27 (31, 35, 38), pm, k1 (center st of chart), pm, knit to last st, M1L, k1 = 59 (67, 75, 81) sts. Continue stripe pattern and anchor pattern (see Intarsia-Knitted Anchor Pattern below and chart on page 253) until body measures approx. 9¾ (11, 12¼, 13½) in / 25 (28, 31, 34) cm. BO 2 sts for armholes at beginning of next 2 rows = 55 (63, 71, 77) sts rem. Work back as for front, including the chart if desired.

Front

Continue as est until armhole depth measures 3¼ (3½, 4, 4¼) in / 8 (9, 10, 11) cm or body measures approx. 13 (14½, 15¾, 17) in / 33 (37, 40, 43) cm. BO the center 21 (21, 23, 25) sts for front neck as follows: K17 (21, 24, 26) (left shoulder), BO 21 (21, 23, 25) sts, knit to end of row (right shoulder). Each shoulder now has 17 (21, 24, 26) sts. Work each shoulder separately.

Shape neck as follows: BO 2 sts at neck edge once, then 1 st once = 14 (18, 21, 23) sts rem for shoulder. Continue straight until piece measures 14½ (17, 18¼, 19¼) in / 37 (43, 46, 49) cm. BO rem sts. Make second shoulder the same way, decreasing at neck edge to mirror shaping.

Back

Continue as est until body measures approx. 14¼ (16¼, 17¼, 18½) in / 36 (41, 44, 47) cm. BO for back neck as follows: K17 (21, 24, 26) (right shoulder), BO 21 (21, 23, 25) sts, knit to end of row (left shoulder). Each shoulder now has 17 (21, 24, 26) sts. Work each shoulder separately, continuing shaping at edge, as follows: BO 2 sts at neck edge once, then 1 st once. Continue straight up until piece measures 14½ (17, 18¼, 19¼) in / 37 (43, 46, 49) cm. BO rem sts. Make second shoulder the same way, decreasing at neck edge to mirror shaping.

Shoulders

Seam right shoulder with Kitchener st.

German Short Rows

Work up to the stitch where you will turn and work it. Sl st just worked st and turn work—the st is now on the right needle together with sts not worked. Hold working yarn over the right needle and pull up until the "knot" lies centered on the right needle. The yarn should now lie over the right needle. Work back over the sts that were already worked on previous row. The slipped st now has two legs, which sit together like a type of knot on the needle. When that st is worked later on, work the two legs together as one st.

Sleeves

Begin with right sleeve. The sleeves are worked from the top down, shaped with German Short Rows (see above). Beginning on front at the top of the first stripe at base of armhole, with MC pick up and knit about 22 (24, 28, 28) sts, pm at top (t-marker), then pick up and knit another about 22 (24, 28, 28) sts after t-marker down to last stripe at base of armhole. Purl until 5 sts after t-marker; sl and turn. Knit until 5 sts past t-marker; sl and turn. *Purl until 5 sts past last turn; sl and turn. Knit until 5 sts past last turn; sl and turn*; rep from * to * until you've turned a total of 4 (4, 5, 5) times on each side of t-marker. You should now be on WS; cut yarn.

Continue on RS of sleeve. With MC, work 2 rows Stockinette. Now begin stripe pattern (see Stripe Pattern). Change to stripe color, pick up and knit 2 sts along armhole in stripe, knit to end, pick up and knit 2 sts. Work 1 row Stockinette and then begin working in the round: Pick up and knit 1 st in

first stripe of armhole, knit, pick up and knit 1 st in last stripe at base of armhole = 50 (54, 62, 62) sts total.

Pm between last 2 sts that were picked up at underarm (BOR). The sleeve shaping will be on each side of this marker. Knit for about ¾ in / 2 cm and then begin decreasing; decrease the same way every ¾ in / 2 cm, 8 (10, 11, 11) times as follows: K1, k2tog, knit until 3 sts before marker, k2tog tbl, k1 = 34 (34, 40, 40) sts rem. Continue as est until sleeve measures 8¼ (9, 10¼, 11½) in / 21 (23, 26, 29) cm from underarm or desired length. On next rnd, decrease 6 (6, 8, 8) sts evenly spaced as follows: (K3, k2tog) 6 (6, 8, 8) times, k4 (4, 0, 0) = 28 (28, 32, 32) sts rem. With MC, work k2, p2 ribbing for 1¼ in / 3 cm. BO with your favorite stretchy BO method. Make second sleeve the same way.

Finishing Knitted Anchor

If you decided on a knitted anchor, seam open side edges of front and back to armholes using mattress st into outer half of sts.

Shoulders

Seam right shoulder with MC and Kitchener st over BO sts. For the button band on left shoulder, join sleeve by sewing the first 2 sts together with Kitchener st over the BO sts at armhole before picking up and knitting sts for bands.

Buttonhole/Button Bands

The buttonhole edge is open over the left shoulder. The buttonhole band is worked on the front as follows: With smaller-size circular needle and MC, pick up and knit approx. 14 (18, 21, 23) sts through edge sts, bringing yarn through from WS. Work 3 rows in Stockinette and then make 3 buttonholes spaced about ⅝ (¾, 1, 1¼) in / 1.5 (2, 2.5, 3) cm apart. For each buttonhole: Yo twice, k2tog. Work 3 rows Stockinette. Purl 1 row (fold line). Work 3 rows in Stockinette and then make 3 buttonholes spaced about ⅝ (¾, 1, 1¼) in / 1.5 (2, 2.5, 3) cm apart. Work 3 rows Stockinette. BO loosely on WS. A fourth buttonhole for sizes 4, 6, and 8 yrs will be made in the neckband.

Work button band on back. With smaller-size circular needle and MC, pick up and knit approx. 14 (18, 21, 23) sts through edge sts, bringing yarn through from WS. Work 1 row in Stockinette. BO on WS. Fold buttonhole band in half at fold line and sew BO edge to pick-up edge. Seam side edges of bands.

Neckband

The neckband is doubled. With smaller-size circular needle, MC and RS facing, starting at the button band, pick up and knit approx. 82 (82, 90, 90) sts around neck and button band edges. Work back and forth in k2, p2 ribbing, beginning and ending with k2 on RS and p2 on WS. After 3 rows in ribbing, for sizes 4, 6, 8 yrs, make a buttonhole at 3rd st from edge as done for buttonhole band. Make another buttonhole after 6 rows at 3rd st from edge. When neckband measures 1½ in / 4 cm, BO in ribbing. Fold the neckband to the WS and sew the edge to the WS.

Finishing

Weave in all ends neatly on WS by sewing into the tops of the sts so the yarn won't show on RS.

Wash sweater following instructions on ball band. Lay sweater on a dry towel, pat it out to finished measurements, and leave until completely dry.

Anchor Chart

Either embroider the anchor with duplicate stitch or knit in intarsia as described in pattern.

CAPTAIN Pattern

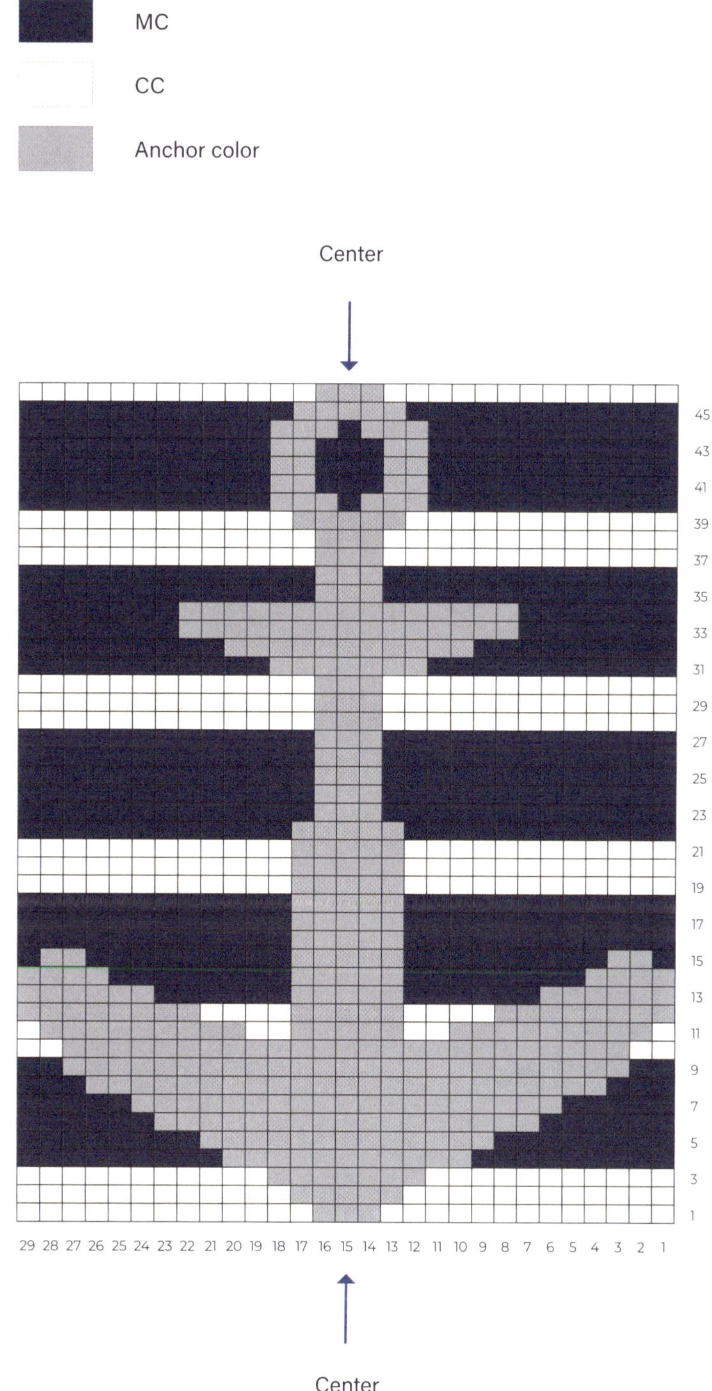

CAPTAIN Stripe Pattern

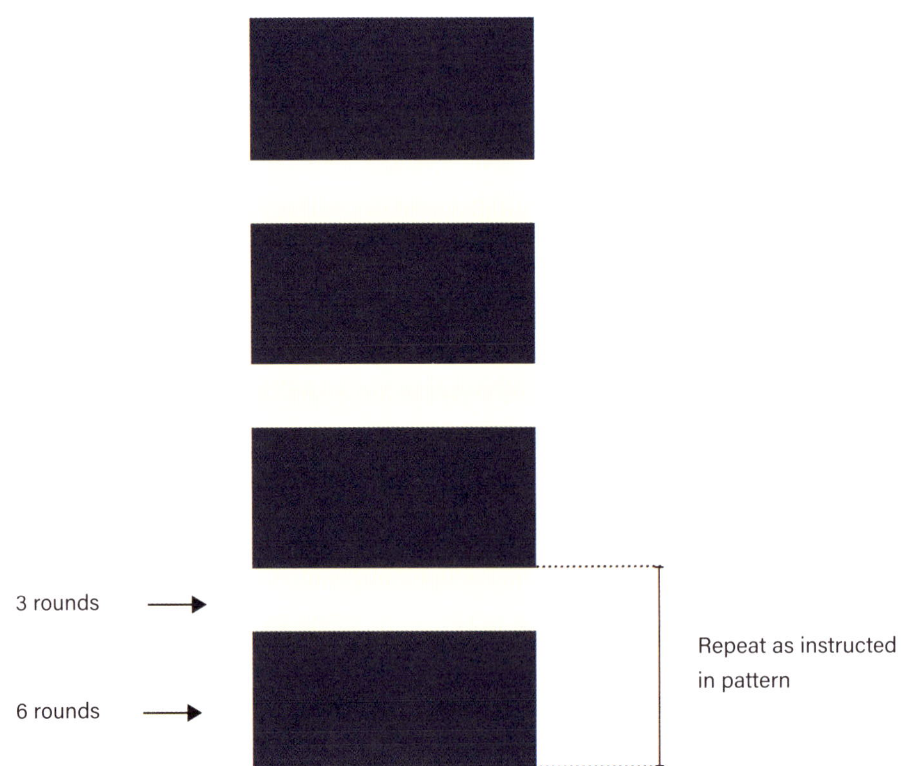

OCEAN

Multicolor Striped Pullover

"You can't cross an ocean unless you have the courage to lose sight of the shore." A wise proverb, and the inspiration behind our OCEAN sweater.

The striped pattern on this pullover is based on four colors and the idea is that you can arrange them in endless ways—an ocean of nuances. Lose sight of shore, let your creativity loosen, and design your own color variation.

OCEAN has raglan sleeves, a doubled neckband, and striped ribbing. It is knit with a 100 percent Merino yarn (not superwash) for good elasticity so the sweater and ribbing will hold their shape.

OCEAN

PATTERN SUITABLE FOR INTERMEDIATE KNITTERS

SIZES 4 (6, 8, 10, 12) years

FINISHED MEASUREMENTS

Chest Circumference 23¾ (26¾, 30, 33, 36¼) in / 60 (68, 76, 84, 92) cm

Length 16½ (17¾, 19, 20, 21¼) in / 42 (45, 48, 51, 54) cm

Sleeve Length 11½ (12¾, 13¾, 15, 16¼) in / 29 (32, 35, 38, 41) cm

GAUGE 23 sts × 33 rnds = 4 × 4 in / 10 × 10 cm in Stockinette with larger-size needles. Make a gauge swatch before you begin knitting to ensure that you are working at the correct gauge. Adjust needle size if necessary to obtain correct gauge.

MATERIALS

Yarn Double Sunday by Sandnes Garn (100% Merino wool, 118 yd/108 m / 50 g)

Yarn Amounts
Color A: 2 (3, 3, 4, 4) skeins
Color B: 2 (3, 3, 4, 4) skeins
Color C: 1 (1, 1, 1, 1) skein
Color D: 1 (1, 2, 2, 2) skein(s)

Needles US sizes 2½ and 6 / 3 and 4 mm: 24 in / 60 cm circulars and sets of 5 dpns if you are not using magic loop

Notions 8 stitch markers

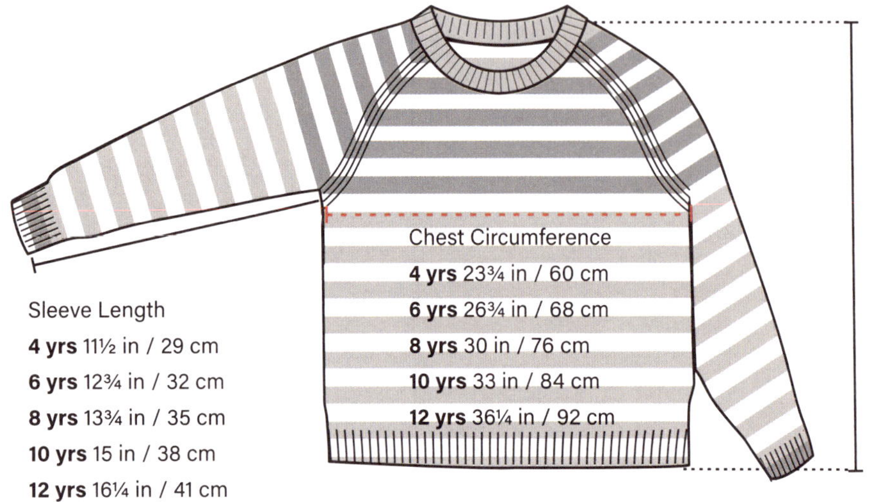

Garment Construction

The OCEAN pullover is worked from the bottom up in the round. The body is worked first and then the sleeves are each worked in the round. The body and sleeves are joined on a circular needle and knit with raglan shaping for the yoke.

Body

With larger-size circular needle and Color B, CO 136 (156, 176, 196, 212) sts. Join to work in the rnd, being careful not to twist cast-on row. Begin ribbing while placing markers: Pm (BOR), work k2, p2 ribbing for 68 (78, 88, 98, 106) sts, pm, work ribbing to end of rnd. Work a total of 5 rnds in ribbing. Change to Color A. Continue in ribbing until piece measures 1¼ in / 3 cm. Knit 1 rnd.

Change to Stockinette and, *at the same time*, continue in stripe pattern as follows. *Change to Color B, knit 5 rnds, change to Color A, knit 5 rnds*; rep from * to * a total of 7 (8, 9, 10, 10) times.

When body measures approx. 9 (10¼, 11½, 11¾, 13¾) in / 23 (26, 29, 30, 35) cm, ending with 2 rnds in a stripe, shape underarms: At beginning of rnd, BO 4 sts, k60 (70, 80, 90, 98), BO 8 sts, knit to last 4 sts of rnd, BO 4 sts. Cut yarn = 120 (140, 160, 180, 196) sts rem. Set body aside while you knit sleeves. Make note of where you are in stripe pattern.

Sleeves

With larger-size dpns and Color B, CO 36 (36, 40, 44, 44) sts. Divide sts onto dpns and join to work in the rnd, being careful not to twist cast-on row. Pm for BOR and work k2, p2 ribbing for 5 rnds. Change to Color A. *Work 5 rnds, change to Color B, work 5 rnds, change to Color A*; work from * to * until cuff measures 1¼ in / 3 cm. Knit 1 rnd.

Change to Stockinette. Pm after first and before last st. Begin shaping sleeve as follows: Knit, increasing 1 st with M1 outside each marked st. Increase the same way every ¾ in / 2 cm 11 (12, 13, 14, 16) times = 58 (60, 66, 72, 76) sts. *At the same time*, continue stripe pattern as described above until sleeve measures 11½ (12¾, 13¾, 15, 16¼) in / 29 (32, 35, 38, 41) cm, ending with same color and row of stripe pattern as on Body. BO 8 sts for each underarm = BO 4 sts on each side of center underarm = 50 (52, 58, 64, 68) sts rem. Set sleeve aside while you make second sleeve the same way.

Join Body and Sleeves

Arrange body and sleeves on larger-size circular needle so you can begin the yoke with raglan shaping. Begin by placing 8 markers. Continue with stripe pattern as est, with the rnd beginning at left shoulder on back of sweater:

Marker 1: K1, pm, knit to last st before next join of body and sleeve.
Marker 2: Pm, k1, yo, k1.
Marker 3: Pm, knit until 1 st before next join of body and sleeve.
Marker 4: Pm, k1, yo, k1.
Marker 5: Pm, knit until 1 st before next join of body and sleeve.
Marker 6: Pm, k1, yo, k1.
Marker 7: Pm, knit until 1 st before next join of body and sleeve.
Marker 8: Pm, k1, yo.

The yoke now has a total of 224 (248, 280, 312, 336) sts, including yos. On next rnd, work yos as k1tbl. Begin decreasing for raglan at each marker (see Raglan Shaping). The rnd and first raglan decrease begin on left shoulder on back of sweater.

Raglan Shaping

Working Stripe Pattern (see Stripe Pattern on Yoke), work raglan decreases at each stitch marker every 3rd rnd a total of 15 (17, 21, 24, 27) times, as follows: Knit until 2 sts before marker, sl 1, k1, psso, k3, k2tog = 8 sts decreased.
NOTE: The raglan decreases are worked differently on the WS so they will look the same on RS: P2tog, p3 (raglan sts), p2tog tbl.

Neck Shaping

At the same time, after 10 (12, 16, 19, 22) rnds of raglan decreases [= 144 (152, 152, 160, 160) sts rem], begin neck shaping while continuing with raglan shaping and stripe sequence.

To shape neck, bind off on a rnd without raglan decreases, as follows: Knit to marker 3, BO the center 16 (18, 19, 20, 20) sts for front neck, knit to end of rnd. Cut yarn. Now work back and forth in Stockinette. *At the same time*, BO 2 sts at beginning of next 2 rows, then 1 st at beginning of next 10 rows. After last raglan decrease, BO rem sts.

Stripe Pattern on Yoke

Knit 5 rnds, change to color B. Knit 5 rnds and then change to color D. Rep these 10 rnds a total of 0 (1, 1, 2, 3) time(s).

Knit 5 rnds and then change to color C. Knit 5 rnds and then change to color D. Knit 5 rnds. Rep these 10 rnds 3 times. Change to color C. Knit 5 rnds.

Neckband

The neckband is doubled. With smaller-size circular needle, Color C, and RS facing, pick up and knit approx. 96 (96, 96, 104, 104) sts around neck. Work k2, p2 ribbing for 1½ in / 4 cm. BO in ribbing.

Finishing

Weave in all ends neatly on WS by sewing into the tops of the sts so the yarn won't show on RS.

Seam underarms with Kitchener st over bound-off sts. Fold neckband and sew down on WS.

Wash sweater following instructions on ball band. Lay sweater on a dry towel, pat it out to finished measurements, and leave until completely dry.

OCEAN Color Sequence

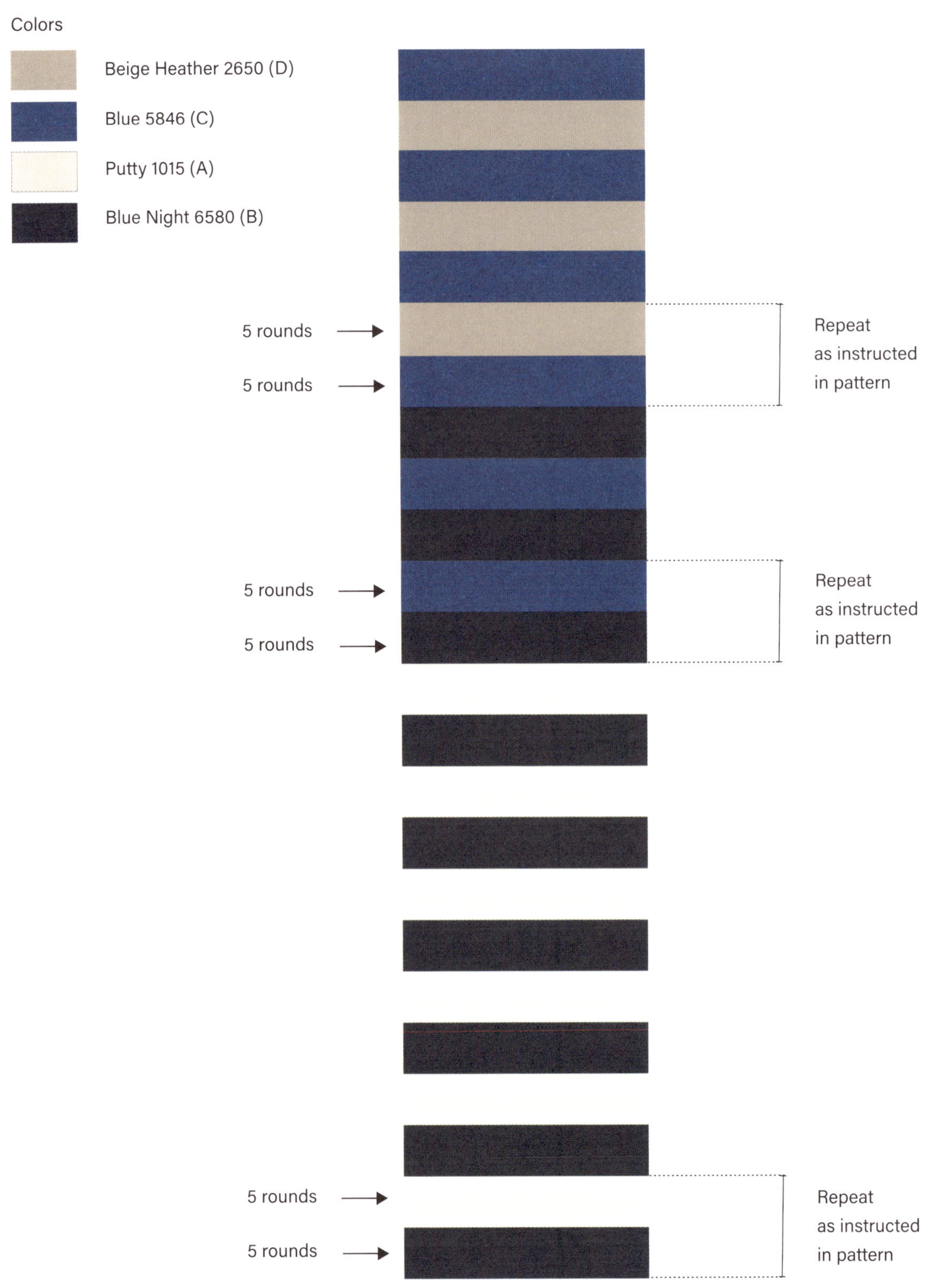

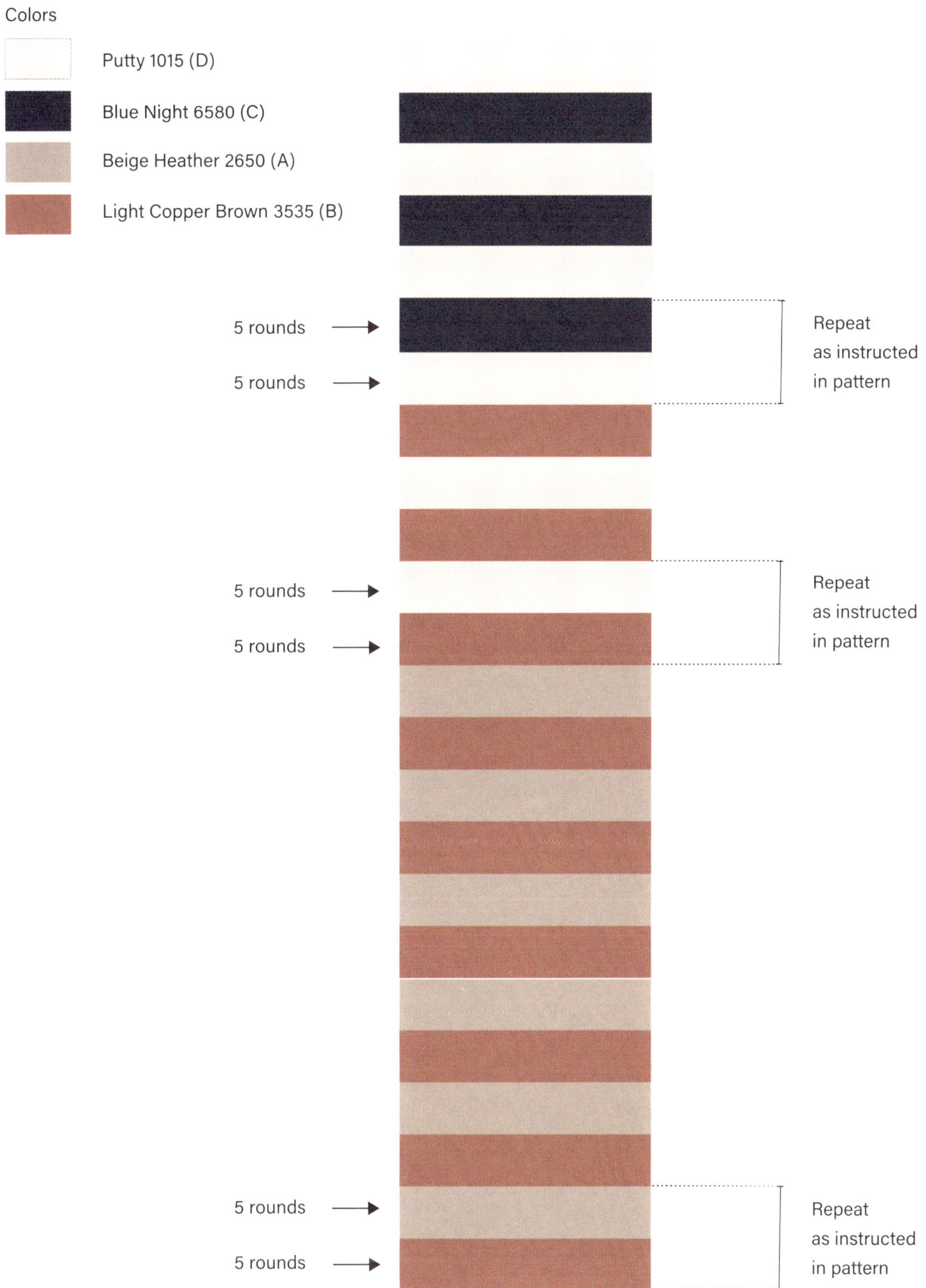
Colors
Putty 1015 (D)
Blue Night 6580 (C)
Beige Heather 2650 (A)
Light Copper Brown 3535 (B)
5 rounds
5 rounds
Repeat
as instructed
in pattern
5 rounds
5 rounds
Repeat
as instructed
in pattern
5 rounds
5 rounds
Repeat
as instructed
in pattern

COUSTEAU

Brioche Cap

The name and design of this cap were inspired by Jacques Cousteau, the French explorer, ocean researcher, and photographer. Cousteau was often shown wearing a little red cap as he traveled the world.

COSTEAU, knit with Norwegian wool yarn, is worked in brioche stitch with a folded brim. Wool is a temperature-regulating fiber that holds warmth even when damp. It is also antibacterial, so wool garments do not need to be washed too often—an airing-out is usually sufficient.

This cap, knit in the round, is cool and quite comfortable. The cap pattern can be varied endlessly. Make it with one color, two colors, or leftover yarns in many colors.

COUSTEAU is perfect for a beach baby or a mermaid as well as any aged seafarer.

COUSTEAU

PATTERN SUITABLE FOR EXPERIENCED KNITTERS

SIZES	Child (Adult)
FINISHED MEASUREMENTS	
Circumference	12¾ (17¼) in / 32 (44) cm
Length	8¼ (9¾) in / 21 (25) cm with folded brim
Brim	1½ (2½) in / 4 (6) cm
GAUGE	24 sts × 30 rnds = 4 × 4 in / 10 × 10 cm in brioche. Make a gauge swatch before you begin knitting to ensure that you are working at the correct gauge. Adjust needle size if necessary to obtain correct gauge.
MATERIALS	
Yarn	Finull by Rauma (100% Norwegian wool, 191 yd/175 m / 50 g)
Yarn Amounts	2 (2) skeins
Needles	US size 1½ / 2.5 mm: 16 or 24 in / 40 or 60 cm circular and set of 5 dpns if you are not using magic loop
Notions	4 stitch markers

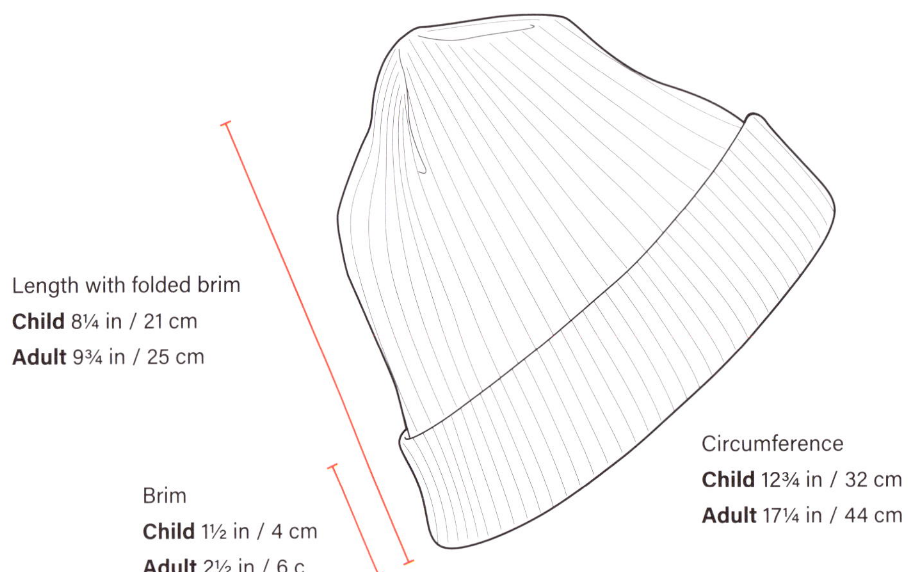

Garment Construction

The cap is worked from the brim up in brioche stitch for a nice, smooth-flowing texture. It begins with the brim, then the cap body is worked straight up until the crown is shaped with decreases.

Cap

With circular needle, CO 80 (112) sts, placing 4 markers with 20 (28) sts between each marker. Join to work in the rnd, being careful not to twist cast-on row. Work in brioche (see Brioche Pattern). You can make the cap with a single color or stripes. For a striped cap, see the illustrations of striped caps for inspiration.
NOTE: The first round in the stripe pattern corresponds to rounds 2 and 3 in Brioche Pattern.

Brioche Pattern

Beginning Rnd
Rnd 1: *Yo, sl 1 purlwise, k1*; rep from * to *.

Purl Brioche Rnd
Rnd 2: *P1 (work slipped st together with yarnover), yo, sl 1 purlwise*; rep from * to *.

Knit Brioche Rnd
Rnd 3: *Yo, sl 1 purlwise, k1 (work slipped st together with yarnover)*; rep from * to *.
Rep Rnds 2 and 3 until cap measures 1½ (2½) in / 4 (6) cm. Purl 1 rnd (fold line). Continue in Brioche Pattern until cap measures 6¾ (7½) in / 17 (19) cm.

Crown Shaping

Begin decreasing to shape crown with left- and right-leaning decreases before and after each marker. Begin on Rnd 3 (a knit rnd) as follows: Sl 1 knitwise, k1, decrease 2 sts by passing slipped st over, put st back on left needle, pass next st over, move st to right needle (= **right-leaning decrease**). *Work in brioche until 3 sts before next marker, sl 1, k2tog, psso (= **left-leaning decrease**), sl 1 knitwise, k1, psso, move st to left needle, pass next st over, move st to right needle (= **right-leaning decrease**); rep from * to * until 3 sts rem before last marker, sl 1, k2tog, psso (= **left-leaning decrease**) = 16 sts decreased. Decrease the same way on every Rnd 3 of the Brioche Pattern, with 2 sts fewer between decreases on each rnd until 16 (16) sts rem. Work 1 rnd without decreasing and then work a final decrease rnd, decreasing only at every other decrease point = 8 (8) sts rem.

Cut yarn and draw end through rem 8 (8) sts; tighten.

Finishing

Weave in all ends neatly on WS by sewing into the tops of the sts so the yarn won't show on RS.

Wash cap following instructions on ball band. Lay cap on a dry towel, pat it out to finished measurements, and leave until completely dry.

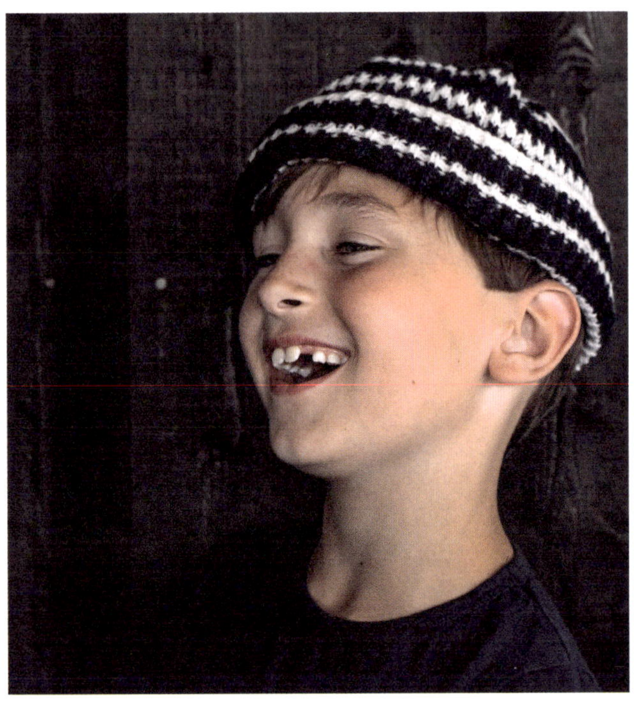

COUSTEAU Stripe Pattern

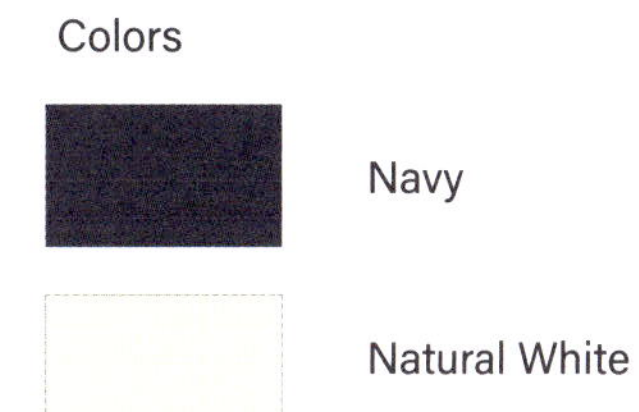

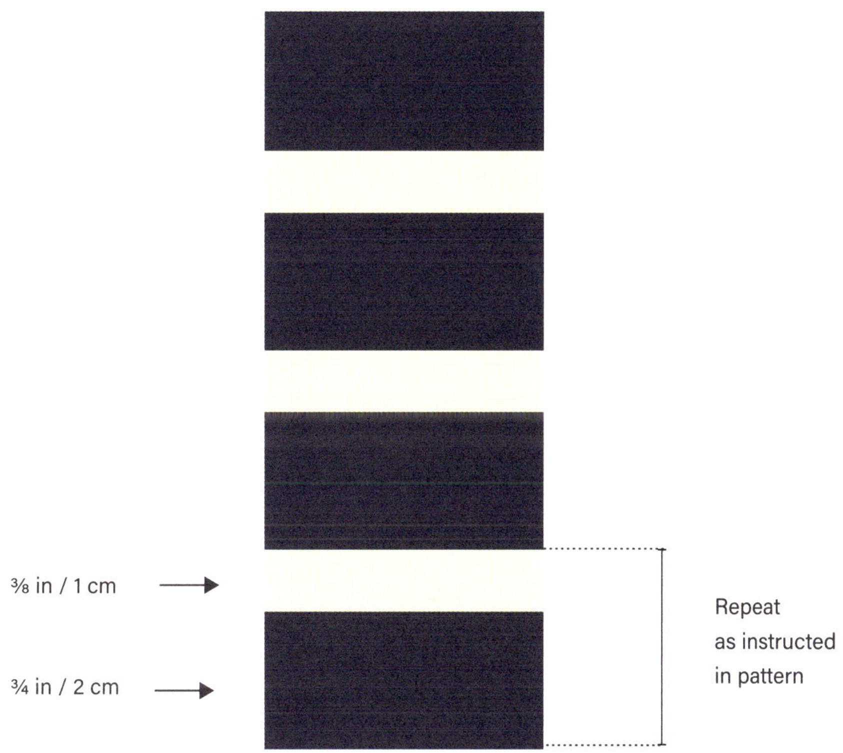

PARTNERS

We have had the great pleasure of working with a number of partners who made their unique products and materials available to us, contributions that enabled us to confidently sail this book project through the seas.

Yarn Sources

Filcolana
@filcolana
filcolana.dk

Isager
@isageryarn
isagerstrik.dk

Krea Deluxe
@kreadeluxe
kreadeluxe.com

Rauma
@raumagarn
raumagarn.no

Sandnes Garn
@sandnesgarn
sandnesgarn.dk

Historic Photographs

M/S Maritime Museum of Denmark
(M/S Museet for Søfart)
@maritimemuseumofdenmark
mfs.dk

Materials and Accessories for Photos

YKK Denmark A/S, Ikast (zippers)
ykk.dk

Lakor (clothing)
@lakorsoulwear
lakor.dk

By LOHN (bags)
@bylohn
by-lohn.dk

ACKNOWLEDGMENTS

Thank you to our photographer, Sibel Rønstrup, for your unique contributions to this knitting book. Your fantastic photographs have captured the essence we wished to convey through our designs. Each picture tells a history and creates a connection to the maritime universe in a way that would not have been possible without your passion and competence.

Thank you to the M/S Maritime Museum of Denmark and Henriette Gavnholdt Jakobsen, who helped us access the many wonderful historic photos on seafaring. These pictures have been the foundation for this book. They have given us unique insights into a profession that has been and is still undergoing great change, as well as the conditions under which seafarers worked in the past.

Thank you to Thorbjørn Thaarup, museum inspector at the M/S Maritime Museum, who wrote the foreword. We greatly value your words and your good input, which we got at our exciting meeting at the M/S Maritime Museum.

Thank you to Isager, Krea Deluxe, Filcolana, Rauma, and Sandnes Garn for contributing such lovely yarns for the designs in the book. A big thank-you for your dialogue and engagement in the creation of this book.

Thank you to Stine Møller-Madsen, YKK Denmark, for contributing their zippers for our designs.

Thank you to By LOHN for the knitting bags.

Thank you to Lakor for loaning us their maritime garments for the models.

Thank you to all the models: Arben Berisha (Beni Café Vitus), Matias Holze, Per Reinholdt, Fredrik Elmegaard Almöf, Louise Marie Olsen, Peter Tjellesen, Camilla Tjellefsen, Kirsten Solis, Troels Hoffmann, Cathrine Pedersen, Emile Lassen, Christian Lassen, Ditte Birch, Ane Bendix Madsen, Rasmus Krogh, Michael Erlang-Nielsen, Lisa Gyldenlund Mikkelsen, and the parents who gave Sibel Rønstrup permission to photograph their lovely children. Thank you to the children: Norma, Martha, Wilbur, Svend, Gerda, Molly, Johanne, Arthur, Erik, Lander, Hjalmer, Otto, Dagmar, and Ingrid.

All the knitwear has become even more special because you wore it so beautifully and naturally. Without you, this book would never have been possible, and your dedication and enthusiasm have made every single design completely special.

Thank you to all our test knitters and garment knitters: Troels Hoffmann, Britt Rauff Laursen, Mariane Flyvholm, Heidi Brunhøj, Annemette Halskov, Lise Lotte Madsen, Jette Sørensen, Yvonne Bech, Jeannie Stubtoft, Hanne Vinding, Jette Schwartz, Helle Hytting Hansen, Dorthe Vestergaard, Malene Sliger, Dorthe Hansen, Birgit Larsson, Anette Kaa, Camilla Holm Veie, Malou Rolin, Janni Riemenschneider, Astrid Skov Midtiby, Pia Rotbøl, Anja Nielsen, Josefine Maigaard, Anna Laurberg, Inger Søndergaard, Amelia Luise Lyngfeldt Larsen, Permille Ebstrup Bitsch, Christina Palm Nielsen, and Nicoline Christensen, who knit all the samples in various sizes and colors. Not only did you make your time and skills available, but your feedback and input were invaluable.

Thank you to our graphic designer, Jørn Rasmussen, for making this book so utterly special and beautiful. Thank you to publisher Ulrik T. Skafte at Bogoo Publishing, who made it possible to create this book. Thank you also for the inspiring collaboration. Thank you to editor Emilie Tholstrup and Julie Pedersen for our collaboration and your valuable contributions to this work. You took such great care with the text and contributed perspectives that strengthened the contents for our readers, in addition to seeing details and relating them in a clear and insightful way.

Last, but not least, we wish to express our heartfelt and loving thanks to our families and friends. Your support and backing have been a wonderful part of this exciting journey. In the long hours of work and preparation, your patience and understanding were invaluable. It was your encouraging words and faith in us that carried us forward.

KØBENHAVN

ABOUT THE AUTHORS

Lotte Rahbek has a background in IT and has worked in the development of knitting patterns for five years. She is the author of one previous book: *Du er min øjesten*, published in English as *Knits for Little Ones* (2025).

Gitte Verner Jensen has worked in industrial design and fashion, including knitwear, for thirty years. She is employed by the Louisiana Museum of Modern Art in Humlebæk, Denmark.

Editor: Shawna Mullen
Designer: Darilyn Lowe Carnes
Managing Editor: Lisa Silverman
Production Managers: Alison Gervais and Kathleen Gaffney

Library of Congress Control Number: 2025931145

ISBN: 978-1-4197-7871-1
eISBN: 979-8-88707-509-9

All of the historical photos were kindly made available by the M/S Maritime Museum of Denmark, which has all rights to the photographs. Details are listed for the following photographs:

Front endpapers—Photographer unknown, CC-BY-NC-SA
Back endpapers—Sibel Rønstrup, specialmoments.dk
Archive photo collage, pages 18–19:
Boy at tiller—Photographer unknown, CC-BY-NC-SA
Boys pulling rope—Photographer: Henning Thalund, formerly, mate, CC-BY-NC-SA
Men in black smoking—Photographer unknown, CC-BY-NC-SA
Sailor with dove on shoulder—Photographer unknown
Boys in front of wooden boat—Photographer: Henning Henningsen, CC-BY-NC-SA
Smoking captain, leaning against a door—Photographer unknown, CC-BY-NC-SA
Sail—Photographer unknown, CC-BY-NC-SA
Men on S/S London, page 21: Photographer unknown, CC-BY-NC-SA
Fishermen, page 35: Photographer unknown, CC-BY-NC-SA
Mate, page 57: Photographer unknown, CC-BY-NC-SA

Chapter collage, page 81:
Sailor in white—Photographer unknown, CC-BY-NC-SA
Watercolor of ship—Photographer unknown, CC-BY-NC-SA
Sailors, page 95: Photographer unknown, CC-BY-NC-SA
Martha, page 107: Photographer unknown, CC-BY-NC-SA
Maren, page 119: Photographer unknown, from National Archief, 252-8836
Men on ship, with Wellington boots, page 129: Photographer: Henry Frederiksen, CC-BY-NC-SA

Chapter collage, page 135:
Man holding a ladder—Photographer unknown, CC-BY-NC-SA
Young man scraping a boat—Henning Thalund, formerly, mate
Danstrup boatsmen with life buoys—Photographer unknown, CC-BY-NC-SA
Sailor, page 137: Photographer unknown, CC-BY-NC-SA
Ship, page 151: Photographer unknown, CC-BY-NC-SA
Women, page 177: Photographer unknown, CC-BY-NC-SA
Ship, page 199: Photographer: Per Benny Paulsen, CC-BY-NC-SA
Chapter collage, page 205:
Nice sailor—Photographer unknown, CC-BY-NC-SA
4 children—Photographer unknown, CC-BY-NC-SA
Seaman, page 207: Photographer Jes Salling, CC-BY-NC-SA
Sailor with model ship, page 235: Photographer unknown, CC-BY-NC-SA
Anchor, page 247: Photographer: H. Hauch, CC-BY-NC-SA
Man with pipe, page 273: Photographer: Henry Frederiksen, CC-BY-NC-SA

The photographs on pages 16 and 17 are reproduced with permission from *Visserstruien*, a book published by Forte Creatief, an imprint of Unieboek, and Het Spectrum, Amsterdam

Originally published in Danish in 2023 as *Et hav af masker* by Bogoo, Aarhus, Denmark

Printed and bound in China
10 9 8 7 6 5 4 3 2 1

ABRAMS The Art of Books
195 Broadway, New York, NY 10007
abramsbooks.com

ABRAMS is represented in the UK and Europe by Abrams & Chronicle Books, 1 West Smithfield, London EC1A 9JU and Média Participations, 57 rue Gaston Tessier, 75166 Paris, France.
abramsandchronicle.co.uk and media-participations.com
info@abramsandchronicle.co.uk